COOKING from the
HEART of SPAIN

Also by Janet Mendel

Cooking in Spain
The Best of Spanish Cooking
Traditional Spanish Cooking
Shopping for Food and Wine in Spain
Great Dishes from Spain
My Kitchen in Spain

COOKING *from the* HEART *of* SPAIN

FOOD OF LA MANCHA

JANET MENDEL

wm
WILLIAM MORROW
An Imprint of HarperCollinsPublishers

Portions of this book have appeared in somewhat different form in *Foods from Spain News*, *Spain Gourmetour*, and *Living Spain*.

Translations of extracts of *Don Quijote de la Mancha* by Miguel de Cervantes are by the author.

HarperCollins books may be purchased for educational, business, or sales promotional use. For information please write: Special Markets Department, HarperCollins Publishers, 10 East 53rd Street, New York, NY 10022.

FIRST EDITION

Designed by William Ruoto
Map by Gordon Studio

Printed on acid-free paper

Library of Congress Cataloging-in-Publication Data
Mendel, Janet.
    Cooking from the heart of Spain : food of La Mancha / Janet Mendel.
      p. cm.
    ISBN-13: 978-0-06-075174-6
    ISBN-10: 0-06-075174-6
    1. Cookery, Spanish. 2. Cookery—Spain—Mancha. I. Title.

    TX723.5.S7M443 2006
    641.5946—dc22   2005053384

06 07 08 09 10   WBC/QW   10 9 8 7 6 5 4 3 2 1

To Luella

La mejor salsa del mundo es la hambre.

Hunger is the best sauce.

—Miguel de Cervantes

CONTENTS

Acknowledgments

Many thanks to Amanda Clark and Donna Ellefson, two good friends who joined me on my culinary travels in La Mancha and helped me so much in sourcing ingredients in the United States. I really could not have put these recipes together without them.

I want to thank photographer Jean Dominique Dallet, who let me ride shotgun on his forays through La Mancha. He was a good guide on the Quixote trail.

Thanks to Donna Daniels Gelb and Marlene Parrish, who helped with recipe testing. Thanks, too, to Robert Wolke, for consulting on the science; to writer Gerry Dawes for contacts in the wine world; and to Ed Owen of Madrid, journalist, my personal tapa guide.

Many more assisted me along the way as I collected recipes and stories in La Mancha. I especially would like to thank the following:

Sisters Maria Victoria and Blanca Morras of Monasterio San Benito, Clarisas-Franciscan nuns in El Toboso (Toledo) who shared recipes for convent sweets.

José Rosell Villasevil, president Sociedad Cervantina, Toledo.

Dionisio de Nova of Bodegas Dionisos, Valdepeñas (Ciudad Real).

Javier Alegria, El Tablazo, Villalba de la Sierra (Cuenca).

Manuela Sevilla Mompó, librarian, Quintanar de la Orden (Toledo), and her mother, Francisca Mompó.

Carlos Falcó, Marqués de Griñón, winemaker, Malpica de Tajo (Toledo).

Iñigo Valdenebro, producer of extra virgin olive oil, Toledo.

Roberto Arcos, knife maker, Albacete.

Pepe Expósito, knife maker, Albacete.

Pedro Condés Torres, director, Manchego Cheese Board, Valdepeñas (Ciudad Real).

Pilar Martínez, Azafrán Bealar, Motilla del Palancar (Cuenca).

Ana Beatriz Callejas, Saffron Board of La Mancha, Camuñas (Toledo).

Juan Pacheco Parra, president, Garlic Cooperative, Las Pedroñeras (Cuenca).

Adolfo Muñoz, Restaurante Adolfo, Toledo.

Manuel de la Osa, Restaurante Las Rejas, Las Pedroñeras (Cuenca).

Ian Gibson, author, Madrid.

Juan Carlos Palomino, Taller Gastronómico, Los Yébenes (Toledo).

Apelio García Sánchez-Horneros, Los Yébenes (Toledo).

Amelia Moreno Rosilla and David Cohn, Quintanar de la Orden (Toledo).

Samuel del Coso Román, Sephardic Center, Toledo.

I am indebted to several cookbooks in the Spanish language that pointed the way in my recipe gathering. Some are noted in specific recipes. All are listed in the bibliography at the end of this book.

Many thanks to my agent, Fred Hill, for finding just the right place for my work. Thanks to Susan Friedland, formerly of HarperCollins, the editor who started me on this book.

And *mil gracias* to Harriet Bell, my editor at William Morrow, who edited the book with taste and saw it through to fruition. Thanks to editorial assistant Lucy Baker; Chris Benton, for careful copyediting; Luca Pioltelli, who took the jacket photograph; Don Harris of La Tienda, who provided the foods for the photograph; Roberto de Vicq de Cumptich, who designed the jacket; and Bill Ruoto, for putting together a handsome book.

Special thanks to my good friends Harry and Charlotte Gordon, who not only shared many Manchegan meals and wines with me but contributed to the book by designing the map of La Mancha.

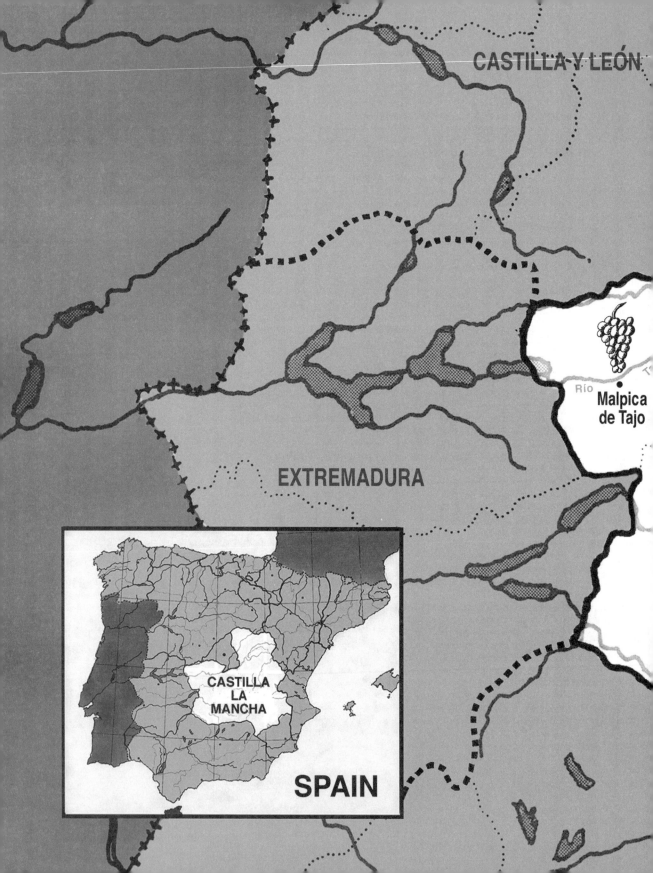

ARAGÓN

GUADALAJARA

MADRID

Villalba
de la Sierra

TOLEDO

Júcar

CUENCA

CASTILLA

Campillo
de Altobuey

Los
Yébenes

El Toboso

Las
Pedroñeras

LA

VALENCIA

Alcázar
de San Juan

CIUDAD REAL

MANCHA

ALBACETE

Almagro

La Solana

Valdepeñas

ANDALUCÍA

MURCIA

La Mancha,
the Heart of Spain

Against wide open spaces and big skies, shepherds move herds of sheep across stubbled fields. Windmills appear on ridge tops like a line of cavalry. The occasional castle with its medieval battlements looks for all the world like a movie set from *El Cid*. In the autumn, Spain's central *meseta*, high plateau land, surprises with bursts of color—russet leaves of vineyards, poplar trees by riverbanks spangled with golden leaves, sweet green of new wheat springing up. Plowed earth is a strong mineral red. Sunsets above the vast plains streak the sky with violet, pink, and periwinkle. Ruffled by wind, the leaves of olive trees shimmer silvery green.

I first visited La Mancha in the fall to write an article about saffron, the aromatic spice grown in Spain's central region. I discovered a region of contrasts, old and new, brilliant color, savory food, delectable sweets.

In the saffron fields I followed the pickers down the rows as they filled their baskets with tiny saffron crocuses. Later I sat with the women who opened the petals and pulled out the stigma—three orange-red wisps—which, dried, becomes the spice we know. While they worked, they told me about traditional dishes cooked with saffron, which I later tasted in a local tavern.

From there I traveled to the hilltop town of Alarcón, where I stayed in an eighth-century fortress (now a hotel belonging to the national network of paradors) and dined on succulent baby lamb roasted in a wood-fired oven. The meat, redolent of wild herbs that fueled the fire, was meltingly tender. At the nearby Roman ruins of Valera, I found saffron flowers popping up between the foundations of walls built in the first century. Stopping in a small village for a bite to eat, I encountered a weekly street market set up in the central plaza. A gypsy woman selling snails from a wheelbarrow told me how to cook them.

At country *ventas,* the sort of roadside eateries where Don Quixote had his mix-ups, I sampled rustic country stews, hearty garlic soups, big, satisfying salads, and splendid vegetable dishes such as *pisto,* the forerunner of ratatouille.

I love these foods that frankly reveal their roots in the local soil—sausages made on a local farm, bread baked daily from wheat ground at a nearby mill, cheese made from the milk of sheep that graze springtime pastures, wine lovingly made from the grapes of the region and aged in caves hacked from the limestone earth. It is ancient, yet it is fresh.

While the straightforward simplicity of this food is so appealing, I also thrill to the innovation of a new generation of chefs and winemakers in La Mancha, the *vanguardistas* of twenty-first-century cuisine. Who ever would have imagined Syrah varietal wines in the middle of La Mancha? (They are marvelous!) What would Sancho Panza have thought about cold jellied garlic soup topped with foam of pimentón? (I bet he would have chuckled heartily.) While salt cod is very old stuff in La Mancha, it surely has a new lease on life as interpreted today in several of La Mancha's finest restaurants. And I love the nerve of a chef who dares to match plebeian beans, cooked to a creamy smoothness with saffron, and seared foie gras, which, when cut, releases its juices into the beans.

On subsequent visits to La Mancha, I joined a master confectioner of almond marzipan in his Toledo *obrador* and spent a day with a shepherd and maker of artisanal Manchego cheese. I ate trout pulled from cold streams in Cuenca and partridge taken in the hills of Toledo. I sampled La Mancha in all seasons, squelching through mud in asparagus fields to cut spring's first spears and sweating in the vineyards of Valdepeñas during the late-summer *vendimia,* grape harvest. I savored every minute of it.

🌾 THE LAY OF THE LAND

La Mancha is an upland plateau in the very center of Spain. The Arabs who conquered most of Spain in the eighth century called it Al-Manchara, meaning "arid land." Known as Moors, they took over towns and strongholds previously held by Visigoths and Romans before them (the city of Toledo, the Roman Toletum, was founded in 190 B.C.). The conquering Moors left an indelible mark on culture, architecture, and, of course, cooking.

The Arabs, who came from the crossroads of the great spice routes to the East, brought to Spain a treasure chest of aromatics—cinnamon, nutmeg, pepper, aniseed, sesame, cumin, coriander, ginger, caraway, saffron. They introduced the cultivation of almonds, eggplant, bitter oranges, pomegranates, rice, and sugarcane. They extended the olive groves, which had been planted by the Romans, and devised complex irrigation systems.

In those medieval times, Jewish communities also resided in central Spain. Legend relates that the Hebrew peoples had lived in Spain since the time of King Solomon and the voyages of the Phoenician traders. What is certain is that communities of Jews existed in what is now Spain from the first century, during the time of the Roman Empire. They called their country Sepharad. During periods of benevolent Moorish rule, Spain's Jews enjoyed a "golden age," participating at court as doctors, linguists, and diplomats.

During several centuries of Reconquest, as successive Christian kings struggled to take back land lost to the Moors, La Mancha was the battlefield. Military-religious orders, such as the Knights of Calatrava, Knights of San Juan, and Knights of Santiago, moved into the region, building fortifications—castles—to secure fiefdoms wrested from the Moors. Thus La Mancha acquired its other name—Castilla, or Castile, meaning "castle." By the end of the twelfth century, Christian rulers had regained much of La Mancha, whereas in the south of Spain, in Andalucía, the last Moorish king was not routed until 1492.

After the Reconquest and until the fateful year of 1492, when Jewish and Muslim inhabitants were forced to convert to the Catholic Church or else were expelled from Spain, La Mancha enjoyed several centuries of fitful *convivencia,* fairly peaceful coexistence among Moors, Jews, and Christians. The Islamic culture contributed hugely to architecture, literature, science and medicine, agriculture, and the culinary arts. This influence deeply imbues Spanish cooking, which, beneath its sturdy simplicity, wafts an aroma of refinement, of a delicate complexity left from those medieval times—savory dishes with subtle sweet and sour flavors, crushed almonds for richness, lavish pastries spiked with cinnamon, saffron, rose water.

The sixteenth century ushered in Spain's Golden Age, when conquistadors brought glory and riches to Spanish shores—along with new foods from a new world, such as chocolate, beans, peppers, potatoes, squash, and, eventually, tomatoes. Carlos V, who ascended the Spanish throne in 1519 and became Holy Roman Emperor as well, made Toledo his imperial capital. This king expanded Spain's influence throughout Europe, bringing under a single crown most of Spain, the Hapsburg domains of Austria, parts of Italy, the Spanish colonies in America, parts of France, Belgium, and the Netherlands. When he abdicated in 1556, his son, Felipe II, succeeded him and later moved the capital to Madrid.

It was during the second half of this century that Miguel de Cervantes Saavedra, born in the town of Alcalá de Henares near Madrid, came of age. By 1592, a hundred years after Columbus's first voyage and the discovery of the Americas, Cervantes' writing career was beginning to flourish (he was earlier an enlisted soldier, a prisoner captured by Barbary pirates, and a government commissary officer). During his lifetime, there were amazing exploits by Spanish explorers in the Americas. Cervantes himself unsuccessfully petitioned the Council of the Indies for a post in the West Indies. Cervantes' most famous work, *Don Quijote de La Mancha,* was first published in 1605.

En un lugar de la Mancha, de cuyo nombre no quiero acordarme, no ha mucho tiempo que vivía un hidalgo de los de lanza en astillero, adarga antigua, rocín flaco y galgo corredor. Una olla de algo más vaca que carnero, salpicón las más noches, duelos y quebrantos los sábados, lentejas los viernes, y algún palomino de añadidura los domingos, consumían las tres partes de su hacienda. . . . Frisaba la edad de nuestro hidalgo con los cincuenta años: era de complexión recia, seco de carnes, enjuto de rostro, gran madrugador y amigo de la caza.

> *In a certain place in La Mancha, whose name I don't wish to remember, there lived not so long ago a gentleman of the landed gentry, the sort who kept a lance in the rack, an old shield, a thin nag and a racing greyhound. An olla—boiled dinner—with somewhat more beef than mutton, salpicón—leftovers—on most nights, duelos y quebrantos—eggs and brains—on Saturdays, lentils on Fridays and some squab on Sundays for good measure, used up three-quarters of his income. . . . Our gentleman was getting on for fifty: he was of robust constitution, lean, gaunt-faced, an early riser and aficionado of hunting.*

It was four hundred years ago that Don Quixote sallied forth from his La Mancha village in search of adventure. Wearing a rusty suit of armor and a bashed-up helmet, he partook of a meager meal of salt cod at a roadside inn and was unceremoniously beknighted by the innkeeper with a thwack on the shoulder.

The story opens with a description of what Don Quixote ate most days of the week. Throughout the book, Cervantes feeds us morsels about life and food at the end of the sixteenth century. Don Quixote proves an excellent guide to the foods and cooking of present-day La Mancha, for the lay of the land has changed very little.

⁑ LA MANCHA TODAY

Modern-day La Mancha belongs to the autonomous region of Castilla–La Mancha, situated in central Spain, which has its seat of government in the enchanting city of Toledo. The culture of Castilla–La Mancha falls somewhere between the austerity of Aragón and Old Castile and the flamboyance of Andalucía.

Castilla–La Mancha incorporates the provinces of Toledo, Ciudad Real, Cuenca, Albacete, and Guadalajara (all with provincial capital cities of the same names). These provinces border on every other region of Spain, with the exception of two archipelagos, Catalonia, La Rioja, Navarra, and those bordering the northern Bay of Biscay. La Mancha, an inland region, has no seaport but—surprise!—is famous for its seafood.

Ciudad Real in the south shares some traditional dishes with adjoining Córdoba and

Jaén. Toledo on the west borders Extremadura, land of the conquistadors. Rough *dehesa*, scrubland, of holm oaks and low stone walls, extends from one region into the next. Iberico pigs thrive here, fattening on the acorns. The *accidentado*—rough—terrain of the Montes de Toledo shelters partridge and other game.

To the north, Castilla–La Mancha touches the frontier of Old Castile (now Castilla y León). The food, grave and simple like the land, seems ancient—shepherds' stews whose recipes are almost biblical; ham and sausages cured as they have been for centuries; fresh trout from fast-flowing mountain streams.

Cuenca in the east makes an abrupt transition into Aragón and the Levant of Valencia. Albacete, once part of the kingdom of Murcia, continues to share with that Mediterranean region in the cultivation of paella rice.

Madrid también es La Mancha—Madrid is La Mancha too. Long before it was the capital of a united Spain, Madrid was a dusty town on the La Mancha plateau, a crossroads for migrating flocks of sheep. The food of this vibrant and cosmopolitan city, which today encompasses flavors from every region of Spain and the world, reveals its rustic past in favorite tapa bar foods and wines.

I have lived in Spain for many years and love its food from the inside out. La Mancha, for me, is the "real" Spain—not Andalucía, not Catalonia, not Basque, not Galicia, nor Asturias. This is Spanish cooking true to its roots and enticing in its future. The heart of Spain.

✺ USING THESE RECIPES

Most dishes included in this book are authentic and traditional. Some recipes I have modified to make them either more user-friendly or more healthful (less lard, more olive oil). Where ingredients may be hard to come by for American cooks, I suggest alternatives. A few recipes are creative ways to use typical Manchegan products. Some are my own invention; others have been adapted from dishes presented by modern-day chefs. An example is saffron ice cream, which incorporates La Mancha saffron in a nontraditional dessert.

Here is a glossary of ingredients and utensils used in the recipes. For sources, see the list at the end of the book.

BROTH   In recipes that call for chicken broth, use homemade broth (page 94) or canned low-sodium broth. For fish broth use homemade broth (page 135), bottled clam juice, or water.

CAZUELA   A cazuela is an earthenware casserole, glazed on the inside, unglazed on the outside bottom, that can be used on top of the stove and in the oven. It is much used in Spanish cookery, though a heavy skillet, sauté pan, or enameled cast-iron casserole can be used instead. Cazuelas come in many widths, though they generally are not very deep (for example, a 10-inch cazuela is 3 inches deep). Big ones are heavy and not easy to maneuver in and out of the oven. Small ones, *cazuelitas,* are perfect for individual servings.

The advantage of cazuela cooking is that earthenware holds a slow, steady heat, letting food cook gently and evenly. It's even possible to sauté or brown foods in a cazuela, by adding enough oil to cover the bottom surface, slowly heating it until very hot, and adding food to be browned without crowding.

When purchasing a new cazuela, soak it in water for twenty-four hours to help leach out the raw clay taste, though frequent use is the best method of curing. Don't heat a cazuela empty and take care not to set a hot one down on a very cold surface or it will crack.

CHILE (*GUINDILLA*)   Hot chile peppers are used sparingly in Spanish cooking. Mild green pickled chiles, much like peperoncini, are a favorite accompaniment to bean dishes. Dried red chiles of medium hotness, such as cayenne, are sliced or minced to add to some dishes. The best substitute is hot red pepper flakes.

CHORIZO   This is the most emblematic sausage in all of Spain. Made of chopped pork and pork fat and seasoned with garlic and pimentón (paprika), it is dry-cured, not smoked. Spanish chorizo is ready to eat without cooking (unlike Mexican chorizo, which is a raw sausage). In Spain chorizo is produced in two types—a hard sausage that is sliced for cold cuts and a softer sausage with more fat content that is tied off in short links, best for stewing with beans and lentils. Spanish chorizo is available in the United States at select markets. If you can't find it, substitute an unsmoked spicy Italian sausage, adding pimentón for color and flavor.

DENOMINACIÓN DE ORIGEN, DO   These initials stand for "denomination of origin," designating wines and foods that have protected status guaranteeing their geographic home and their quality. Castilla–La Mancha presently has eight wine DOs (see page 349), plus DO Aceite de los Montes de Toledo (olive oil), DO Queso Manchego (cheese), DO Cordero Manchego (lamb), DO Ajo Morado de Las Pedroñeras (garlic), DO Melón de la Mancha,

DO Miel de la Alcarria (honey), DO Berenejena de Almagro (pickled eggplant), and DO Azafrán de la Mancha (saffron).

HAM   See Serrano Ham.

MORTAR AND PESTLE   When a recipe calls for freshly ground black pepper, you probably reach for the pepper mill. The traditional Spanish method calls for freshly grinding spices in a small mortar, usually a brass *almirez*. You can use any small stone mortar. Put the saffron in first and crush it to a powder. Then add small, whole spices such as peppercorns, cloves, and cumin seed. Continue with any dried herbs and finish the blend with soft items such as garlic cloves. Last, dilute the mixture with water, broth, or wine before stirring it into the food.

OLIVE OIL   Use olive oil from Spain for the recipes in this book. Choose extra virgin olive oil for sautéing, for salads, for gazpacho, and in other recipes where the oil is not cooked (for instance, drizzled over grilled fish, cooked vegetables, baked potato). For deep-frying, when a large quantity of oil is required, use either extra virgin olive oil (preferably of a varietal such as Picual that is stable at high heat) or one labeled simply *olive oil*. The latter is refined olive oil to which some virgin oil is added for flavor. It is much less expensive than extra virgin oil.

There are some 27 million olive trees in Castilla–La Mancha, which is the second-largest producer of olive oil, after Andalucía, in Spain. Spain has seven protected olive oil denominations of origin, one of which, Montes de Toledo, is in Castilla–La Mancha. DO Montes de Toledo oil is produced from the Cornicabra olive variety, which makes a fresh, fruity oil with aromas of apple and almond and a lovely, buttery texture. (More about olive oil on page 273.)

PIMENTÓN, PIMENTÓN DE LA VERA, SMOKED PIMENTÓN   Pimentón is Spanish paprika. It is produced in two regions, in eastern Spain, where a hot, dry Mediterranean climate allows the peppers to be sun-dried, and also in western Spain in the La Vera region of Extremadura, where the peppers are smoke-dried for 10 to 15 days over smoldering chunks of wild holm oak. The slow smoking fixes the natural carotenoid pigments of the peppers, producing an intensely red spice. It also adds an ineffable natural smokiness that complements many foods. After drying, the peppers are ground to a powder.

Pimentón is produced from the *Capsicum annuum* pepper, the chile pepper discovered by Columbus on his first trip to the New World. Columbus carried peppers and other New World plants back to Spain, where they were cultivated by monks in various abbeys. The Hieronymite monks at the Yuste monastery in La Vera were the first to dry the peppers and use the powder as a flavoring and food preservative.

Emperor Charles V, when he abdicated the Spanish throne in 1555 and retired to the Yuste monastery, got to like the spice (he was a notorious gourmand) and recommended it to his sister, Queen Mary of Hungary. That's where it became known as *paprika*, from the Serbo-Croatian word for "pepper."

Spanish pimentón, smoked or unsmoked, comes in three flavors—*dulce*, sweet; *agridulce*, bittersweet; and *picante*, spicy-hot. Each is made from a different subspecies of pepper. Sweet pimentón, smoked or unsmoked, is the most versatile, while the bittersweet adds complexity to a dish. The spicy-hot is packed with flavor and not fiery. Cayenne can be substituted for hot pimentón.

In Spain, the lion's share of pimentón goes to the sausage-making industry. The most emblematic Spanish sausage, garlicky chorizo, is colored and flavored with it. Pimentón is widely used in home cooking, too, and not just sprinkled for color, but in heaping spoonfuls. Use smoked pimentón with discretion, however, as its earthy, smoky aroma can overwhelm delicate flavors.

Stir pimentón into a little water and blend it to a smooth paste before adding it to a sauce. Or stir it into hot oil in a sauté and immediately add liquid so that the pimentón doesn't scorch. If using pimentón on barbecued food, add it during the last few minutes of grilling so that it doesn't burn. If a recipe calls for smoked pimentón, ordinary pimentón or paprika can be substituted. Sources are listed at the back of this book.

RICE   Spanish rice, used for paella and other rice recipes, is a round, medium-short grain. This variety of rice soaks up the flavors of the foods that are cooked with it—olive oil, garlic, chicken, rabbit, meat. It can be cooked dry, as for paella; *meloso*, juicy; or *caldoso*, soupy. Part of the growing region for Denominación de Origen Calasparra rice is situated in the valleys of the Mundo and Segura rivers, in the southeast of Albacete province, bordering Murcia. Bomba is one of three varieties of rice cultivated there. It is especially valued for cooking in soupy rice dishes, because it doesn't "flower," or open up and become mushy. If Spanish rice is not available, substitute another medium-short-grain rice such as Arborio. When rice is cooked as a side dish or salad (not in a casserole with other ingredients), use your favorite long-grain rice.

SAFFRON (More about saffron on page 160.) Look for saffron with the DO of La Mancha seal. Any other saffron may be imported from other countries. Spanish saffron is usually sold in threads (not powdered) by gram measures. One gram, about one-tenth of one ounce, is a sufficient quantity for about six recipes of paella, risotto, or chicken in saffron-almond sauce. There is no substitute for saffron. Although in Spain artificial yellow coloring is frequently used in place of pricey saffron (especially in paellas served up to tourists), no other yellow spice can take the place of sensuous saffron.

It's not easy to measure strands of saffron. In this book, ¼ teaspoon or ½ teaspoon means lightly filling the spoon, tamping the threads down slightly without crushing the saffron. One-half teaspoon equals about sixty filaments.

For use in cooking, when you want to extract the full flavor and color of the saffron, first crush it in a small mortar. Perfectly dry saffron will crumble easily. If you don't have a mortar and pestle, use the butt end of a knife to crush the saffron in a teacup. It doesn't need to be totally pulverized.

Add enough liquid—wine or hot water, milk, or broth—to cover the crushed saffron. Let it infuse for at least 10 minutes and up to 45 minutes. Stir the crushed saffron and liquid into a sauce toward the end of cooking time so that the aroma doesn't dissipate in long cooking. On the other hand, if you want the golden color to permeate the cooking food, such as for paella and some potato dishes, add the saffron infusion at the very beginning of the cooking time. Saffron can be purchased at many food stores and from the sources listed at the back of the book.

SALT COD (*BACALAO*) Unless otherwise noted in a recipe, salt cod needs to be soaked for at least 24 hours to remove the salt and rehydrate the dried flesh before being incorporated in a recipe. Wash the salt cod in running water. Place in a bowl and cover with cold water. Cover the bowl and refrigerate for 6 hours. Drain, rinse the cod, and cover with fresh water. Change the water once or twice more. After draining, squeeze the cod gently to express moisture. It is now ready to be cooked according to the recipe.

Fresh cod can be substituted for salt cod in recipes, although it will contribute a very different flavor and texture.

SERRANO HAM; IBÉRICO HAM (*JAMÓN SERRANO*) This is a salt-cured ham from Spain that is typically sliced paper-thin and served as a tapa with wine or Sherry. It is not smoked or cooked. *Serrano* means "mountain," because these hams traditionally were cured in highland regions where temperatures and humidity enhanced the curing process. They are now produced in modern processing plants with temperature controls, allowing stable year-round conditions for curing. Castilla–La Mancha is the country's largest producer of serrano ham.

Serrano ham is exported to the United States and can be found in the deli sections of good supermarkets and at specialty shops. (See Sources.)

When the ham comes from a pig of the Iberico breed, a small, brown pig native to western Spain, it is called *jamón ibérico,* Iberico ham, or *pata negra,* "black foot," because it has a black hoof. These pigs roam the *dehesas,* rough pastureland forested with wild oaks, gobbling acorns and wild grasses. Their meat makes the best ham in the world, sweet, nutty, succulent.

Diced serrano ham or scraps of the ham's fat (*tocino*) are used in cooked dishes, almost like a seasoning. They are especially good sautéed with vegetables, omelets, mushrooms, and shrimp. Chunks of ham bone add flavor to a pot of beans or lentils. If serrano ham is not available, use unsmoked Canadian bacon or lean pancetta in cooked recipes, fatty bacon in place of *tocino.* In salads, sandwiches, and croquettes, unsmoked cooked ham could substitute for serrano.

Slice serrano ham immediately before serving. Use a very sharp slicing knife with a long, flexible blade to slice from a whole ham. Cut lengthwise pieces, with the grain, as thinly as possible. (Special racks that clamp the ham tightly make slicing easier.) Presliced, vacuum-packaged serrano ham should be brought to room temperature before the packet is opened.

VINEGAR   White wine vinegar is the most widely used in Spanish cooking. Red wine vinegar may be substituted if the color doesn't matter. Sherry vinegar is more mellow (from maturing), but also more acidic than normal wine vinegar.

USEFUL EQUIVALENTS

1½ pounds baking potatoes = 3 medium potatoes

1 cup chopped onion = 1 medium onion

1 cup chopped bell pepper = 1 large bell pepper

1 cup peeled, seeded, and chopped tomato = 2 medium tomatoes (11 to 12 ounces)

1 cup chopped leek = 1 leek

½ cup diced carrot = 1 carrot

1 teaspoon chopped garlic = 1 medium garlic clove

1 cup coarsely grated cheese (not packed) = 3 ounces

½ cup diced ham or bacon = 3 ounces

Tapas, Starters, and Salads

From a working-class tavern in an agricultural village in the middle of La Mancha, where the lamb fried with whole garlic cloves is unconscionably good, to a trendy wine bar in upmarket Madrid, where lollipops of quails' legs accompany the reserva wines, tapa bars provide the best possible introduction to Spanish cuisine, both traditional and *vanguardista*. What a wonderful assortment of food! Hot dishes and cold ones, fresh and raw or crispy and fried, flavors both simple and exotic, old and new.

I have grouped tapas, starters, and salads together because there is much crossover between them. Many salads, such as Tomato-Tuna Salad, appear at tapa bars, while some tapas, such as Manchego Cheese and Potato Croquettes or Partridge and Chicken Pâté, serve nicely as starters or, accompanied by a salad, as a whole lunch.

Some favorite tapas require no recipe. Serrano ham is simply sliced paper-thin from a whole ham. Olives are dipped from a jug. Aged Manchego cheese is sliced and served with bread. Almonds are heaped in a bowl. If you are preparing a tapa party, be sure to include some of these.

Throughout this book are many more recipes for dishes that might also be served in a typical tapa bar. For example, the Spanish Potato Tortilla in the next chapter, Codfish Balls with Walnuts in the fish chapter, or Spiced Pork Loin in Confit in the meat chapter can be served in small portions as a tapa. Similarly, recipes in other chapters—in particular those for vegetable dishes—are frequently served as starters.

Tapas were invented to go with wine. In the taverns of La Mancha and Madrid, red wine is the preferred drink with tapa foods. (See page 347 for more about the wines of La Mancha.) But equally acceptable are white wine, fino Sherry, and beer.

THYME-MARINATED OLIVES

Aceitunas con Aliño de Tomillo

At a small inn in Los Yébenes in the Montes de Toledo, I was served two different sorts of home-cured olives, both prepared by Carmen Sánchez. The olives in one dish were green; those in the second were almost black. Both were of the same variety, cornicabra, an oval olive with a curved tip, the same olive that is pressed for the region's extra virgin oil. And both had been picked green. Carmen explained that one batch had been prepared in a soda-lye solution and the other had been soaked for two months in only water. The soda-lye fixes the green color and sweetens whole olives in only twenty-four hours. They are then washed thoroughly and placed in seasoned brine. The dark olives had been sliced to the pit—Carmen showed me a little gadget with four thin blades for incising the olives, one by one—then soaked in frequent changes of water for two months until all the bitterness was removed. Then the olives were placed in the flavored brine. Carmen used thyme and garlic to flavor the brine.

Give ordinary bottled olives a home-cured flavor by marinating them with thyme, garlic, and lemon.

MAKES 2 CUPS

2 cups drained, bottled manzanilla olives	1 tablespoon salt
½ teaspoon dried thyme	2 garlic cloves, slivered
1 bay leaf	½ lemon, sliced
2 teaspoons wine vinegar	1 fresh thyme sprig (optional)

Rinse the olives and soak them in water for 1 hour. Drain again.

Combine 3 cups water in a saucepan with the thyme, bay leaf, vinegar, and salt. Bring to a boil. Remove from the heat and allow to cool. Strain the liquid into a 1-quart nonreactive glass jar. Add the drained olives, garlic, lemon, and thyme if you're using it. Combine well. Cover tightly and allow to marinate, refrigerated, for 7 days.

Store the olives in the refrigerator for up to 2 months.

TOASTED NUTS and SEEDS

Cañamones

La Cocina del Quijote (The Cuisine of the Quixote) by Lorenzo Díaz, an authentic Manchego, is a book about the traditional dishes of the region, many of which were known in Don Quixote's era. The author tells of a special treat that he enjoyed as a child, *cañamones*, handfuls of toasted seeds and nuts. *Cañamones* are hemp seeds, but they were mixed with wheat berries, dried chestnuts, and nuts. Here is one version—without hemp seeds, but including sunflower seeds, which are famous in the province of Cuenca. Walnuts, pine nuts, linseeds, chestnuts, figs, and raisins could be added as well, but do not fry the chestnuts, figs, or raisins.

MAKES 5 CUPS

1 cup dried chickpeas, soaked overnight	1 cup almonds
1 cup wheat berries, soaked overnight	1 cup sunflower seeds
¼ cup olive oil	½ teaspoon aniseeds
1 cup hazelnuts	1 teaspoon coarse salt

Drain the chickpeas and wheat berries and pat dry. Heat the oil in a deep skillet. Fry the chickpeas over medium-high heat until golden brown and crisped, 5 minutes. Skim them out and drain on paper towels.

Fry the wheat berries until golden, 2 minutes. Tilt the pan so oil drains to one side and skim out the wheat. Drain.

Continue frying the hazelnuts and almonds, each for about 1 minute. Pour off the remaining oil and toast the sunflower seeds with the aniseeds in the same skillet, about 1 minute.

Combine all the toasted seeds and nuts and sprinkle with salt. When completely cool, store in an airtight container. Keeps for up to 2 weeks.

CRISP-FRIED TURNOVERS *with* TUNA FILLING

Empanadillas de Atún

I once made hundreds of these little turnovers for a big party, stashing them in the freezer a week before the event. Happily, I had help in the kitchen when it came time to fry them. Served hot and crisp, the turnovers just flew off the trays, disappearing within minutes.

The tuna filling is both delicious and convenient, but chicken, fish, shredded beef, and pork are other good choices. In Toledo, empanadillas are filled with thin slices of fried pork loin in tomato sauce.

MAKES FIFTY-SIX 3-INCH TURNOVERS OR FORTY 3½-INCH TURNOVERS

FOR THE DOUGH

2¼ cups all-purpose flour, plus flour for the board

1 teaspoon salt

¼ teaspoon fennel seeds, coarsely ground

8 tablespoons (1 stick) cold unsalted butter, cut into ¼-inch pieces

⅓ cup plus 1 tablespoon cold dry white wine

FOR THE FILLING

1 cup drained canned tuna

¼ cup Tomato Sauce, homemade (page 26) or canned

1 hard-cooked egg, chopped

1 tablespoon chopped fresh flat-leaf parsley

1 tablespoon brandy

⅔ cup finely chopped manzanilla or pimiento-stuffed olives

2 tablespoons minced onion

Salt and freshly ground black pepper

1 teaspoon wine vinegar or fresh lemon juice

Pinch of cayenne

Olive or vegetable oil for deep-frying

Combine the flour, salt, and fennel seeds in a food processor. Add the butter and pulse until the mixture resembles coarse meal. Add the wine and process for 30 seconds, until the flour begins to clump.

Turn the dough out onto a lightly floured board. Push it together into a ball, then stretch it once, twice, then press it into a ball again. Cover with plastic wrap and refrigerate for at least 2 and up to 24 hours.

Combine all the filling ingredients in a bowl, taste, and add more salt, vinegar, or cayenne if necessary. It should be strongly seasoned.

Divide the ball of dough in half. Keep one half refrigerated and place the other half on a lightly floured board. Pat it down with the rolling pin until it is slightly softened and flattened enough to start rolling. Roll the dough out as thinly as possible, sprinkling board and rolling pin with flour as needed.

Use a cookie cutter to cut 3-inch, 3½-inch, or larger circles. Gather up scraps, press them together, and refrigerate. Place a spoonful of the filling on the bottom half of each round of dough. Dip a finger in water and moisten the edges of the bottom half. Fold the top half of the circle over the filling and press the edges together. Use the flat butt end of a knife to crimp the edges. Place each empanadilla, as filled, onto a tray.

When all of the circles are filled and sealed, roll out the second half of the dough in the same manner. Cut circles, fill, and seal the empanadillas. Then roll out the remaining scraps of dough, cut circles, and fill.

Heat the oil in a deep pan to a depth of at least 1 inch, or in a deep fryer, until shimmering but not smoking (about 360°F). Fry the empanadillas, a few at a time, until they are golden brown, 5 to 6 minutes. Remove with a skimmer and drain on paper towels. Continue frying the remaining empanadillas. Serve hot or at room temperature.

NOTE: *To freeze uncooked turnovers, place them in a single layer on a tray in the freezer until frozen. Then pack them in layers separated with plastic wrap in a covered freezer container. Remove them from the freezer about 15 minutes before frying. Fry them without defrosting, allowing about 2 minutes more time in the hot oil.*

The turnovers can be fried up to 2 hours in advance of serving and reheated in a 400°F oven for 5 minutes.

VARIATION: *To bake the turnovers, preheat the oven to 375°F and place the turnovers on an ungreased baking sheet. Brush the tops with beaten egg and bake until golden, 20 to 25 minutes.*

PUFFY SHRIMP FRITTERS

Buñuelos de Gambas

Serve these tasty fritters with drinks. They are best hot out of the oil.

MAKES 20 FRITTERS

½ cup all-purpose flour

½ teaspoon baking powder

Pinch of celery seeds

Pinch of cayenne

¼ cup minced green garlic shoots or scallions

2 tablespoons chopped fresh parsley

1 egg, separated

¼ cup lager beer

2 cups chopped peeled shrimp (about 9 ounces)

½ teaspoon salt

About 2 cups olive oil for deep-frying

Combine the flour, baking powder, celery seeds, and cayenne in a bowl. Stir in the minced garlic shoots or scallions, parsley, egg yolk, and beer to make a paste.

Shortly before frying the fritters, stir the shrimp into the batter. Beat the egg white until stiff. Beat in the salt. Fold the egg white into the batter.

Heat the oil to a depth of about 1 inch in a deep skillet until shimmering. Drop heaping teaspoons of the shrimp batter into the oil and fry, turning once, until golden on both sides, 2 to 3 minutes.

Drain on paper towels and serve immediately.

TAPA HOPPING IN MADRID

It was just about 8:00 P.M. when three of us walked into our first tapa bar, the nineteenth-century Taberna de Antonio Sánchez in the old section of Lavapies of Madrid. We ordered red wine from Valdepeñas and the house tapa, *morcilla*, blood sausage, with pine nuts and raisins. In Madrid, 8:00 is a good hour to start out on a tapa crawl—early, with shops just closing and supper still a couple of hours away.

We moved on to Cava Baja, Madrid's best-known tapa street. At Lucio's adjunct, we enjoyed eggs scrambled with potatoes and ham. Yes, scrambled eggs. That simple.

Another couple joined our group. We moved along to La Carta, where the *pincho*, tomato, cheese, and anchovy speared on a toothpick, was served free with our glasses of red wine. We ordered *revuelto de habitas*, tiny fava beans sautéed with ham.

By the time we got to La Casa del Abuelo, yet another couple joined the group. We were speaking English, Spanish, and French. The *gambas al ajillo*, shrimp sizzled with garlic, were delicious. We passed right by Café Brava, home of the famous *patatas brava*, crisp-fried cubes of potato in a spicy sauce. At Freiduria de Gallinejas, which specializes in innards and organs, I had to try a La Mancha specialty, *zarajos*, lamb tripe twisted around grapevine skewers and roasted. It was tender and delicious.

At 1:00 A.M., in the Plaza de Santa Ana, we flagged taxis to go home. By that hour tapa bars were closed, but thousands of young people thronged the plaza. The night was young. But we weren't.

Madrid, one of the world's great capital cities, may not be where the tapa custom originated (that would be in the wine bars of Andalucía). But it's where tapas consolidated as an expression of social, cultural, artistic, and culinary life. Today, life in Madrid would not be the same without the convivial rituals of the *tapeo*, the meeting and greeting, eating and imbibing. Part of the attraction of the *tapeo* is the *paseo* and the *movida*. It is a movable feast—you stop at one bar to taste its specialty, then stroll up the street to another, around the corner for a third round. Then you bump into another group of friends and move on to a different locale. The movement is part of the entertainment. And—this is important—you don't sit down at a table. Tapas are best on foot, standing at the bar or balancing wineglass and tapa on a little shelf.

The variety of tapas is quite stunning. Most tapa bars serve ten to twenty different dishes, but some specialize in just one. So, for instance, a particular bar may serve only ham and sausages, another only *bacalao* dishes, others exclusively shellfish or snails. Tapas range from very traditional home cooking to innovative and trendy.

Tapas divide into roughly four categories: ready to eat, salads and cold dishes, fried foods, and *tapas de cocina,* hot cooked dishes. It's perfectly acceptable to mix and match them in any order.

Ready to eat includes olives, toasted almonds, aged cheese, and the special Spanish ham, *jamón serrano.* In many tapa bars these hams hang from the beams alongside sausage links and garlands of garlic. The ham is very thinly sliced and served raw. One type of serrano ham, made from the breed of Iberico pig, is especially esteemed and justifiably expensive. Some bars serve a *surtido de ibérico,* an assortment of Iberico ham, cured loin, and sausages. Others feature *pinchos*—tidbits such as pickles, anchovies, and eggs speared on toothpicks.

Salads and cold dishes run the gamut from stuffed eggs, potato salad, and bean salad to seafood cocktail, marinated mussels, and fish roe. *Tortilla de patatas,* a thick potato omelet cut into squares and served cold, is a classic. Fried foods are among the glories of tapa bars—batter-fried shrimp, golden croquettes, crisp eggplant.

Tapas de cocina may be served in *cazuelitas,* earthenware ramekins. They include meatballs, notably in an almond-saffron sauce; tripe stew; chicken sautéed with garlic; kidneys in Sherry sauce. Almost any dish—beef stew to braised partridge—can be and is served in tapa-size portions. Some are cooked to order on a *plancha,* griddle.

Tapas are not necessarily finger food, as some stews and sauced foods may require a spoon or fork. Bread accompanies tapas, a must for mopping up delicious sauces. A tapa is a small individual portion; a *ración* is a larger portion suitable for sharing.

Tapas have their pace, which is leisurely. Spaniards can put away quite a lot of food while just standing at the bar, sipping wine, and having an animated conversation with friends.

La Mancha and its wines are deeply embedded in Madrid's tapa culture. By the nineteenth century, Valdepeñas had become the wine of choice for the taverns of Madrid, supplied by muleteers who hauled it to the capital in wineskins. With the coming of the railroad in 1861, a daily "wine train" delivered carloads of wine to the capital. To this day, Madrid *tascas* feature wines and foods of La Mancha.

MANCHEGO CHEESE *and* POTATO CROQUETTES

Croquetas de Queso

Pass a tray of these cheesy croquettes at your next wine party. They are sure to be a hit. The recipe is adapted from a book about Manchego cheese, *La Mancha y el Queso Manchego*, published by the department of agriculture of Castilla–La Mancha. For authenticity's sake and flavor too, use true Manchego. However, a sharp Cheddar could be substituted.

Cooking the potatoes unpeeled prevents them from absorbing a lot of cooking water. They will be almost as flaky as a baked potato.

MAKES FIFTY 1½-INCH CROQUETTES

1½ pounds baking potatoes (3 medium)	½ teaspoon salt
1 tablespoon olive oil, plus about 4 cups for deep-frying	Pinch of dried thyme
	Pinch of hot pimentón or cayenne
6 ounces Manchego, grated (about 2½ cups)	4 eggs
1 tablespoon minced scallion	1 teaspoon wine vinegar
¼ cup finely chopped fresh flat-leaf parsley	1 cup fine dry bread crumbs

Cook the unpeeled potatoes in boiling water until tender, about 30 minutes. Drain thoroughly. Split them in half and scoop the flesh into a bowl, discarding the skins. Add 1 tablespoon oil and mash the potatoes with a fork or potato masher until fairly smooth.

Stir the cheese into the potatoes. Add the scallion, parsley, salt, thyme, and hot pimentón.

Separate 2 eggs. Place the whites in a clean bowl. Stir the yolks into the potato mixture.

At high speed, beat the whites until stiff. Beat in the vinegar.

Fold half of the egg whites into the potato mixture until thoroughly combined. Fold in the remaining whites.

Beat the remaining 2 eggs in a shallow bowl. Spread the bread crumbs on a tray.

Use a teaspoon to scoop up a mound of potato-cheese. Drop it into the beaten egg and roll it to coat all sides. Lift it out with the spoon and a fork, allowing excess egg to drain off. Place the croquette in the crumbs. Continue shaping croquettes until the tray is filled. Spoon some of the crumbs over the croquettes and, using a fork, roll them to coat all sides.

Lift the croquettes out of the crumbs, patting very gently to shape each into a ball. Place them on another tray as they are shaped.

Place enough oil in a deep skillet to reach a depth of ¾ inch. Heat the oil until it is shimmering but not smoking (360°F). Fry the croquettes in 4 or 5 batches, turning them once, until they are golden brown, 1½ to 2 minutes. Skim out and drain briefly on paper towels. Serve hot.

NOTE: *Croquettes can be fried up to 4 hours in advance and kept at room temperature. Place them on a baking sheet and reheat them in a preheated 400°F oven until hot, 10 minutes. Fried croquettes can be frozen for up to 1 month. Remove them from the freezer 15 minutes before heating. Place on a baking sheet and bake in a preheated 375°F oven for 15 minutes.*

"DOUBLE" EGGS

Huevos Dobles

Double eggs, because there are eggs on the inside and eggs on the outside. These are fun, though time-consuming, to prepare. The coating is thicker and crisper if the eggs are dipped twice in flour, egg, and crumbs.

Serve each person one egg. Tomato sauce makes a good accompaniment.

The recipe makes more stuffing mixture than needed for the 6 egg whites. Any leftovers make a fine sandwich spread.

SERVES 6 AS A STARTER

6 hard-cooked eggs

1 tablespoon olive oil, plus about 2 cups for frying

¼ cup finely chopped onion

¼ cup minced serrano or cooked ham

¾ teaspoon salt

Pinch of caraway seeds

½ teaspoon Dijon mustard

Pinch of hot pimentón or cayenne

1 tablespoon plus 1½ cups milk

2 tablespoons butter

5 tablespoons flour, plus ½ cup for dredging

1 to 2 eggs

1 cup fine dry bread crumbs

Tomato sauce, homemade (page 26) or canned, for serving (optional)

Peel the eggs and pat them dry. Cut each in half lengthwise. Transfer the yolks to a small bowl.

Heat 1 tablespoon oil in a small skillet. Sauté the onion and ham over medium heat until the onion is softened, 5 minutes. Scrape the mixture into the bowl with the yolks. Add ¼ teaspoon of the salt, the caraway seeds, mustard, pimentón, and 1 tablespoon of the milk. Mash the yolks until smooth. Press the yolk mixture into the hollows of the egg whites.

Cover a tray with a layer of plastic wrap. Place the egg halves, stuffed side down, 2 inches apart in a single layer. Refrigerate.

Melt the butter in a saucepan. Stir in 5 tablespoons flour and stir until smooth over low heat. Remove the pan from the heat and stir in the remaining 1½ cups milk very gradually, until the mixture is smooth. Return to medium heat. Cook, stirring, until the sauce is thick and smooth, 5 minutes.

Spoon the hot sauce over the egg halves, napping them smoothly with the sauce. Refrigerate the eggs until the coating is chilled and solidified, at least 3 and up to 24 hours.

Roll one egg half over, stuffing side up. Pick up another egg and place it on top, so the stuffing is enclosed. Repeat with the remaining eggs. Return the tray to the refrigerator.

Place flour for dredging in a shallow pan. Beat 1 or 2 eggs in a shallow dish. Place half the bread crumbs in another shallow pan.

Dredge each egg in flour. Pat off the excess and gently press the 2 halves together. Roll the eggs in beaten egg. Place them in the tray of bread crumbs. Sprinkle the remaining half of the crumbs over the eggs. Roll or pat the eggs so they are completely covered with crumbs. Allow to dry on a tray for 15 minutes.

If desired, repeat the breading, dredging the eggs first in flour, then eggs, then in crumbs.

Heat oil to a depth of ¾ inch in a deep skillet until shimmering but not smoking (360°F). Fry the eggs, turning to brown all sides, 4 to 5 minutes. Remove with a slotted spoon and drain on paper towels. Serve hot or warm, accompanied by tomato sauce if desired.

NOTE: *The eggs can be stuffed and fried up to 24 hours in advance and refrigerated. Bring them to room temperature while you preheat the oven to 400°F. Place in an oven pan and heat in the oven for 8 to 10 minutes.*

TOMATO SAUCE *Salsa de Tomate Frito*

This is a basic smooth tomato sauce that can be served as an accompaniment to cooked foods, such as the Double Eggs in the previous recipe, or as a cooking medium for foods such as Piquant Cocktail Meatballs (page 31). You can vary the flavor of the sauce by adding other herbs or by using smoked pimentón.

Makes 1½ cups

  2 cups drained canned plum tomatoes
  2 tablespoons olive oil
  1 cup chopped onion
  2 garlic cloves, chopped
  ¼ cup chopped fresh flat-leaf parsley
  1 teaspoon sweet pimentón
  Pinch of ground cumin
  1 bay leaf
  Salt and freshly ground black pepper

Cut out the stem end of the tomatoes and break the tomatoes up slightly.

Heat oil in a saucepan and sauté the onion and garlic over medium heat until the onion begins to turn golden, 5 minutes. Add the parsley and pimentón and stir for 30 seconds. Add the tomatoes, cumin, bay leaf, and salt and pepper to taste.

Bring to a boil, cover, and simmer until the tomatoes are thickened, 25 minutes.

Puree the sauce in a blender. If desired, strain sauce to remove any remaining seeds.

Serve the sauce hot or at room temperature.

SALT COD *and* ROASTED PEPPER TOASTS

Tiznao

Tiznao means "blackened," for the cod and vegetables are charred over hot coals or under the broiler. Roasting gives the peppers a bittersweet edge that contrasts nicely with the salty cod. In this recipe, the salt cod is soaked after grilling, not before. If salt cod does not appeal to you, try this recipe using water-packed canned tuna, well drained, in its place. In La Mancha, tiznao is usually served as a starter in small *cazuelitas,* individual earthenware ramekins, with plenty of bread on the side. It makes a fine appetizer, heaped on toasted slices of baguette.

꿎 MAKES **18** TOASTS, ENOUGH TO SERVE **6** AS A STARTER

¾ pound salt cod, to make 1 to 1½ cups flaked cod, or drained water-packed canned tuna

2 medium onions

2 red bell peppers

3 large tomatoes

1 head of garlic

3 tablespoons extra virgin olive oil

2 teaspoons sweet pimentón

Hot red pepper flakes

Freshly ground black pepper

¼ teaspoon ground cumin

Salt

18 baguette slices, toasted, for serving

¼ cup black olives, pitted

Preheat the broiler.

Place the cod on a sheet of heavy-duty foil. Roll up the edges to make a rim. Place on a broiler rack and broil about 4 inches from the heat until the surface is lightly toasted, 10 minutes. Turn the piece of cod (drain off and discard any liquid that accumulates in the foil packet) and broil until toasted, about 10 minutes. Remove the cod from the oven, discarding the foil, and place it in a bowl. Add water to cover and soak for at least 1 and up to 4 hours, changing the water twice.

Place the onions, peppers, tomatoes, and garlic on the broiler rack and toast them under the broiler, about 4 inches from the heat, turning occasionally, until the tomato skins are split, the peppers and onions charred. The tomatoes will take 8 to 10 minutes, the onions, garlic, and peppers 20 to 25 minutes.

As they are roasted, transfer the vegetables to a pan and cover with a lid. When cool enough to handle, peel the tomatoes, discarding seeds. Chop coarsely.

Peel the peppers, discarding the seeds and stem. Cut the peppers into thin strips.

Peel the onions, cut them into quarters, and then sliver them. Slit open the garlic cloves and unwrap the softened garlic cloves. Cut them lengthwise into quarters.

Drain the soaked cod. With your fingers, separate it into flakes or crumbs, discarding all skin and bones.

Heat the oil in a skillet or cazuela. Add the tomatoes and cook over high heat for 5 minutes, until they have sweated out most of their liquid. Add the peppers and cook for 2 minutes. Then add the onions and garlic and season with pimentón, red and black pepper to taste, and cumin. Reduce the heat to low and cook, covered, for 15 minutes. Stir in the cod flakes. Remove from the heat and let stand, covered, for at least 30 minutes or up to 2 hours. Add salt to taste.

Serve the tiznao heaped on toasted baguette slices or on individual plates, accompanied by toast. Scatter olives on top.

GARLICKY SALT COD DIP

Atascaburras

Atascaburras means "to choke a donkey." This cod and potato puree should be that thick. Serve it as an appetizer dip or in individual ramekins as a starter, accompanied by toast or bread sticks. Start this at least a day before serving, to allow the salt cod to soak for 24 hours.

SERVES 4 TO 6

½ pound salt cod

1¼ pounds baking potatoes, peeled and quartered (about 3)

4 garlic cloves, peeled

¼ cup plus 1 tablespoon extra virgin olive oil

¼ cup walnut halves

1 hard-cooked egg, sliced

Toast Crisps (page 30) or bread sticks for serving

Rinse the pieces of cod to remove excess salt. Cover with water and soak for 24 hours, changing the water 3 times. Drain and rinse the cod.

Put the potatoes in a pot with water to cover. Bring to a boil, then reduce the heat to simmer. Add the cod and cook, covered, very gently until the potatoes are tender, about 20 minutes. Drain, saving 1 cup of the cooking liquid.

Crush the garlic in a large mortar or bowl. Gradually add the cooked potatoes, mashing them to a smooth paste. Beat in ¼ cup oil and enough of the reserved liquid to make a stiff puree, about ½ cup.

With your fingers, flake the cod, discarding all skin and bones. Stir the flaked cod into the potato puree.

Spread the puree in a shallow bowl or in individual ramekins, smoothing the top. Drizzle the remaining tablespoon of oil over the puree. Garnish with walnuts and sliced egg. Serve with Toast Crisps or bread sticks.

❧ TOAST CRISPS *Tostaditas Crujientes*

Slice the bread very thinly, so it crisps in the oven. The crisps keep for several days in an airtight container. They are also good served with soup or pâté.

❧ Makes 24 small toasts

Twenty-four ¼-inch baguette slices
½ garlic clove
1 tablespoon extra virgin olive oil

Preheat the oven to 375°F.

Trim off the bread crusts if desired, then place the slices on a baking sheet.

Cut a crosshatch on the cut side of the garlic clove. Scrub the cut garlic on one side of each bread slice. Brush the slices with oil.

Bake until the bread is golden and crisp, about 8 minutes.

PIQUANT COCKTAIL MEATBALLS

Pinchos de Albondiguillas

You can make these versatile meatballs with ground pork, veal, turkey, chicken, lamb, or beef. Quickly fried (a light flouring prevents them from splattering while frying), they can be served piping hot or at room temperature. These are nicely spiced and accented with piquillo peppers, so they require no dipping sauce. Piquillo peppers are tiny sweet red peppers with just a hint of piquancy. They are grown in northern Spain, roasted, and canned, providing a handy flavor boost. If you can't find piquillos (see the back of the book for sources), use any roasted pimiento. The meatballs also may be simmered in Tomato Sauce (page 26) and served with pasta or rice as a main dish.

MAKES **60** BITE-SIZED MEATBALLS, ENOUGH TO SERVE **20** AS A TAPA

2 pounds ground pork butt

2½ teaspoons minced garlic

½ cup minced onion

½ cup chopped fresh flat-leaf parsley

2 teaspoons salt

¼ teaspoon cayenne

1 teaspoon sweet smoked pimentón

1 teaspoon sweet pimentón

½ teaspoon ground cumin

¼ teaspoon dried thyme

½ teaspoon dried oregano

¼ teaspoon freshly ground black pepper

Grating of fresh nutmeg

1 tablespoon wine vinegar

About ¼ cup all-purpose flour for dredging

About ½ cup olive oil for frying

10 piquillo peppers, from a 7.6-ounce jar, drained and patted dry

Place the pork in a bowl. Add the garlic, onion, and parsley.

In a small bowl, combine the salt, cayenne, smoked pimentón, sweet pimentón, cumin, thyme, oregano, pepper, and nutmeg. Add the vinegar and stir to make a smooth paste. Sprinkle the spice mixture into the meat. Knead the meat with your hands to distribute the seasonings evenly.

Allow the meat to stand at room temperature for 1 hour or cover and refrigerate it for up to 24 hours.

Form the mixture into 1-inch balls. Dredge the meatballs in flour, patting off the excess.

Heat enough oil to cover the bottom of a large heavy skillet. Fry the meatballs over medium heat in 2 batches, turning to brown them on all sides, until browned and cooked through, about 5 minutes. Transfer the meatballs to paper towels to drain.

Cut each piquillo pepper into 6 strips. Fold a strip into thirds, spear it with a toothpick, and skewer a meatball. Place on a serving platter and serve hot or at room temperature.

NOTE: *The meatballs can be prepared up to 4 hours in advance and reheated on a pan in a 375°F oven for 8 minutes.*

PARTRIDGE and CHICKEN PÂTÉ

Paté de Perdiz y Pollo

The partridge pâté served in La Mancha restaurants is a smooth, creamy version. No partridge? No problem. Make this pâté with all chicken or substitute quail, veal, or pork. Use both white and dark chicken in the mix. And if truffles aren't available or within your budget, simply eliminate them from the recipe. Fresh pork belly, which is uncured bacon, keeps the pâté juicy.

Serve slices of the pâté at room temperature on salad greens accompanied by Scarlet-Pickled Onions (page 282) and toasts. A fine reserva red Tempranillo wine from La Mancha is the appropriate accompaniment.

SERVES 16 TO 20

1 pound boned partridge

1 pound boneless, skinless white and dark chicken

½ pound fresh pork belly

2 eggs, separated

½ cup milk

¼ cup brandy

¼ cup dry or medium Sherry (fino or amontillado)

1 tablespoon salt

½ pound chicken livers

1 teaspoon freshly ground black pepper

½ teaspoon dried thyme

¼ cup finely chopped fresh flat-leaf parsley

½ cup grated onion

½ ounce black truffles, chopped (optional)

8 slices bacon

Cut the partridge, chicken, and pork belly into cubes. Puree the meat in 2 batches in a processor or blender, adding 1 egg yolk and ¼ cup milk to each batch.

Combine the paste with the brandy, Sherry, and salt in a bowl. Chop the chicken livers in the processor or blender and mix thoroughly into the paste. Season with pepper, thyme, parsley, and onion. Refrigerate the mixture, covered, for at least 1 and up to 8 hours.

Preheat the oven to 350°F.

Beat the egg whites until stiff. Stir a third of the whites into the partridge paste. Fold in the remaining whites.

Place half the mixture in a 6-cup loaf pan (or in two 3-cup terrine molds). Scatter the chopped truffle on top, if you're using it. Spread the remaining pâté mixture over. Top with bacon slices. Place the mold in a pan and add boiling water to come halfway up the sides of the mold. Cover the top with foil. Bake until the pâté is set (internal temperature of 180°F), about 1 hour (50 minutes for the smaller terrines).

Allow the pâté to cool, then refrigerate. Unmold the pâté, draining off excess liquid, and slice to serve. The pâté keeps, refrigerated, for up to 2 weeks.

LIVER and GAME PÂTÉ, CUENCA STYLE

Morteruelo de Cuenca

This country pâté, somewhat like rillettes, is made with pork liver, partridge, hare, and chicken and spiced with an exotic combination of cinnamon and caraway. In the province of Cuenca, outdoorsmen—lumberjacks and shepherds—wrap the potted pâté in straw and bury it in a snowdrift to keep during the winter.

Partridge and hare give the pâté a deep color and flavor, but the dish is just as delicious made with chicken.

I prefer to cook the pork liver separately, so it doesn't overwhelm the flavors of the chicken and game. Don't like liver? Leave it out and increase the amount of chicken.

The pâté is tastiest when piping hot. It can be served in individual ramekins as a starter, with toasted bread crusts as dippers; as a sandwich filling; as hash, alongside fried eggs; or as an appetizer, spread on toasts and broiled with a topping of pine nuts or chopped walnuts.

✺ MAKES 24 TOASTS, ENOUGH TO SERVE 24 AS AN APPETIZER OR 6 AS A STARTER

¾ pound pork liver

3 teaspoons salt

1 pound boneless chicken legs, hare, partridge, or rabbit

½ pound fresh pork belly (uncured pancetta)

1 small onion

4 cloves

1 celery stalk

1 bay leaf

4 country bread slices, crusts removed, toasted

1 teaspoon sweet pimentón

¼ teaspoon ground cinnamon

1 teaspoon coarsely ground black pepper

½ teaspoon caraway seeds

Pinch of ground cloves

½ teaspoon dried oregano

2 garlic cloves, crushed

¼ cup pine nuts or coarsely chopped walnuts

2 teaspoons olive oil

24 baguette slices, toasted

Fresh parsley leaves for garnish

Put the pork liver in a pan and cover with salted water. Soak for 1 hour and drain. Bring the liver to a boil in fresh water to cover and simmer for 10 minutes. Drain. Cover with fresh water and 1 teaspoon of the salt. Bring to a boil and simmer until the liver is very tender, about 30 minutes. Allow the liver to cool in the cooking liquid.

Place the chicken in a pan with the pork belly. Cover with 2 quarts water. Add the onion stuck with the cloves, celery, remaining 2 teaspoons of salt, and bay leaf. Bring the water to a boil and cook the chicken and pork belly until very tender, 2 hours. Drain, saving all the liquid.

When the meat is cool enough to handle, strip off any skin, bone, and rind and discard. Chop or shred the meat and reserve.

Drain the cooked liver and chop it finely. Combine the liver with all the meat in a large bowl (making about 4 cups).

Break the toasted country bread into pieces and grind it coarsely in a food processor (making 1½ cups). Stir the bread crumbs into the chopped meat.

Combine the pimentón, cinnamon, black pepper, caraway, ground cloves, oregano, and garlic in a small bowl. Stir in ½ cup of the reserved broth. Stir the spice mixture into the meat and bread crumbs. Add 2½ cups more of the reserved broth to the meat mixture.

Place the mixture in a large nonstick skillet over medium heat. When the mixture begins to bubble, reduce the heat and cook, stirring frequently, until it is very thick, 30 minutes. The pâté can be cooled and kept, covered and refrigerated, for up to 1 week.

To serve, lightly brown the pine nuts in the olive oil in a small skillet over medium heat, about 2 minutes.

Preheat the broiler.

Spread a heaping tablespoon of pâté on each of the baguette toasts. Sprinkle with ½ teaspoon toasted pine nuts, pressing them into the pâté. Place the toasts on a broiler pan and broil until hot and lightly browned, 2 to 3 minutes. Garnish each toast with a parsley leaf.

BEAN SALAD *with* CHORIZO

Ensalada de Alubias con Taquillos de Chorizo

La Mancha is a land of legumes. Beans, chickpeas, and lentils are grown here and not just for an occasional soup. They are favored fare in everyday meals, all year-round. When there are leftover cooked beans, they go into a tasty salad such as this. In Spain, this salad would be served as a first course, but it makes a good side with summer barbecue.

SERVES 6 TO 8 AS A STARTER OR SIDE DISH

1 pound dried pinto or red kidney beans, soaked overnight

1 bay leaf

Salt

½ cup chopped fresh flat-leaf parsley

½ teaspoon dried oregano

⅛ teaspoon cumin seeds

½ cup chopped onion

¼ cup chopped red bell pepper

1 cup Spanish hard chorizo or salami in ¼-inch dice (¼ pound)

¼ cup olive oil

¼ cup wine vinegar

Freshly ground black pepper

¼ cup Spanish empeltre or other black olives

2 hard-cooked eggs, quartered

Sliced radishes and lettuce leaves for garnish

Drain the beans and put them in a pot with water to cover, the bay leaf, and 1 teaspoon salt. Bring to a boil, skim, then reduce the heat and simmer, covered, until the beans are tender, 1 to 2 hours. Drain the beans and place in a bowl.

Add the parsley, oregano, cumin seeds, onion, bell pepper, chorizo, oil, and vinegar. Add salt and pepper to taste and combine well. Cover and refrigerate for at least 2 and up to 24 hours.

Remove the beans from the refrigerate and let stand at room temperature for 30 minutes. Transfer the beans to a platter and garnish with olives, quartered eggs, radishes, and the lettuce leaves tucked around the beans.

BEEF and HAM SALAD

Salpicón de Carne

Salpicón—essentially leftovers from the midday *olla*, the great stewpot—is what Don Quixote ate for supper most nights. Salpicón (*sal* = salt, *picar* = to chop) is a cold hash made by chopping together the leftover meat and vegetables from the pot and dressing them with salt, olive oil, and vinegar. In this rendition, I've stuck close to sixteenth-century foodways—no tomatoes, peppers, or potatoes. However, in present-day Madrid tapa bars, a dish also called salpicón is made with chopped tomatoes, green peppers, and shellfish.

You may use boiled beef from the olla, leftover pot roast, or roast beef from the deli for this recipe. It can be heaped on greens on individual salad plates, or, if you like a molded effect, fill a 3-inch cylinder (such as a biscuit cutter) with a quarter of the salad mixture, press it down firmly, then press it out of the mold onto a plate. Repeat with the remaining three servings. You can also serve the mixture hot—stir the beef and ham into the sautéed onions, heat thoroughly—and call it hash.

SERVES 4

1½ cups chopped or shredded cooked beef	½ teaspoon freshly ground black pepper
1 cup diced cooked ham	½ teaspoon dried oregano
1 cup diced cooked carrot	¼ cup wine vinegar
½ cup chopped fresh flat-leaf parsley	¼ cup mayonnaise
3 tablespoons olive oil	1 teaspoon Dijon mustard
1 cup chopped onion	1 tablespoon extra virgin olive oil
⅓ cup chopped celery	1 tablespoon drained capers
1 garlic clove, chopped	1 hard-cooked egg, chopped
1 teaspoon salt	Lettuce or other greens for serving

Combine the beef, ham, carrot, and parsley in a bowl.

Heat the olive oil in a skillet over medium heat and sauté the onion, celery, and garlic until softened, about 5 minutes. Add to the beef along with the salt, pepper, oregano, and 3 tablespoons of the vinegar. Cover and marinate at room temperature for 1 hour or in the refrigerator for up to 4 hours.

While the beef mixture marinates, prepare the sauce. Whisk the mayonnaise until smooth. Stir in the mustard, extra virgin olive oil, and remaining tablespoon of vinegar.

Right before serving, fold the capers and chopped egg into the beef salad. Arrange the salad on lettuce or other greens. Serve with the sauce spooned over the salad.

TOMATO-TUNA SALAD

Pipirrana

I visited the town of Alcázar de San Juan (province of Ciudad Real), famous for wine and cheese, in early September when it was celebrating a local fiesta. At midday groups of friends gathered in the huge central plaza, in the shade of the town hall, where they set up folding tables to prepare this *pipirrana*. Each group had an enormous earthenware bowl in which were combined tomatoes, onions, hard-cooked eggs, tuna, olives, and olive oil to make a soupy salad. Invited to partake, I was instructed to scoop it up on chunks of bread. Those with country know-how speared the bread on the tip of a pocketknife and dipped it into the pipirrana.

Pipirrana—also known as *moje*, dunk, because it's soaked up with bread—traditionally was made with fresh or home-canned tomatoes. Now folks use canned tomatoes from the grocery store, which are surprisingly good with the addition of tuna and fine olive oil. Choose a quality brand of tomatoes.

SERVES 6

---

4 cups drained canned tomatoes (save the juice for another use)

1 cup finely chopped onion

4 hard-cooked eggs, chopped

1 cup drained canned tuna in olive oil in chunks

1 cup sliced pitted green and/or black olives

1½ teaspoons salt

Up to ⅓ cup extra virgin olive oil

Lettuce leaves for serving (optional)

Chopped fresh basil or dried oregano for garnish (optional)

Bread for serving

Core the tomatoes and cut them into pieces. Place them in a large bowl and add the onion, eggs, tuna, olives, and salt. Combine the oil drained from the tuna with additional extra virgin olive oil to make ⅓ cup. Add to the salad and combine gently. Let the salad stand at room temperature for 30 minutes before serving.

Line shallow bowls or ramekins with lettuce if desired. Spoon the salad mixture into the bowls. Garnish with chopped basil or a pinch of oregano, if desired. Serve with bread for dipping into the juicy salad.

LEMON SALAD *with* SHRIMP

Ensalada de Limones con Gambas

In Alcázar de San Juan, a town right in the middle of La Mancha, this is served as a lunchtime dish on fiesta days. In Alcázar and elsewhere in La Mancha, where it is also called *moje,* it's served in a big bowl with lots of bread for dipping into the tangy juices—as is the preceding recipe. The traditional lemon salad does not contain shrimp—that was my idea. It makes a surprisingly good shrimp "cocktail." Some chopped avocado is a good addition, too.

SERVES 4

3 medium lemons

½ cup chopped scallion

½ cup pitted black olives, halved lengthwise

¼ teaspoon salt

3 hard-cooked eggs, chopped

2 tablespoons extra virgin olive oil

¼ pound peeled small shrimp

Lettuce or other salad greens for serving

Chopped fresh cilantro for garnish

Slice off both ends of the lemons. Set a lemon on end on a cutting board. With a sharp knife, slice down, removing both peel and pith in one cut. Turn the lemon and continue peeling it in this manner. Slice the lemon crosswise and discard any seeds. Chop the lemon. Repeat with the remaining 2 lemons. Put the chopped lemon in a bowl.

Add the scallion, olives, salt, and eggs to the lemon. Stir in the oil. Let the salad stand for 1 hour.

Cook the shrimp in boiling salted water for 2 minutes. Drain and rinse in cold water.

Line salad plates with lettuce leaves or other greens. Spoon the lemon mixture on top. Scatter the shrimp over the lemon. Garnish with cilantro and serve.

SHEEPSHEARERS' RICE SALAD with HAM and CHEESE

Ensalada de Esquileo

This recipe is adapted from *Guisos, Viandas y Otras Pócimas* by Joaquín Racionero Page. Although he doesn't say why the salad is the sheepshearer special, I suspect it's because the rice and its accoutrements could be prepared in advance and packed in a pouch to be carried to the country where the shearers worked. According to Pedro Condés, administrator for the Manchego Cheese Board, the sheep still have to be sheared every year, although the wool is worth nothing.

SERVES 6 AS A STARTER OR 4 AS A MAIN COURSE

2 cups cooked Spanish round-grain rice

½ cup diced cooked ham

½ cup cooked peas

¼ cup diced cooked carrot

½ cup diced Manchego

¼ cup diced flame-roasted red pepper, preferably piquillo

½ cup chopped scallion

½ cup diced peeled fresh tomato

¼ cup sliced green olives

¼ teaspoon whole-grain mustard

¼ teaspoon dried oregano

2 tablespoons wine vinegar

Salt and freshly ground black pepper

3 tablespoons extra virgin olive oil

Salad greens for serving

Combine the rice in a mixing bowl with the ham, peas, carrot, cheese, red pepper, scallion, tomato, and olives.

Mix the mustard, oregano, vinegar, ½ teaspoon salt, and pepper to taste together in a small bowl. Whisk in the oil until dressing is emulsified. Stir into the rice salad and mix well. Let stand at room temperature for at least 15 minutes or up to 2 hours.

Serve the rice salad heaped on salad greens.

SALAD OF PICKLED PARTRIDGE *or* CHICKEN

Ensalada con Escabeche

Partridge in spiced escabeche is one of La Mancha's emblematic dishes. If you find pickled partridge at gourmet shops, serve it in this delectable salad. The salad is almost as good made with Chicken Wings in Escabeche. Strip the meat from the bones, discarding most of the skin too. You'll need the meat from about 8 wings (16 wing pieces) to serve 4. Use some of the carrots from the marinade in the salad too. The salad can be garnished with pickled mushrooms and onions. Or omit the pickles and scatter pomegranate seeds over the salad.

SERVES 4

4 cups mixed salad greens

3 cups boned pickled partridge or Chicken Wings in Escabeche (page 170) plus pickling liquid

8 hard-cooked quail eggs, halved, or 4 hard-cooked eggs, quartered

Cherry tomatoes or sliced plum tomatoes

¼ teaspoon dried oregano

2 tablespoons chopped scallion

Pickled Mushrooms, (page 281; optional)

Scarlet-Pickled Onions, (page 282; optional)

Olives or capers

1 tablespoon plus 1 teaspoon extra virgin olive oil

Chopped fresh flat-leaf parsley

Divide the salad greens among 4 salad plates. Top with the boned partridge or chicken. If there are carrot pieces in the escabeche, scatter them around the partridge or chicken.

Garnish the partridge with hard-cooked eggs, tomatoes, oregano, scallion, pickled mushrooms and onions, if you're using them, and olives or capers.

If the escabeche liquid is jellied, heat it briefly in a microwave or a saucepan to liquefy. Drizzle 2 teaspoons of the pickling liquid over each salad. Drizzle 1 teaspoon oil over each. Garnish with chopped parsley.

TOMATOES STUFFED *with* POTATO-CAPER SALAD

Tomates Rellenos con Ensaladilla Rusa

Ensaladilla rusa—"Russian" salad—is a classic in Madrid tapa bars. Besides potatoes and carrots, it usually contains peas. In this version, tangy capers replace the peas and boost the flavor. This recipe makes only enough potato-caper salad to stuff the tomatoes. You can quadruple the quantities to make a fine luncheon salad.

Chilling the potato for several hours makes it easy to dice.

SERVES 4

1 medium baking potato (½ pound)

1 carrot, peeled

Salt

1 tablespoon white wine vinegar

4 medium tomatoes (1½ pounds)

¼ cup diced red or green bell pepper

1 tablespoon chopped scallion

1 tablespoon chopped fresh parsley

1 heaping tablespoon drained capers

¼ cup mayonnaise

2 tablespoons extra virgin olive oil

Pinch of hot smoked pimentón (optional)

Lettuce leaves for serving

Cook the potato and carrot in boiling water until they are fork-tender, about 15 minutes for the carrot, 25 minutes for the potato. Drain and chill them for 4 hours.

Peel the potato. Cut the potato and carrot into ⅜-inch dice. Place in a bowl and sprinkle with ½ teaspoon salt and the vinegar.

Cut the tops off the tomatoes and scoop out the seeds and pulp, leaving tomato shells. Salt them and leave upside down to drain.

Add the bell pepper, scallion, parsley, and capers to the potato and carrot. In a small bowl, whisk the mayonnaise until smooth. Then whisk in the olive oil, little by little, until the mayonnaise is smooth and glossy. Stir the mayonnaise into the potato salad.

Fill the tomato shells with the salad. Sprinkle with pimentón if desired. Serve the tomatoes on lettuce leaves.

MANCHEGAN SALAD *with* CHEESE

Ensalada a la Manchega

Fresh salads are extremely popular in Castilla–La Mancha. Simple ones may serve as a side dish with a meat entree, in place of cooked vegetables. This salad is usually presented as a starter, placed in the center of the table. Someone does the honors of liberally anointing the salad with good olive oil and wine vinegar, a sprinkle of salt, and it's ready to enjoy. At a family meal, everyone helps himself directly from the platter.

SERVES 4

1 garlic clove, crushed

½ teaspoon salt

1 teaspoon Dijon mustard

⅓ cup chopped scallion

3 tablespoons wine vinegar

5 tablespoons extra virgin olive oil

2 tablespoons chopped fresh parsley

6 cups torn leaf lettuce, escarole, or mixed salad greens

1 large tomato, cut into wedges

1 cup peeled and diced cucumber

¼ pound Manchego, cut into ½-inch dice

1 hard-cooked egg, quartered

½ cup drained canned tuna

12 black or green olives

4 canned white asparagus spears (optional)

Combine the garlic, salt, mustard, scallion, and vinegar in a small bowl and whisk to combine. Whisk in the oil until the dressing is emulsified. Stir in the parsley.

Spread the lettuce on a large platter. Place tomato wedges around the edges. Scatter the cucumber and cheese over the top. Put the egg wedges on top. Scatter the tuna and olives over. Arrange the asparagus on the salad if you're using it.

Whisk the dressing again and drizzle it evenly over the salad. Serve immediately, without tossing.

GREEN BEAN SALAD with GRAPES and ANISE

Ensalada de Judías Verdes con Uvas

Fermented grape juice makes wine. Distilled wine makes *aguardiente*, a clear, strong alcoholic beverage usually flavored with aniseeds. In La Mancha it is customary to preserve fruits such as grapes and cherries in aguardiente, which becomes subtly infused with the fruit. In bars and restaurants you will see beautiful decanters and flasks of the liqueur with fruit. It is served in tiny glasses as a digestive. The fruit can be drained and served separately.

This salad, incorporating grapes in aguardiente, was inspired by a recipe in a little book, *La Cocina Tradicional en la Provincia de Toledo*, prepared by a chef at the national parador of Oropesa (Toledo). Paradors are a national network of hotels, often situated in monumental castles, monasteries, and ancestral palaces. The original recipe calls for serving the salad with sautéed scallops of venison. It's equally good with chicken breast or lamb.

Add the dressing to the beans immediately before serving so the vinegar doesn't leach the bright green from the beans.

SERVES 4

½ cup seedless red grapes, halved

2 tablespoons *aguardiente de anís* or anisette

1 pound green beans

⅓ cup thinly sliced celery

¼ cup thinly sliced scallion

1 hard-cooked egg

1 garlic clove, crushed

½ teaspoon Dijon mustard

1 tablespoon wine vinegar

2 tablespoons extra virgin olive oil

½ teaspoon salt

Red leaf lettuce for serving

Place the halved grapes in a small bowl and add the aguardiente or anisette. Allow to macerate for 2 hours. Drain the grapes and discard the aguardiente.

Cut off the tops and tails of the beans and either sliver them lengthwise or cut crosswise into 2-inch pieces. Cook the beans in boiling salted water until crisp-tender, 7 to 8 minutes. Drain and refresh in cold water. Drain.

Place the beans in a bowl and add the celery, scallion, and grapes.

Cut the egg in half. Transfer yolk to a small bowl. Dice the white into the bowl with the beans.

Mash the yolk with the garlic, mustard, vinegar, oil, and salt. Stir the dressing well. Immediately before serving, toss the dressing with the beans. Garnish a serving bowl with the lettuce or divide the salad among 4 individual serving dishes, garnishing each with a few lettuce leaves.

Tortillas,
Egg *and* Cheese Dishes,
Savory Pastries,
and Sandwiches

The story of Don Quixote's adventures is essentially the world's first road-trip novel. On the road with Rocinante. Zen and the art of windmill tilting. Travels with Sancho Panza.

After one of their early adventures together, Sancho (*panza* means "belly") proffers his humble repast of onion, cheese, and bread, slyly suggesting that it wouldn't suit the likes of a valiant knight like Don Quixote. Don Quixote, quite hungry by this point, declares that, though it's a point of honor with knights errant not to eat but once in a month, when they do eat, he declares, they take what's nearest to hand, except for the occasional sumptuous banquet, of course. So the two share the humble meal companionably.

Another time they sup with shepherds—Don Quixote seated on an upturned watering trough—on braised goat meat, cheese, and edible acorns.

When I was on the road in La Mancha, I frequently stopped at roadside ventas for a morning breakfast or midafternoon snack. To go with coffee I ordered tortilla, a thick potato omelet, or a plate of cheese accompanied by bread and olive oil. Simple pleasures, filling food.

The recipes in this chapter are especially suitable for light meals—brunch, lunch, supper, and snack. In Spain, egg dishes—and they range from the beloved tortilla, an omelet with potatoes, to vegetable-egg combos, casseroles, and timbales—are rarely served for breakfast. They are favored for tapas and snacks, light suppers, sometimes starters.

Manchego is Spain's best-known cheese—so famous that its name is illegally "borrowed" by cheeses made elsewhere. Cheese is principally enjoyed on its own, as a tapa with red wine or sandwiched in a crusty roll as a snack. However, in combination with eggs, cheese makes some delicious luncheon dishes, such as Baked Eggs with Cheese, Cheese Flans with Ham, and Chard and Cheese Pie.

Savory pastries, some of which overlap with egg and cheese dishes, also make appetizing lunch or supper dishes. Add a salad and the meal is complete.

You'll find here a basic recipe for Spanish bread, so delicious when freshly baked with good flour. Enjoy it fresh with meals and for sandwiches. Because it contains no fat and no preservatives, it doesn't stay fresh long. However, stale bread is a primary ingredient in Spanish cookery—toasted and drizzled with fine olive oil for a *tostada* (page 85), crumbled and fried with bacon bits as in *migas* (page 275), or soaked in broth to thicken garlic soup.

SPANISH POTATO TORTILLA

Tortilla de Patatas

Here is the classic all-time favorite Spanish egg dish, *tortilla de patatas*. A Spanish tortilla is in no way even remotely related to the Mexican flat corn or flour wrapper—except that both are round. In Spain, a tortilla is a round cake of eggs and other ingredients, a sort of omelet. But neither is a tortilla the same thing as a frittata. For one thing, it's never baked. And, to make a tortilla properly, you need a lot of olive oil to slowly, slowly poach the potatoes.

You will find tortilla served in chunks at just about every Madrid tapa bar, the perfect accompaniment to a glass of wine, but it's also good for breakfast, lunch, supper, or a picnic.

Use a well-seasoned omelet pan or lightweight nonstick skillet for the tortilla. A cast-iron pan will be too heavy for turning the tortilla.

Cook the potatoes in lots of olive oil and drain it off. Return only a spoonful of oil to the skillet to cook the tortilla and save the remainder for another use.

SERVES 4 FOR LUNCH, 20 AS A TAPA

½ cup olive oil

2 pounds baking potatoes (about 4 medium), peeled and chopped into 1-inch pieces

1 teaspoon salt

2 tablespoons chopped onion

6 eggs

Heat the oil in a 10-inch skillet over medium heat. Add the potatoes and turn them in the oil to coat them thoroughly. Reduce the heat to medium-low and cook the potatoes very slowly, stirring frequently, without browning, for 10 minutes. Sprinkle them with ½ teaspoon of the salt.

Add the onion and continue cooking, stirring frequently, until the potatoes are fork-tender, 20 minutes more.

Beat the eggs in a large bowl with the remaining ½ teaspoon salt.

When the potatoes are tender, place a plate over the skillet and tip the pan to drain excess oil into a small heatproof bowl.

Stir the potatoes into the beaten eggs.

Return a little of the reserved oil to the skillet and pour in the potato-egg mixture. Cook over medium heat until the omelet is set, about 5 minutes, adjusting the heat so the tortilla does not brown. Shake the skillet to keep the tortilla from sticking.

Place a flat lid or plate on top of the skillet. Hold it tightly and tip to drain out any excess oil into the heatproof bowl. Then invert the tortilla onto the plate.

Add a little reserved oil to the pan and slide the tortilla back in to cook on the other side, about 3 minutes more. Slide it out onto a serving dish and serve hot or at room temperature. For tapa servings, cut the tortilla into 2-inch squares, making 20 pieces. For lunch servings, cut it into wedges, serving 4.

TORTILLA *with* ARTICHOKES *and* HAM

Tortilla con Alcachofas

You would need to cut up dozens of fresh artichokes to have enough for this recipe. Frozen artichoke hearts make prepping easy. They acquire a great flavor from slow cooking in olive oil with ham.

SERVES 4 TO 6

¼ cup plus 1 tablespoon olive oil

1 cup chopped onion

2 garlic cloves, chopped

Three 9-ounce packages frozen artichoke hearts or bottoms, thawed (about 5 cups)

3 ounces serrano or cooked ham, chopped (about ½ cup)

1 teaspoon salt

Freshly ground black pepper

6 eggs

1 tablespoon chopped fresh parsley

Heat ¼ cup of the oil in a well-seasoned 10-inch omelet pan or nonstick skillet over medium heat. Sauté the onion and garlic until softened, 5 minutes.

If the artichoke hearts are whole, cut them into quarters or eighths or into roughly 2-inch pieces. Add them to the skillet and sauté for 10 minutes. Add the ham, ½ teaspoon of the salt, and pepper to taste. Cook, covered, for 8 to 10 minutes more, until the artichokes are very tender.

Beat the eggs in a large bowl with the remaining ½ teaspoon salt and the parsley. Add the cooked artichoke mixture to the eggs and stir well to combine.

Heat the remaining tablespoon of oil in the skillet and pour in the egg-artichoke mixture. Smooth the top, but do not stir. Cook over medium heat until the eggs are almost set, without allowing the bottom of the tortilla to brown too fast, about 8 minutes. Use a spatula to firm the sides of the tortilla as it cooks.

Remove the pan from the heat. Place a flat lid or plate on top of the tortilla. Holding it tightly, reverse the skillet and turn the tortilla out on the plate. Slip the edge of the spatula under it and edge it back into the pan, uncooked side down. Don't worry if a few pieces of artichoke escape. Cook until the bottom is set, 3 to 4 minutes longer.

Slide the tortilla out onto a clean serving plate. Serve hot or at room temperature, cut into 4 to 6 wedges.

CAPUCHIN TORTILLA *with* ASPARAGUS

Tortilla Capuchina

This tortilla is so much more delicious than the simple ingredients might suggest. Something crisp and green on the side is all you need for a fine lunch.

SERVES 4 TO 6

2 cups asparagus in 1-inch pieces (about 1 pound)

6 tablespoons olive oil

2 cups peeled, diced potatoes (about ¾ pound or 2 medium)

1½ teaspoons salt

½ cup chopped onion

¼ cup chopped bacon (optional)

1½ cups coarse fresh bread crumbs (from 3 to 4 slices of bread)

6 eggs

1 tablespoon chopped fresh parsley

Cook the asparagus in boiling water until just tender, about 4 minutes. Drain, refresh in cold water, and drain well. Set aside.

Heat 5 tablespoons of the oil in a nonstick 10-inch skillet. Add the potatoes and sprinkle with ½ teaspoon salt. Cook the potatoes over medium heat, turning them frequently, until almost cooked, 5 to 10 minutes, adjusting the heat so the potatoes do not brown.

Stir in the onion and bacon, if you're using it, and continue to sauté over medium heat for 5 minutes. Add the asparagus and bread crumbs and sauté for 3 minutes. Remove from the heat.

Beat the eggs, parsley, and remaining teaspoon of salt in a mixing bowl.

Stir the contents of the skillet into the beaten eggs. Wipe out the skillet so no bits are stuck to the surface. Add the remaining tablespoon of oil and heat. Pour the egg mixture into the skillet. Use a spatula to spread it evenly, but do not stir. Cook over medium heat until the tortilla is nearly set, about 3 minutes. Shake the skillet slightly to keep the tortilla from sticking on the bottom.

Working over a bowl to catch any possible drips, place a flat plate or pan lid on top of the tortilla. Hold it tightly and invert the skillet, turning the tortilla out onto the plate. Slide the tortilla back into the skillet, uncooked side down. Cook until set on the bottom, 2 minutes.

With a spatula, lift the edge of the tortilla while tipping the skillet and slide the tortilla out onto a serving dish. Serve hot or at room temperature, cut into 4 to 6 wedges.

CRACKLY FRIED EGGS

Huevos Estrellados

Spanish fried eggs are a very special category. The egg should emerge from immersion in hot olive oil with the white a little crackly around the edges—*estrellada*—and the yolk still unset. The procedure is more like poaching, only the medium is oil, not water. The eggs must be very fresh and at room temperature. Fry them one at a time. Fried eggs accompany *migas*, fried bread crumbs (page 275), and *pisto*, vegetable medley (page 245).

❧ SERVES 4

⅓ to ½ cup olive oil

4 eggs

2 garlic cloves, coarsely chopped

Salt and freshly ground black pepper

Place enough oil in an 8-inch skillet to measure ⅜ inch. Heat the oil over medium-high heat until it is shimmering, almost smoking.

Break one egg into a saucer or small cup. Slip it into the hot oil. Add a quarter of the chopped garlic. The egg white will bubble up around the yolk. Use a heatproof spoon or skimmer to spoon hot oil over the top of the egg. The edges of the egg white will turn brown and crackly. The egg will cook in less than 1 minute.

Skim the fried egg out of the oil. Continue frying the remaining eggs in the same oil, adding garlic to each egg. Sprinkle with salt and pepper.

EGG, POTATO, and GARLIC SCRAMBLE

Revuelto de Huevos y Patatas con Ajo

I first tasted this at an olive oil mill, where it was served as part of *desayuno molinero*, a typical olive miller's breakfast. It was called *huevos mal educados*—badly behaved eggs—because the eggs, instead of being perfectly fried disks, are broken up into the potatoes and fried with garlic.

In this recipe, whole unpeeled cloves of garlic cook with the potatoes and flavor the oil. You can choose whether or not to squeeze out and eat that nugget of flavor.

SERVES 4

2 pounds baking potatoes (about 4)

6 garlic cloves

⅓ cup olive oil

⅓ cup chopped spring onion or scallion

½ cup chopped green bell pepper

Pinch of hot red pepper flakes or cayenne

1 teaspoon salt

¼ teaspoon ground cumin

4 eggs

2 tablespoons chopped fresh parsley

Peel the potatoes. Cut them lengthwise into quarters, then slice them ¼ inch thick. Crush the garlic with the flat side of a knife. Slice off the root end, but do not peel them.

Heat the oil in a large nonstick skillet. Add the potatoes and garlic and sauté over medium-high heat for 5 minutes. Don't let the potatoes brown. Add the onion, green pepper, red pepper flakes, salt, and cumin. Sauté over high heat for 1 minute. Cover and lower the heat. Cook, stirring occasionally, until the potatoes are tender, about 10 minutes.

Push the potatoes to one side and break an egg into the pan. Move the potatoes again and add another egg. Likewise, add the remaining 2 eggs. Let the eggs cook over medium heat for 2 minutes, until the whites are set. Sprinkle with parsley.

With a wooden spatula, scoop up and turn the potatoes, breaking up the eggs. Make 4 or 5 turns. Remove the pan from the heat. Cover and allow the eggs to finish cooking in the heat from the potatoes, 2 minutes. Serve hot.

EGGS *with* FAVA BEANS

Revuelto con Habas

This egg and bean scramble is frequently made with canned favas, available at any time of year, but it's best with fresh fava beans in the spring.

Choose young, freshly picked favas. Cook them in boiling water, then drain and plunge into cold water. This keeps the outer skins tender. You will need almost 6 pounds of favas in their shells to get 4 cups shelled beans.

SERVES 4

4 cups shelled fava beans	½ cup bread in very small dice
2 tablespoons olive oil	½ cup grated tomato pulp (page 62)
⅓ cup diced bacon	½ teaspoon salt
½ cup chopped onion	Freshly ground black pepper
1 garlic clove, chopped	5 eggs

Cook the beans in boiling water to cover until tender, 15 minutes. Drain and cover them with cold water.

Heat the oil in a large skillet over medium heat. Sauté the bacon, onion, and garlic for 3 minutes. Add the diced bread and sauté for 2 minutes. Stir in the tomato pulp.

Drain the beans and add them to the skillet with the salt, pepper to taste, and ½ cup water. Cook, covered, for 10 minutes. Uncover the skillet and cook for 5 minutes more, leaving a little liquid with the beans.

Break the eggs into the skillet. Cook for 2 minutes, until the whites begin to set. Stir the whites to mix with the beans and cook for 2 minutes. One by one, stir the yolks into the beans. Cook just until they are softly scrambled, 2 minutes.

Serve hot.

SATURDAY EGGS *and* BACON

Duelos y Quebrantos

This tasty dish of eggs scrambled with bacon is what Don Quixote ate on Saturdays. Roughly translated, *duelos* means "toils and travails" or "grief" (a duelo is a wake preceding a funeral too), and *quebrantos* means "afflictions" or "cracked." The dish may have originated in the old custom in some places of La Mancha for shepherds to deliver to their masters any animals that died or were injured during the week. The meat was salted and dried to make sheep or goat jerky (*tasajo*), and the bones were cracked and cooked in the olla to make a Saturday stew thickened with eggs. Presumably, it was the master who had lost his stock who suffered the duelos—and ate them.

But some Cervantes scholars declare the addition of bacon or salt pork contrary to the custom of Cervantes' time, for Saturdays were days of semiabstinence, when fatty meat and salt pork were not allowed, but animal "parts" were permitted. A soup of offal—chicken feet, gizzards, lamb's brains, tripe—would be thickened with beaten eggs. From that is derived another interpretation of the dish as eggs with lamb's brains, often with the addition of bacon—a modest venial sin in exchange for a great deal of pleasure.

SERVES 4

3 tablespoons olive oil	6 eggs
¼ cup chopped onion	1 tablespoon chopped fresh parsley
½ cup diced bacon, pancetta, or fatty ham	Freshly ground black pepper
½ cup diced Spanish soft chorizo (1 link, 2½ ounces)	Triangles of bread fried in olive oil for serving (optional)

Heat the oil in a large skillet over medium heat. Add the chopped onion, bacon, and chorizo and fry for 4 minutes.

Beat the eggs with the parsley. Pour the eggs into the skillet and stir until softly set. Serve immediately with a little black pepper. Accompany the eggs with fried bread if desired.

GARLICKY ASPARAGUS *and* EGGS

Ajo de Espárragos

In Spain this vegetable dish with eggs probably would be presented as a first course or as the main dish for a light supper. It's also an ideal brunch dish. Serve it with toast "buttered" with extra virgin olive oil.

⁂ SERVES 4

4 cups chopped thin asparagus (about 1¾ pounds)

3 tablespoons olive oil

1 cup chopped onion

3 garlic cloves, chopped

1 bay leaf

½ cup chopped serrano ham (about 3 ounces)

2 teaspoons sweet pimentón

2 tablespoons all-purpose flour

1 teaspoon salt

Freshly ground black pepper

4 eggs

Pinch of hot smoked pimentón or cayenne

Cook the asparagus in boiling salted water until crisp-tender, about 3 minutes. Drain, saving the liquid.

Heat the oil in a skillet or cazuela over medium heat and sauté the onion, garlic, and bay leaf until the onion is softened, 3 minutes. Add the ham and asparagus and sauté for 3 minutes. Remove and discard the bay leaf.

Remove the pan from the heat and stir in the sweet pimentón and flour. Return the pan to medium heat and stir in 1⅓ cups of the reserved cooking liquid. Season with salt and pepper. Stir the asparagus and cook until the sauce thickens slightly, about 3 minutes.

Lower the heat so the sauce just simmers. Break the eggs on top of the asparagus. Sprinkle them with hot pimentón. Cover the skillet and poach the eggs until the whites are set but the yolks still runny, 4 to 5 minutes. Remove the pan from the heat and let stand, covered, until the eggs are set, 1 minute more. Serve in shallow soup plates.

Instant Tomato Puree

Over the years I've learned many tricks from Spanish cooks, such as this one for quickly preparing pureed tomatoes. Cut the tomatoes in half and grate them on the coarsest side of a box grater. Collect all the pulp and juices. Discard the flattened skin—which also serves as a shield for your knuckles! You will need about 1½ pounds tomatoes to make 2 cups of grated tomato pulp.

EGGS POACHED in TOMATO PUREE with CHEESE

Huevos Escalfados en Puré de Tomate con Queso

Not all cheese in La Mancha is Manchego with DO. Several excellent cheeses are made of a combination of milks—cow, sheep, and goat. Some are marketed fresh and uncured, so they are fairly soft and creamy. Such a soft cheese would be perfect for this dish of eggs poached over a bed of tomato puree. Fresh mozzarella would be a good substitute. Serve the eggs with plenty of fresh bread for dunking.

SERVES 4

3 tablespoons olive oil

2 cups grated tomato pulp (from 1½ pounds tomatoes) (page 62)

1 teaspoon salt

Freshly ground black pepper

8 thin slices cheese (¼ pound)

2 ounces serrano ham, thinly sliced (optional)

8 eggs

⅛ teaspoon hot smoked pimentón or a pinch of cayenne

Heat the oil in a 12-inch skillet over high heat. Add the tomatoes and season with ½ teaspoon of the salt and pepper to taste. Cook for 1 minute, lower the heat to medium, and cook the tomatoes for 10 to12 minutes. Quite a lot of liquid will remain.

Remove the pan from the heat. Lay the slices of cheese on top of the tomato puree. Divide the ham, if you're using it, into 8 pieces. Place them on top of or between the slices of cheese. Break the eggs, one by one, into a small cup and slide them into the pan on top. Sprinkle with the remaining ½ teaspoon salt and the pimentón.

Cover the skillet and place over high heat for 1 minute. Reduce the heat to medium and cook gently until the whites are just set but the yolks are still runny, 6 to 7 minutes. Let stand for 1 minute before serving.

Use a large spoon to lift eggs, cheese, and tomato sauce out of the skillet. Serve in shallow soup plates.

EGGS BAKED *in* SPINACH NESTS

Huevos en Nidos de Espinacas

When this egg dish is part of a larger menu, one egg per person is fine. But if it's to be the whole meal, use 2 eggs for each. The eggs can be baked in metal or ceramic ramekins or in individual earthenware cazuelas. Cazuelas are slow to heat, but they retain heat after being removed from the oven. Remove the cazuelas when the whites are barely set and the eggs will finish cooking from residual heat.

Use Manchego or a smoky cheese such as San Simón from Galicia in northwest Spain or Idiazábal from the Basque Country.

SERVES 4

5 cups shredded spinach (about ¾ pound)	1 cup diced tomato
3 tablespoons olive oil	1 teaspoon salt
¼ cup chopped onion	Freshly ground black pepper
1 garlic clove, chopped	4 to 8 eggs
¼ cup diced bacon (optional)	¼ cup grated cheese

Preheat the oven to 400°F.

Cook the spinach in boiling water until wilted, 2 to 3 minutes. Drain and press out excess liquid.

Heat the oil in a medium skillet over medium heat and sauté the onion, garlic, and bacon, if you're using it, for 2 minutes. Turn the heat to high and add the tomato, salt, and pepper to taste. Reduce the heat to medium and cook until the tomatoes are thick, about 10 minutes. Add the spinach to the tomatoes and cook for 3 minutes.

Divide the spinach mixture among 4 lightly oiled ramekins or individual cazuelas. Use a spoon to make 1 or 2 indentations in the spinach. Break 1 or 2 eggs into each ramekin. Sprinkle cheese over the eggs.

Bake until the whites are set but the yolks are still runny, about 10 minutes. Serve immediately.

BAKED EGGS *with* CHEESE

Costrada Manchega

This makes an admirable luncheon or supper dish, serving four with two eggs each or up to eight with one egg per person. Manchego is preferred, but the recipe works with any flavorful cheese, such as Gruyère or Cheddar.

SERVES 4 TO 8

8 slices sandwich bread

3 tablespoons olive oil

10 ounces cheese, grated, preferably Manchego (about 3 cups)

½ cup dry white wine

⅛ teaspoon cumin seeds

⅛ teaspoon minced fresh rosemary

8 eggs

Salt and freshly ground black pepper

1 garlic clove, sliced crosswise

Chopped fresh parsley

Preheat the oven to 375°F.

Remove the crusts from the bread and lightly toast the slices. Arrange them in a single layer in an oiled baking pan. Brush them with 1 tablespoon of the oil.

Combine the cheese, wine, and cumin seeds. Spread the cheese mixture over the bread. Scatter the rosemary on top. Break an egg on top of each slice of bread. Sprinkle with salt and pepper to taste.

Heat the remaining 2 tablespoons oil in a small skillet and sauté the garlic until golden. Spoon the oil and garlic over the eggs and cheese.

Bake until the whites are set but the yolks are still runny, about 10 minutes. Sprinkle with chopped parsley to serve.

"FRIDAY PIE" with FISH

Pastel de Viernes

On Fridays during Lent, housewives prepare meatless meals—thus the name of this tasty dish, Friday pie. It is traditionally made with *bacalao,* dry salt cod, first soaked, then flaked. I have substituted canned tuna, making this "pie" easy to prepare and a delicious lunch any day of the week. Accompany it with Tomato Sauce (page 26) and a fresh salad.

You probably will not need additional salt—taste the mixture after adding the tuna and before incorporating the eggs.

SERVES 4 TO 6

---

2 tablespoons olive oil

½ cup chopped onion

1 tablespoon all-purpose flour

1 cup 2% or whole milk

Freshly grated nutmeg

Freshly ground black pepper

2 cups drained canned tuna (one 16-ounce can)

¼ cup sliced black, green, or pimiento-stuffed olives

4 eggs, beaten

1 tablespoon fine dry bread crumbs

Preheat the oven to 350°F.

Heat the oil in a saucepan over medium heat and sauté the onion until softened, 3 minutes. Stir in the flour and cook for 1 minute. Whisk in the milk and cook, stirring constantly, until the mixture thickens, 4 minutes.

Remove from the heat and add nutmeg and pepper to taste, the tuna, olives, and eggs.

Coat a 9-inch pie pan with cooking spray. Sprinkle with the bread crumbs. Pour the tuna mixture into the pan and spread evenly.

Bake until the pie is set and a skewer inserted comes out clean, about 45 minutes. Serve hot or at room temperature.

EGGPLANT TIMBALE

Cuajado de Berenjenas

Spanish cooking has a number of variations on *cuajado*, a sort of timbale with vegetables, eggs, and cheese. Precursors of the ever-so-popular *tortilla*, made of eggs with potatoes or other vegetables, and somewhat like the Italian frittata, the cuajados come from Spain's medieval Sephardic Jewish culture, where an all-dairy meal (no flesh) was served on some holidays. In fact, modern-day Sephardim call these meatless meals by the Spanish word *desayuno*, or "break-fast"—meaning a substantial brunch or lunch.

This eggplant timbale indeed makes a delightful brunch dish or an elegant starter. It looks quite special, with its shiny black skin. I like to serve it sliced, on greens with a sharp, tangy dressing (such as yogurt with Dijon mustard and Sherry vinegar) to highlight the richness of the cheese and eggplant.

SERVES 6 TO 8 AS A STARTER

4 medium eggplants (2 to 2½ pounds)

1 tablespoon grated onion

3 eggs

2 cups fresh bread crumbs

2 cups grated cheese, such as Manchego

1 teaspoon salt

½ teaspoon freshly ground black pepper

1 tablespoon wine vinegar

Olive oil for the pan

Preheat the broiler.

Pierce the bottoms of the eggplants twice with a skewer (to prevent steam from accumulating as they heat). Roast them under the broiler (or over charcoal, in the oven, or in a microwave), turning once, until they are soft when tested with a skewer, about 10 minutes per side. Do not let the skin char. Remove and cool slightly.

Preheat oven to 375°F.

Remove and discard the eggplant stems. Cut the eggplant open lengthwise and scoop out the flesh, reserving the skins. Puree the flesh in a blender or food processor with the onion and eggs.

Place the pureed eggplant in a bowl and fold in the bread crumbs, cheese, salt, pepper, and vinegar.

Oil the bottom and sides of a 2-quart ovenproof casserole or an 8-inch cake pan. Place the eggplant skins, shiny side down, on the bottom of the pan, overlapping them slightly and allowing them to extend partway up the sides. Spoon the eggplant and cheese mixture into the pan, smoothing the top. Cover with a lid or foil. Place the pan in a larger container and add boiling water to reach halfway up the sides of the baking dish. Carefully place in the preheated oven.

Reduce the oven heat to 350°F. Bake the timbale until set and a skewer inserted in the center comes out clean, about 55 minutes. Remove and let cool for 15 minutes.

Loosen the sides of the timbale. Place a serving plate on top and carefully invert the timbale onto the plate. Serve warm or cold.

NOTE: *The timbale can also be baked in a loaf pan without the eggplant skins.*

CHEESE FLANS *with* HAM

Flan de Queso con Jamón

Egg whites folded into the custard give these flans a delicate mousselike texture. Serve them with steamed broccoli or grilled asparagus as a luncheon entree or with shrimp or crab and greens as a starter. Prepared with milk plus cream, these flans are very rich. For a lighter version, use all milk. Manchego works best, but any well-flavored cheese can be used instead.

SERVES 8

2 tablespoons olive oil

3½ tablespoons all-purpose flour

2 cups milk

1 cup heavy cream

½ cup tomato sauce, homemade (page 26) or canned (not concentrate)

4 eggs

½ pound cheese, grated (about 2 cups)

½ cup chopped serrano or cooked ham (3 ounces)

Pinch of cayenne

Pinch of dried oregano

1 teaspoon salt

Freshly ground black pepper

Preheat the oven to 350°F. Oil eight 1-cup custard cups or individual flan molds and set them in a baking pan.

Heat the oil in a saucepan over medium heat and stir in the flour. Cook, stirring, for 1 minute. Whisk in the milk and cream and cook until the custard begins to thicken, 5 minutes. Whisk in the tomato sauce and cook, stirring, for 2 minutes.

Separate 2 of the eggs, putting the whites in one bowl and beating the yolks with the whole eggs in another. Whisk the beaten eggs and yolks into the sauce. Remove from heat and stir in the cheese, ham, cayenne, oregano, salt, and pepper to taste.

Beat the egg whites until they hold stiff peaks. Beat a third of the whites into the custard mixture. Fold the remaining whites thoroughly into the custard.

Ladle the custard mixture into the custard cups, filling them only three-quarters full. Pour enough hot water into the baking pan to come halfway up the cups. Carefully transfer the pan to the oven. Bake until the custards are set (a skewer inserted in the center will come out clean), 40 to 45 minutes.

Remove the flans from the baking pan and let them cool for at least 15 minutes. Loosen the sides with a knife and unmold the flans onto individual plates. Serve warm or at room temperature.

AN ARTISANAL CHEESEMAKER
IN LA MANCHA

Sheltered in a barn from the fierce sun of a La Mancha summer, two hundred sheep of the Manchega breed are baaing politely, waiting for lunch. The sheep were milked at 5:00 A.M. and taken out to graze the golden, stubbled wheat fields on the farm. José Araque Carrascosa, former shepherd, now a master cheesemaker, is proud of his stock.

José's father before him was a shepherd in the small town of La Solana. And his granddad, his great-granddad, and his great-great-grandfather too were shepherds. They tended flocks of sheep in the upland plains of central Spain.

"They say La Solana breeds shepherds," says José. La Solana means "a place in the sun." A few centuries ago this was a favored wintering destination for great herds of sheep that moved in a seasonal migration from the northern provinces to the south. From medieval times the sheep were a source of fantastic wealth for their wool. Now the wool is virtually worthless, but the cheese—once a by-product, made by shepherds to conserve the milk—is like gold.

Cheesemaking was a cottage industry—literally made in the family home—and the cheeses were sold locally. In 1990 José decided to register the family business with the Consejo Regulador de la Denominación de Origen Queso Manchego, the regulating board that authenticates all cheese with the Queso Manchego label.

With his wife, Paqui, who learned cheesemaking from her mother-in-law, José continued making artisanal cheese from the milk from his own ewes. When his cheeses started taking prizes at important gastronomy and livestock fairs, José and Paqui decided to expand their cheesemaking capacity and moved the operation to a shiny new facility with the latest equipment.

His cheese, labeled artisanal Manchego, is made from raw, unpasteurized milk. The milk comes from several family herds, all within a fifteen-mile radius—close enough so that he can monitor the milk's quality and sanitation.

José and Paqui make cheese every other day, so the milk is held for up to two days in refrigerated tanks. Then it is piped to a big temperature-controlled vat where it is warmed to 30°C (86°F). Paqui monitors the process. When the temperature is right, she weighs out the *cuajo,* rennet, a curdling agent.

When the milk begins to thicken into curds, Paqui sets in motion the *lira* (lyre), a mechanical arm with steel threads that rotate, cutting the curds into smaller and smaller bits. In former times the curds had to be cut by hand, a slow process requiring patience. With mechanization, she can process as much as fifteen hundred gallons of milk in one go, almost single-handedly.

The whey is drawn off from the vat of clabbered milk. It is piped to holding tanks, then to tanker trucks, and sold to the baking industry. A small part of the whey Paqui heats gently to make *requesón*, cottage cheese, for local consumption (delicious drizzled with honey and sprinkled with a few walnuts). She also separates the *nata*, the rich, sweet cream that rises to the top of the whey. Ewes' milk is highly valued for cheesemaking because it is much richer in fat, protein, and milk solids than cows' milk. It takes 5 liters (4¾ quarts) of sheep's milk to make 1 kilogram (2.2 pounds) of cheese.

José scoops out some fresh curds from the new batch of cheese to taste. They are sweet, almost sunny.

The next step requires all hands—two of the couple's sons and a niece. The curds sluice through various funnels on their way to becoming cheese. The molds used are high-tech plastic with tiny holes that facilitate the release of whey. They are imprinted with a crosshatch pattern that mimics the woven *esparto* grass strips with which Manchego cheese traditionally was molded.

Curds are heaped into the molds. As the molds emerge on the miniature conveyor belt, Paqui slaps each one with the disk that identifies it officially as Manchego. The curds in their molds go to a press that squeezes out the remaining whey.

During this alchemy, as fresh milk becomes solid, the two sons, Antonio and José Manuel, take charge of removing the fresh cheeses made two days before from the saltwater bath where they have been submerged. A cheese elevator lifts them from the brine and sends them to the end of the line, where they are stacked in crates.

José moves the cheeses to the *secadero,* drying room, where they are stacked and turned for thirty days. From the secadero the cheeses move to a cold curing room, *maduración.* Here they stay for a minimum of sixty days. The aroma begins to mellow, smells of cheese. The cheese develops a light coating of mold, which favors the maturing process. Later they will be brushed to clean off the mold. Then they move to a keeping chamber. Or, in the case of José's aged cheeses, some of them are submerged in olive oil, which keeps them even longer.

After the minimum sixty-day aging, and after sample cheeses are tested in the laboratory of the Manchego regulating board, the board issues the official label. This is authentic Queso Manchego.

The Manchego found in American delicatessens and supermarkets is primarily industrial. All of the requirements are the same—the milk must come from certified ewes of the Manchega breed and be produced within the designated areas of La Mancha (parts of the provinces of Ciudad Real, Toledo, Cuenca, and Albacete). Only coagulant and salt can be added to the cheese. The cheese must be matured for a minimum of sixty days. The only difference is that industrial Manchego cheese is produced from pasteurized milk with the addition of natural ferments. The cheese is subjected to the same lab analysis and meets all the size and flavor specifications of the regulating board. Only cheese authenticated as Denominación de Origen Queso Manchego can carry the official logo with the silhouette of Don Quixote.

CHARD and CHEESE PIE

Torta de Acelgas con Queso

Fresh white cheese, *queso fresco*, often made from goat's milk, makes a solid filling between the two layers of chard. It has a mild flavor of fresh milk, quite unlike cured cheeses. If unavailable, use crumbled ricotta in its place. Bacon adds a subtle smokiness, but if you prefer a vegetarian pie, omit it.

❦ SERVES 6 TO 8

---

1 recipe Flaky Pastry Dough (page 79)

Flour for rolling the dough

2 pounds chard, stems chopped and leaves shredded (12 cups)

2 tablespoons olive oil

¼ cup pine nuts

¼ cup chopped bacon (3 slices; optional)

1 cup chopped onion

2 garlic cloves, chopped

1 egg

½ teaspoon freshly ground black pepper

⅛ teaspoon freshly grated nutmeg

⅛ teaspoon ground ginger

Pinch of ground cinnamon

1 teaspoon salt

2 tablespoons raisins (optional)

¾ pound fresh white cheese, such as *queso fresco*, sliced ¼ inch thick

---

Roll out the pastry dough on a lightly floured surface. Fit it into a 12-inch tart pan with a removable rim. Trim off any excess dough and reserve it. Chill the shell.

Cook the chard in boiling salted water until tender, 15 minutes. Drain and refresh in cold water. Drain very well, pressing to eliminate all liquid.

Preheat the oven to 350°F.

Heat 1 teaspoon of the oil in a skillet over medium-high heat and sauté the pine nuts until they are lightly toasted, about 30 seconds. Skim them out and reserve.

Add the remaining oil to the skillet. When hot, sauté the bacon, onion, and garlic until the onion is softened, 5 minutes. Add the chard and sauté for a few minutes more.

Beat the egg in a bowl with the pepper, nutmeg, ginger, cinnamon, and salt. Add the chard mixture along with the raisins, if you're using them. Combine well.

Pour half of the chard mixture into the tart shell. Arrange the sliced cheese on top. Cover with the remaining chard. Scatter the toasted pine nuts over the top and press them gently into the chard.

Roll any remaining pastry dough into cords to crisscross the top of the pie. Pinch them to the edges of the shell.

Bake the pie until the pastry is light golden, 35 to 40 minutes. Cool on a rack for 10 minutes. Release the pastry from the sides of the tart pan. Remove the outer ring and cut into wedges. Serve warm or cold.

EMPANADAS FILLED *with* SPICY CHICKEN

Empanadas Rellenas con Pollo

Pack these tasty empanadas for a picnic lunch.

※ MAKES 5 EMPANADAS

---

2 tablespoons olive oil

½ cup finely chopped onion

1 garlic clove, chopped

½ boneless, skinless chicken breast, diced (½ pound)

1 roasted and peeled red bell pepper, canned or fresh, chopped

2 tablespoons tomato sauce, homemade (page 26) or canned

2 tablespoons dry white wine or water

½ teaspoon salt

¼ teaspoon dried oregano

Cayenne

¼ teaspoon ground cumin

1 hard-cooked egg, chopped

Flaky Pastry Dough (page 79)

Flour for rolling the dough

1 egg yolk

Heat the oil in a skillet over medium heat and sauté the onion and garlic until softened, 5 minutes. Add the diced chicken and sauté until the chicken loses its pink color, 2 minutes. Stir in the roasted pepper, tomato sauce, wine, salt, oregano, cayenne to taste, and cumin. Cook, covered, for 8 minutes. Uncover and cook to reduce the liquid, but leave the mixture juicy, not dry. Stir in chopped egg.

Preheat the oven to 400°F.

Roll out the pastry dough on a floured surface. Cut four 6-inch circles. Gather up the dough scraps, roll out, and cut one more circle.

Place about ¼ cup of the chicken filling on one half of each circle. Brush the edge of the circle lightly with water and fold the dough over the filling. Crimp or roll the edges to seal the empanadas. Place them on a baking sheet. Combine the egg yolk with 2 teaspoons water and brush the tops of the empanadas with it. Bake until golden, about 30 minutes. Serve hot or at room temperature.

ASPARAGUS TART

Torta de Espárragos

The classic version of this tart is made with silky canned white asparagus. I much prefer the stand-up flavor of fresh green asparagus. Cook it laid flat in a skillet of boiling salted water until tender. Any flavorful cheese, such as Gruyère or Cheddar, can be used in place of Manchego for the gratin topping.

SERVES 6 TO 8

1 recipe Flaky Pastry Dough (page 79)

2 tablespoons all-purpose flour, plus flour for rolling the dough

4 tablespoons (½ stick) unsalted butter

½ cup finely chopped onion

½ teaspoon smoked pimentón

2 cups whole milk

1 teaspoon salt

Pinch of dried thyme

Freshly ground black pepper

2 egg yolks

4 pounds asparagus (2 to 4 dozen spears, depending on thickness), trimmed to 6 inches and cooked

1 large mushroom, thinly sliced

½ cup coarsely grated Manchego

Preheat the oven to 350°F.

Roll out the pastry dough on a lightly floured surface to a 14-inch circle and fit it into a 12-inch tart pan with a removable rim. Line the dough with foil and weight with dried beans or rice. Place on a baking sheet and bake until the edges are lightly colored, 15 minutes. Remove the foil and beans. Return the tart shell to the oven and bake for 8 to 10 minutes longer, or until the crust is pale gold and just begins to pull away from the sides of the pan. Allow to cool.

Heat the butter in a saucepan over medium heat. Add the onion and sauté until softened, 5 minutes. Stir in the 2 tablespoons flour and cook for 1 minute. Stir in the pimentón. Whisk in 1¾ cups of the milk and cook, stirring constantly, until the mixture begins to bubble and thicken. Add the salt, thyme, and pepper to taste. Reduce the heat to very low and cook, stirring frequently, for 5 minutes.

In a heatproof bowl, combine the egg yolks with the remaining ¼ cup milk. Whisk in some of the hot milk mixture, then stir the yolk mixture into the pan. Cook, stirring constantly, until the mixture thickens and begins to simmer. Lower the heat and cook for 5 minutes, stirring frequently.

Preheat the broiler.

Spread half of the custard in the baked tart shell. Arrange the spears of asparagus, tips out, on top, in spokes. Cover with the remaining custard mixture. Press the mushroom slices lightly into the custard. Sprinkle with grated cheese.

Place the pie on a baking sheet about 4 inches from the heat and and broil until the top is bubbly and lightly browned, about 5 minutes. Serve hot or at room temperature.

FLAKY PASTRY DOUGH

Pasta Quebrada

Use this dough for empanadas and both sweet and savory pies. Be sure to let it rest at room temperature for at least 1 hour. The dough works well whether the crust is filled with raw ingredients and baked or baked "blind" and then filled with a cooked filling. The dough freezes well. Thaw completely before rolling out on a floured board.

MAKES ENOUGH DOUGH FOR AN 11-INCH CRUST OR FIVE 6-INCH EMPANADAS

1¾ cups all-purpose flour, plus flour for rolling the dough

1 teaspoon baking powder

½ teaspoon salt

4 tablespoons (½ stick) unsalted butter, cut into small pieces

2 egg yolks

¼ cup olive oil

Sift the flour, baking powder, and salt into a mixing bowl. Rub the butter into the flour until the mixture is crumbly.

Combine the egg yolks and oil. Make a well in the flour and pour in the yolks. Use a fork to blend the flour into the yolks. Add 3 tablespoons cold water to make a soft dough that can be patted into a ball.

Turn the dough out onto a pastry board and knead it very briefly. Cover and let it stand at room temperature for 1 hour before rolling out on a floured board.

NOTE: *To double the recipe for pastry dough, making 10 empanadas, use the following proportions:*

3½ cups flour, plus flour for rolling the dough

1½ teaspoons baking powder

1 teaspoon salt

8 tablespoons (1 stick) unsalted butter

½ cup olive oil

3 egg yolks

7 tablespoons water

BASIC BREAD DOUGH

Masa para Pan

One ¼-ounce envelope quick-rise yeast

1 teaspoon sugar

1 teaspoon salt

4½ cups bread flour

1½ cups warm (120°F) water

Olive oil for the bowl

Combine the yeast, sugar, salt, and 4 cups of the flour in a large mixing bowl. Make a well in the center and add the warm water. Mix with a wooden spoon. Turn the dough out onto a board and knead the remaining ½ cup flour into it. Knead the dough until smooth and elastic, about 8 minutes. Pat into a ball.

Oil a clean bowl. Place the ball of dough in it and turn the dough to coat all sides with oil. Cover the bowl with a dampened cloth and place in a warm, draft-free place to rise until doubled in bulk, about 1 hour.

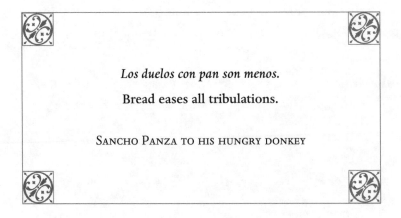

Los duelos con pan son menos.

Bread eases all tribulations.

SANCHO PANZA TO HIS HUNGRY DONKEY

The dough is now ready for use in any recipe that requires bread dough. If the dough is to be baked as bread, shape the loaves, place them on a floured baking sheet, and cover with a dry cloth. Allow to rise until not quite doubled in bulk about 1 hour.

Preheat the oven to 425°F. If you're using a baking stone, place it in the lower third of the oven and preheat.

When the loaves have risen, use a baker's peel or a thin baking sheet to slide under the risen loaves and ease them onto the preheated stone. Otherwise, bake them directly on the baking sheets.

Bake for 15 minutes, lower the oven temperature to 350°F, and bake until the loaves are golden brown and have a hollow sound when tapped on the bottom, 15 to 20 minutes longer, depending on the shape.

PICNIC ROLLS with PORK, SAUSAGE, and EGG

Hornazos de Romería

A *romería* is a pilgrimage to a saint's shrine in the countryside. It's an occasion to pack a picnic basket full of goodies and head for the hills. This bread roll, with sliced meat and egg baked right into it, is favorite fare for romerías in La Mancha. It's also typical for Carnaval, the Spanish version of Mardi Gras. A variation typical for Easter follows.

✳ MAKES 6 ROLLS

---

1 recipe Basic Bread Dough (page 80), risen once

1 cup all-purpose flour

½ teaspoon baking soda

½ cup plus 3 tablespoons olive oil

6 thin slices boneless pork loin (½ pound)

Salt and freshly ground black pepper

½ teaspoon dried oregano

½ teaspoon wine vinegar

1 small garlic clove, minced

6 thin slices serrano ham (3 ounces)

2 links Spanish hard chorizo (5 ounces), cut into ½-inch slices

Cornmeal for the baking sheet

3 hard-cooked eggs, halved lengthwise

After the bread dough has risen once, punch it down and place it in a large mixing bowl. Combine the flour and baking soda. Add ½ cup of the olive oil to the dough in 3 parts, alternating with the flour. Use your knuckles to work the oil into the dough.

When the dough has absorbed the oil, turn it out on a board and knead until very smooth. As the dough is somewhat slippery, additional flour will not be needed.

Place the dough in a bowl, cover with a damp cloth, and allow to rise in a warm place until doubled in bulk, 1 hour.

Place the sliced pork loin on a plate and sprinkle with salt and pepper to taste, oregano, vinegar, and garlic. Allow to stand for 30 minutes.

Heat the remaining 3 tablespoons oil in a skillet and fry the sliced loin very quickly, about 45 seconds per side. Remove. Quickly fry the ham in the same oil. Do not allow it to crisp. Remove. Fry the sliced chorizo, turning to brown both sides. Remove the skillet from the heat, but leave the chorizo in the oil.

Punch down the dough and divide it into 7 equal pieces (baseball sized, about 5½ ounces). Pat and roll a ball of dough out to a 6-inch circle. Place it on a baking sheet that has been sprinkled lightly with cornmeal. Continue with 5 more dough circles.

Cut the sliced pork loin in half lengthwise. Place half an egg, cut side down, in the center of each circle of dough. Place a strip of loin on either side. Press ham and sliced chorizo around the egg. Drizzle the oil remaining in the skillet over the 6 rolls.

Use the remaining ball of dough to roll thin cords. Cut them into approximate 6-inch lengths and crisscross 2 cords over each roll, pinching to attach them to the edges of the round. Allow the rolls to rise while oven is heating.

Preheat the oven to 400°F.

Bake the rolls for 12 minutes. Lower the oven temperature to 350°F and bake until the crust is golden, 8 to 10 minutes longer. The rolls should sound hollow when tapped on the bottom. Cool them on a rack.

VARIATION: *Hornazos para Pascua. This sugared variation of hornazos has a colored hard-cooked egg baked in the center for Easter. With or without the egg, it makes an excellent breakfast roll.*

Prepare the dough for hornazos as directed. While the dough is rising, prepare the following topping.

1 tablespoon olive oil	½ teaspoon grated orange zest
1 cup coarsely chopped almonds	1 egg
¼ cup plus 1 tablespoon sugar	1 tablespoon milk
1 teaspoon ground cinnamon	

Heat the oil in a small skillet over medium heat and sauté the almonds until toasted, about 40 seconds. Add ¼ cup of the sugar and cook for 1 minute, until the sugar begins to melt. Remove from the heat and add the cinnamon and orange zest.

Divide the dough into 8 balls. Pat them into 4½-inch circles and place on a baking sheet sprinkled with cornmeal. Spread the almond topping on the circles. Beat the egg and milk together. Drizzle a little over the almonds. Sprinkle with remaining sugar.

Bake the rolls as directed.

TOAST *with* OLIVE OIL

Una Tostada

This is my favorite breakfast. In its simplest version, it consists of thickly sliced country bread, grilled or toasted, drizzled with extra virgin olive oil, and sprinkled with a little salt. Some people rub the toast with a cut garlic clove. Vary the toppings—canned sardines or leftover fried fish, anchovies, aged Manchego or fresh goat cheese, raw onion, thinly sliced serrano ham, roasted sweet peppers, grated tomatoes (in La Mancha this is known as *tomatón,* but elsewhere in Spain it's "Catalan toast"). As the savory toppings suggest, you can serve the tostada as an appetizer as well as breakfast.

> Slice bread about 1½ inches thick. Toast it under the broiler or in a preheated hot oven, turning once, until lightly toasted on both sides. Place the toasts on a platter. If desired, rub the toasts with garlic. Drizzle with extra virgin olive oil, allowing 1 to 2 teaspoons oil per slice of bread. Serve with the toppings of your choice.

CRISP HAM *and* CHEESE SANDWICHES

Bocaditos de Jamón y Queso

These crispy fried sandwiches go nicely with smooth tomato soup (page 97) or a sliced tomato salad.

SERVES 4

8 slices bread from a small sandwich loaf

3 ounces cheese, preferably Manchego, grated (about 1 cup)

2 tablespoons minced scallion

1 teaspoon Dijon mustard

Pinch of dried thyme

Freshly ground black pepper

6 tablespoons olive oil

2 eggs

2 ounces serrano or cooked ham, thinly sliced

2 tablespoons milk

⅓ cup fine dry bread crumbs

Remove the crusts from the bread and cut the slices in half diagonally.

Combine the cheese, scallion, mustard, thyme, pepper to taste, and 2 tablespoons of the oil. Beat one of the eggs and add to the cheese mixture. Spread the cheese mixture on half of the bread slices. Top with sliced ham and cover with the remaining bread.

Beat the remaining egg with the milk in a shallow bowl. Place the bread crumbs in another plate. Dip the sandwiches into the egg, letting excess drip off. Dredge them in bread crumbs. Place on a plate.

Heat 2 tablespoons of the remaining oil in a skillet over medium heat. Fry half of the sandwiches until nicely browned, 2 to 3 minutes per side. If possible, balance the sandwiches upright to brown the cut edges too. Add the remaining oil to the skillet as needed and fry the remaining sandwiches. Serve them hot.

Soups,
Potages,
and One-Pot Meals

The *olla* is the great soup pot, source of everything delicious—comfort food from Mother's kitchen, lusty stews with legumes and sausage, delicate broths, and sumptuous meals-in-a-pot. The olla represents both sustenance and jubilation. Every day and fiesta.

In this chapter are some light soups, such as Consommé of Quail and Wild Mushrooms, to be served as a first course; vegetable soups, such as Manchegan Soup with Asparagus, which might be a starter or, in larger portions, a luncheon entree; two versions of Castilian garlic soup; and a fish soup. The olla includes *potajes,* potages, which are hearty stews with legumes, and *cocidos*—one-pot meals in which the broth is served as a soup course followed by all the meat and vegetables that cooked in the pot.

In Spanish home cooking, soups are rarely based on stocks. For example, rustic garlic soup is really no more complicated than olive oil, garlic, bread, and water. Nevertheless, I have suggested a simple broth (page 94) to use for most of these soups. Low-sodium canned chicken broth can be used instead. Some soups, such as Chickpea Puree with Crisp Croutons, are concocted especially to use up leftover *caldo,* broth, from the midday boiled dinner. This is a full-flavored broth from slow cooking with chicken, beef, and ham bone. You can approximate it by adding a piece of unsmoked ham and a beef bone to the recipe for simple broth. Or simply use water.

CONSOMMÉ OF QUAIL *and* WILD MUSHROOMS

Caldillo de Codorniz y Setas

I have served this deeply flavorful consommé as a welcoming libation for a holiday buffet party on a blustery winter day. In lieu of canapés, I passed the soup in demitasse cups with the sautéed breast meat and mushrooms speared on toothpicks.

Begin preparations for the consommé one to three days before serving. Any wild or cultivated mushroom can be used—chanterelles are divine; oyster mushrooms are fine.

Boning the quail breasts is fast and easy, but boned quail are readily available. Use a small sharp knife to slit down along the ridge of the breastbone. Cut through the skin at the neck and release the half-breast where the wing is attached. Cut away the other half-breast in the same manner. Leave the skin attached to the breasts.

Brandy de Jerez (brandy aged in Sherry casks in Jerez de la Frontera) lends a deep, mellow flavor to the soup. Dry fino or amontillado Sherry could be used instead. Sherry is the perfect accompaniment to the consommé.

☙ SERVES 12 TO 16 AS AN APERITIF OR 6 TO 8 AS A SOUP COURSE

---

6 to 8 quail (2¼ to 2½ pounds), breasts removed	Salt and freshly ground black pepper
2 teaspoons olive oil	½ teaspoon dried thyme
½ yellow onion	2 bay leaves
¾ pound wild or cultivated mushrooms	Fresh parsley sprigs or stems
3 quarts chicken broth, homemade (page 94) or low-sodium canned	2 egg whites and crushed egg shells to clarify the broth
1 leek, sliced	½ cup Brandy de Jerez or other brandy
2 carrots, sliced	1½ tablespoons extra virgin olive oil
1 celery stalk	1 cup shredded baby spinach leaves
½ cup chopped tomato	

Preheat the oven to 400°F.

Wrap the quail breasts in plastic wrap and refrigerate them until shortly before serving. Spread the remaining quail carcasses in a roasting pan and drizzle with the 2 teaspoons oil. Place the unpeeled onion in the pan with the quail and roast, turning the quail occasionally, until well browned, about 45 minutes.

Transfer the quail and onion to a large soup pot. Add ¼ cup water to the roasting pan and scrape up all the drippings. Add them to the soup pot.

Set aside 2 ounces (about ⅓ cup) of the mushroom caps or slices to finish the soup. Chop the remainder and add them to the soup pot along with the broth. Bring to a boil and skim off any foam that rises to the top. Add the leek, carrots, celery, tomato, 1 teaspoon salt, pepper to taste, thyme, bay leaves, and parsley. Cover and simmer the broth for 1½ hours. Remove from the heat and cool slightly.

Strain the broth in a colander, pressing on the solids to extract all the liquid. Discard the solids. Cool the broth, then refrigerate, covered, for at least 12 hours and up to 2 days.

Skim off and discard the fat from the top of the broth. Place the broth in a clean soup pot over medium heat and add the egg whites and crushed egg shells. Heat, stirring occasionally, until the broth begins to simmer. Lower the heat so it barely simmers for 15 minutes, without stirring, rotating the pot a quarter of a turn at intervals. Keep a close watch so the broth never boils. As the egg white cooks and floats to the top, it will carry along solids that cloud the broth. Remove from the heat and allow to stand 10 minutes.

Line a colander with 4 layers of damp cheesecloth and place it over a clean pot. Gently push the egg-white froth to one side and carefully ladle the broth into the colander. Discard the foam.

Shortly before serving, place the pot of clarified broth over medium heat and add the brandy. Bring to a simmer.

Sprinkle the quail breasts with salt and pepper to taste. Heat the extra virgin olive oil in a skillet over medium heat and sauté the breasts, skin side down, until browned, about 1 minute. Turn and sauté for 1 minute on the other side. The breasts will be pink in the center. Remove and keep them warm.

Sauté the reserved mushroom caps or slices in the same oil, about 1 minute on each side.

When the broth begins to boil, lower the heat so that it simmers and add the shredded spinach. Cook for 2 minutes, until the spinach is wilted.

Serve the consommé in ½-cup cups with the breast and mushroom cap speared on a toothpick or in shallow soup bowls with the breast and mushroom placed in the bowls. If desired, slice the breast crosswise and fan it out in the bowls.

MANCHEGAN SOUP *with* ASPARAGUS

Sopa Manchega con Espárragos

The rounds of toasted baguette soak up the golden broth and turn into pillowy dumplings. This soup finishes in the oven, so use a 2- or 3-quart cazuela or ovenproof casserole that can go from oven to table.

SERVES 8 AS A FAIRLY DELICATE FIRST COURSE OR 4 AS A MORE SUBSTANTIAL MEAL

¼ teaspoon saffron threads

1 pound green asparagus, preferably thin spears

¼ cup plus 1 tablespoon olive oil

1 onion, finely chopped

¼ cup diced ham (optional; about 1½ ounces)

2 garlic cloves, crushed

6 cups chicken broth, homemade (page 94) or low-sodium canned

Salt and freshly ground black pepper

Eight 1-inch-thick slices day-old baguette

¼ teaspoon caraway seeds, lightly toasted and coarsely crushed

1 egg

Crush the saffron threads in a mortar. Place the powdered saffron in a small bowl and add ¼ cup warm water. Let it infuse for at least 10 minutes.

Break off and discard the ends of the asparagus. Cut off the tips and set aside. Chop the stalks into ½-inch pieces and reserve. Blanch the tips in boiling salted water for 1 minute. Refresh under cold water, drain, and reserve.

Heat ¼ cup of the oil in a soup pot over medium heat. Sauté the onion and ham, if you're using it, until the onion begins to brown, about 8 minutes. Add the crushed garlic and chopped asparagus. Sauté for another 5 minutes.

Add the chicken broth and saffron water. Season with salt and pepper to taste. Bring to a boil, then simmer the soup, covered, for 20 minutes.

Preheat the broiler.

Place the baguette slices on a rack and brush with the remaining tablespoon of oil. Place under the broiler until they are browned on one side. Remove.

Place the baguette slices, toasted side up, in one layer in a cazuela or an ovenproof casserole.

Preheat the oven to 450°F.

When the soup is cooked, stir the crushed caraway seeds into it. Ladle the soup over the baguette slices. Beat the egg with 1 tablespoon water. Dribble it over the tops of the toast. Scatter the blanched asparagus tips on top. Place in the oven until the top is slightly browned, about 20 minutes. Turn off the oven and let the soup stop bubbling, then carefully remove the cazuela. Ladle the soup directly from the cazuela into soup bowls.

❧ SIMPLE CHICKEN BROTH *Caldo Sencillo*

This simple broth can be used for making other soups in this chapter. I find it useful to make the broth in quantity and freeze it in two or three containers, so I always have it handy for soup making.

❧ Makes 2 quarts

2 to 3 pounds chicken carcasses, backs, and wings
1 leek, halved
1 carrot, halved
2 celery stalks, halved
Handful of fresh parsley stems
2 tablespoons wine vinegar
1 tablespoon salt
Freshly ground black pepper
Pinch of dried thyme
2 bay leaves

Place the chicken pieces in a large soup pot. Add 3 quarts water and bring to a boil. Skim off the froth and scum that rises to the top. Add the remaining ingredients and bring back to a boil. Cover and simmer for 2 hours.

Strain the broth into a clean pot, discarding all the solids. Cool the broth, then refrigerate. When chilled, lift off and discard any fat that has congealed on top of the broth.

The broth can be kept, covered and refrigerated, for up to 4 days or frozen for up to 2 months.

CAULIFLOWER-POTATO SOUP *with* CHEESE FLAN

Sopa de Vigilia con Coliflor y Flan de Queso

Vigilia signifies a meatless meal. Some families observe vigilia on Christmas Eve, before attending midnight mass and taking communion. Whether made with water or a richly flavored chicken broth, this soup makes a delightful addition to a special dinner.

SERVES 6 TO 8

FOR THE CHEESE FLAN

3 eggs, beaten

1½ cups whole or 2% milk

Pinch of cayenne

¼ teaspoon dried thyme

1 teaspoon salt

1 cup grated Manchego

Preheat the oven to 350°F.

Combine the flan ingredients and pour into an oiled 6-cup loaf pan. Cover the pan with foil. Place it in a larger pan and partially fill with boiling water. Bake until a skewer inserted in the center comes out clean, 20 minutes. Remove the foil and bake for 10 minutes more.

Keep the flan warm in the pan of hot water while you prepare the soup.

FOR THE SOUP

3 tablespoons olive oil

1 cup chopped onion

1 tablespoon sweet pimentón

Pinch of cayenne

Pinch of ground cumin

1 pound baking potatoes (2 medium), peeled and diced

4 cups cauliflower florets (1 pound)

2 quarts water or broth

1 tablespoon salt

Freshly ground black pepper

1 bay leaf

1 tablespoon wine vinegar

Chopped scallion for serving

Chopped fresh parsley for serving

Heat the oil in a soup pot over medium heat and sauté the onion for 5 minutes. Remove the pot from the heat and stir in the pimentón, cayenne, and cumin. Add the potatoes and cauliflower along with the water. Season with the salt, pepper to taste, bay leaf, and vinegar.

Bring the soup to a boil and simmer, covered, until the potatoes are tender, about 35 minutes. Let it cool slightly. Remove the bay leaf and puree the soup in a blender or with an immersion blender. Reheat the puree gently.

Cut the cheese flan into slices and lift them out of the loaf pan with a spatula, discarding any accumulated liquid. Place a slice in each soup bowl and ladle the soup over. Garnish with scallion and parsley.

NOTE: *If you don't want to turn on the oven to make the flan, you can make it in the microwave, using a microwave-safe ring mold. Microwave on full power for 2 minutes; microwave on ¾ power for 3 minutes. Test with a skewer. If the flan is still not set, microwave for 30 seconds and test again.*

TOMATO SOUP *with* BACON

Sopa de Tomate con Bacón

Bacon and smoky pimentón de la Vera give this simple tomato soup a heady aroma. Use any well-flavored broth—chicken, beef, or lamb. Puree the tomatoes in a blender, then pass the soup through a conical chinois strainer. You will be surprised by how many tomato pips get strained out. Serve the soup garnished with cubes of cheese flan or with croutons of fried bread. Change the venue completely with the addition of peeled shrimp.

SERVES 6

2 tablespoons olive oil

3 slices bacon, chopped (¼ cup)

1½ cups chopped onion

2 garlic cloves, chopped

¼ cup fine fresh bread crumbs

1 teaspoon sweet smoked pimentón

Pinch of hot smoked pimentón or cayenne

4 cups diced peeled fresh plum tomatoes (about 2 pounds) or canned tomatoes, drained, liquid reserved

6 cups chicken broth, homemade (page 94) or low-sodium canned, or any meat broth

Salt and freshly ground black pepper

Pinch of dried thyme

1 tablespoon fresh parsley leaves

Fresh herbs (parsley, basil, cilantro, or mint) for garnish

Cheese flan for garnish, (optional; page 95)

Heat the oil in a soup pot and fry the bacon until lightly crisped. Skim out the bacon and reserve. Add the onion and garlic to the fat and sauté over medium heat until the onion is golden, about 5 minutes. Stir in the bread crumbs and fry for 1 minute longer.

Remove the pot from the heat and blend in the sweet and hot pimentón. Add the tomatoes, return the pot to the heat, and cook over high heat for 5 minutes, stirring frequently, until the tomatoes begin to sweat out their liquid.

Add the broth, salt to taste (depending on the saltiness of the broth), pepper to taste, the thyme, and the parsley. If you're using canned tomatoes, add the reserved tomato juice. Bring to a boil, reduce the heat to a simmer, and cook, covered, for 45 minutes. Let stand for about 20 minutes to cool slightly.

Puree the soup using an immersion blender or in batches in a regular blender. Pass the soup through a chinois strainer, pressing on the solids. Discard the solids.

Reheat the soup before serving. Serve garnished with bacon bits, chopped fresh herbs, and, if desired, cubes of cheese flan.

CREAM OF PUMPKIN SOUP

Crema de Calabaza

This recipe is adapted from one given to me by Carlos Falcó, Marqués de Griñón, who makes superlative wines on his estate, Dominio de Valdepusa, in Toledo province.

Use deep orange pie pumpkin or calabaza for this soup.

Served chilled, pumpkin soup is a refreshing summer luncheon entree. Hot, it makes a fine starter for a festive harvest dinner.

SERVES 6

3 tablespoons olive oil

1 cup chopped onion

½ cup diced carrot

1½ cups chopped red bell pepper

2 garlic cloves, chopped

1¼ pounds pumpkin, peeled, seeded, and cut into 1-inch cubes (2½ cups)

1½ cups peeled diced baking potato

5 cups chicken broth, homemade (page 94) or low-sodium canned

1 tablespoon white wine vinegar

1 strip orange zest

Pinch of dried thyme

1 bay leaf

Dash of ground cloves

½ teaspoon salt

1 cup whole milk or light cream

Chopped fresh mint or diced apple for serving

Heat the oil in a soup pot over medium heat and sauté the onion, carrot, and bell pepper for 5 minutes. Add the garlic and pumpkin and sauté for 5 minutes more.

Add the potato, broth, vinegar, orange zest, thyme, bay leaf, cloves, and salt. Bring the soup to a boil, cover, and simmer until the pumpkin is very tender, 25 minutes.

Remove the orange zest and bay leaf. Puree the soup in a blender or with an immersion blender. Strain it, discarding any remaining solids. Stir in the milk.

To serve hot, reheat the soup without allowing it to boil. Garnish with diced apple. To serve cold, allow the soup to cool, then refrigerate, covered, until chilled and garnish with chopped mint.

GREEN PEA SOUP

Sopa Verde

Make this soup in the spring, when fresh peas arrive in the market. Cooking the pea pods produces a "broth" that intensifies the soup's flavor.

✼ SERVES 6 AS A FIRST COURSE

1 pound chicken carcasses, backs, and wings

1 ham bone or ½ pound unsmoked ham

1 leek, sliced

½ onion, peeled

1 bay leaf

1 teaspoon dried thyme

1 celery stalk

Sprig of flat-leaf parsley

Salt and freshly ground pepper

2 pounds fresh peas in pods

3 tablespoons olive oil

3 slices bread, cut into ½-inch dice

Chopped fresh herbs (parsley, fennel fronds, or mint) for garnish

Chopped scallion for garnish

Put the chicken, ham, leek, onion, bay leaf, thyme, celery, and parsley in a pot with 10 cups water. Add 1 teaspoon each salt and pepper. Bring to a boil, then lower the heat and simmer for 1 hour. Strain and reserve the broth. Discard the chicken and vegetables. If desired, reserve the ham to add to the finished soup.

Shell the peas, reserving the pods. Put the pods in a pot and cover with 3 cups water. Bring to a boil and cook for 15 minutes. Strain and reserve the liquid. Discard the pods.

Return the pea water to the pan and bring to a boil. Add ½ teaspoon salt, another sprig of parsley, and the peas. Cook until the peas are very tender, 10 to 20 minutes, depending on their size. Reserve ¼ cup cooked peas. Puree the remainder in a blender until smooth.

Combine 6 cups of the strained chicken broth and the pureed peas in a soup pot. Bring to a boil and simmer for 15 minutes. Taste for salt. Heat the oil in a small skillet and fry the bread cubes until they are golden and crisp, about 6 minutes. Serve the soup garnished with the chopped herbs, scallion, fried bread cubes, reserved peas, and, if desired, shredded ham.

FIFTEEN-MINUTE FISH SOUP

Sopa al Cuarto de Hora

I tested this classic Madrid recipe against the clock, and it really does work—if you've got the chopping done and the water boiling before you start the timer. Use any firm-fleshed fish, such as monkfish or snapper, in this soup. The clams are opened in the soup, which means you eat them out of the shells. If you prefer, first steam them open, discard the shells, and add them to the soup in the last minute of cooking. The classic version of this soup is made with peas, but I like this variation with chard.

SERVES 6

¼ cup olive oil

½ cup chopped onion

1 cup chopped tomato

1 cup chopped chard or peas

6 cups boiling water or fish stock

¼ teaspoon fennel seeds

1½ teaspoons salt

Freshly ground black pepper

¼ cup chopped ham, preferably serrano

Pinch of saffron threads, crushed (optional)

6 ounces fish fillets, cut into 1-inch pieces

½ pound small clams

1 cup cooked rice

¼ cup dry Sherry

6 ounces peeled small shrimp

Heat the oil in a soup pot over medium-high heat and sauté the onion for 1 minute. Add the tomato, chard, and boiling water. Raise the heat to high and cook for 1 minute. Add the fennel seeds, salt, pepper to taste, ham, saffron, and fish. Let the soup bubble for 10 minutes.

Add the clams, rice, Sherry, and shrimp. Cook for 3 minutes more and serve.

GARLIC SOUP

Sopa de Ajo

I cannot imagine a more heartwarming soup for a blustery winter's day. In La Mancha, this soul-satisfying dish is also appreciated as a hangover cure, to be imbibed after a night of partying.

Chicken broth gives depth of flavor to a soup usually made simply with water. Whole cloves of garlic cook in the broth. Serve them with the soup and let each person squeeze out the softened garlic into the broth.

SERVES 4

Sixteen ⅜-inch baguette slices

4 to 8 garlic cloves

¼ cup extra virgin olive oil

¼ cup finely chopped onion

½ cup diced serrano ham (3 ounces)

2 teaspoons sweet pimentón

¼ cup grated tomato pulp (page 62)

6 cups chicken broth, homemade (page 94) or low-sodium canned

4 eggs

Chopped fresh parsley for garnish

Preheat the oven to 350°F.

Place the sliced baguette on a baking sheet. Bake for 6 minutes and turn the slices. Bake for 6 minutes more, or until golden.

Cut a slit into each of the unpeeled garlic cloves. Heat the oil in a deep skillet, cazuela, or soup pot over medium heat. Add the garlic cloves and fry them for 3 minutes, turning to brown. Skim out the garlic and reserve.

Add the onion and ham to the oil and sauté for 1 minute. Stir in the pimentón, then add the tomato pulp. Cook for 1 minute. Return the garlic to the pan. Add the broth and bring to a boil. Reduce to a simmer, cover, and cook for 10 minutes.

Add the toasted bread to the soup. Cover and cook for 5 minutes. Break the eggs into the soup. Cover and poach until the egg whites are set and the yolks still liquid, 4 minutes.

Serve the soup from the same cazuela, lifting out egg, bread, and broth into individual soup bowls. Garnish with parsley.

No comas ajos ni cebollas,
porque no saquen por el olor tu villanería.

Don't eat garlic or onions,
so that they don't take you for a peasant.

Don Quixote's advice to Sancho Panza when
he goes off to become governor of the island

DOUBLE GARLIC SOUP

Sopa de Ajo Emparejado

Double the flavor—crushed garlic cloves plus green garlic shoots make a heady brew. This recipe is adapted from one in *Guisos, Viandas y Otras Pócimas*, by Joaquín Racionero Page.

SERVES 4

2 tablespoons plus 2 teaspoons olive oil

1 pound potatoes, peeled and cut into ¾-inch dice (3 cups)

¼ cup diced red bell pepper

2 garlic cloves, crushed

2 teaspoons sweet pimentón

Pinch of hot red pepper flakes

1 cup diced drained canned tomato

3 tablespoons all-purpose flour

5 cups chicken broth, homemade (page 94) or low-sodium canned

Salt

1 fresh mint sprig

1 cup chopped green garlic shoots, including green tops

Heat 2 tablespoons of the oil in a soup pot over medium heat. Add the diced potatoes and fry them, stirring frequently, until they begin to brown, 5 minutes. Add the red bell pepper and sauté for 1 minute more. Remove the pot from the heat and stir in the crushed garlic, pimentón, and red pepper flakes. Add the tomatoes and return to medium heat. Cook for 2 minutes, stirring.

Combine the flour and 1 cup water in a jar with a tight lid. Shake the mixture until the flour is thoroughly mixed. Pour it into the soup pot, stirring to blend. Add the broth, little by little, stirring well. Season to taste with salt. Add the sprig of mint. Bring to a boil and simmer the soup, covered, until the potatoes are cooked, 10 minutes.

While the soup is cooking, heat the remaining 2 teaspoons oil in a small skillet. Sauté the chopped green garlic over low heat until softened but not browned, 5 minutes.

Stir the sautéed garlic shoots into the soup. Cook for 5 minutes without stirring, until red-colored oil begins to rise to the top. Discard the mint sprig. Let the soup rest for 5 minutes before serving.

THE GARLIC CAPITAL OF SPAIN

Sturdy garlic soup, a classic peasant dish of Spain's central Castilian region, is simple stuff: fry chopped garlic in olive oil, stir in some red pimentón; add water, salt, and chunks of bread; embellish with poached eggs and serve piping hot. But in the La Mancha town of Las Pedroñeras a singular chef, Manuel de la Osa, has turned garlic soup upside down—and chilled it too.

The garlic soup at Manuel's restaurant, Las Rejas, arrives in a martini cocktail glass. Where the olive would come to rest is a poached egg yolk. A jellied, garlic-infused broth makes the cocktail. On top are a flag of crisp-fried serrano ham, a crouton or two, and a drizzle of parsley-infused olive oil. Sancho Panza—who spurned fancy palace food—might have approved with a wink and a grin.

Las Pedroñeras—literally, rockville—is a village southeast of Madrid, smack in the middle of Don Quixote country. The village lays claim to the title of Spain's capital of garlic. A single growers' cooperative in the town, San Isidro del Santo, produced in one year more than seventeen thousand tons of the fragrant bulb. Most of it is the esteemed *ajo morado,* purple garlic, a variety of hard-necked garlic that has papery white layers enclosing cloves shrink-wrapped in violet skins. Purple garlic is both sweet and pungent, with a powerful bite. The purple garlic of Las Pedroñeras enjoys its own protected denomination of origin.

When Manuel de la Osa created the cold jellied garlic soup for the town's annual garlic fair, it became an instant classic. Although the menu at Las Rejas changes with the seasons and with the chef's inspiration, the garlic soup remains. Like most of his dishes, even the wildest flights of fancy, it is based in the traditional kitchen.

Manuel is one of Spain's most acclaimed chefs (Las Rejas earned a Michelin star in 1994) in a country that boasts some of the top chefs in the world. Nevertheless he is essentially a small-town guy. He grew up in Las Pedroñeras, where his father ran a bar on the central plaza. His grandmother, mother, and aunts did the cooking.

"I am rooted in La Mancha," says Manuel. "In my grandmother's kitchen I took in the smells and tastes that still guide me.

"I take traditional dishes and transform them. I might use advanced techniques, from a long tradition of French cuisine. Or combine flavors and textures in new ways. I liberate the imagination."

Ajo arriero, salt cod in muledriver's style—which is to say with lots of garlic—starts from a simple country dish, but, in Manuel's kitchen becomes more complex in flavor and texture, with the addition of smoked cod, almonds, clams, and a garnish of caviar. He pairs partridge with tuna. Matches fatty pancetta and rare squab breast with a sauce of sweet quince jelly. Airy foam of lemon verbena tops gelatinous cod tripe rolled around flaky cod. An intensely flavored green tomato soup with minted olive oil reflects on Andalusian gazpacho.

Manuel's cooking starts with the finest products of the land—artisanally produced Manchego cheese, extra virgin olive oil from small producers in the highlands of the Montes de Toledo, the finest lamb, garlic from Las Pedroñeras, wild game taken locally. And, of course, superb wines. Las Rejas has an impressive listing of wines with La Mancha denomination of origin. (Vineyards occupy more acreage than garlic fields in Las Pedroñeras.)

He playfully combines the local with the exotic when the result produces something special. So, although neither foie gras nor caviar is a local product, both make an appearance.

"I don't mix just for the sake of mixing," says Manuel. "There is an underlying sense of what works." Which comes through in his *potaje con pulpo,* cabbage and octopus soup. Or a hauntingly earthy combo of puddled cheese (Manchego and Parmesan melted with sheep's milk), truffles, hazelnuts, and tomato jam.

About that garlic soup. Manuel says that garlic is abused in his hometown.

"I use about one-tenth the quantity of garlic as in a traditional garlic soup. Badly treated, garlic *se repite.* It comes back up on you."

Don Quixote had the same advice for Sancho Panza when he went off to become governor of an island.

No comas ajos ni cebollas, porque no saquen por el olor tu villanería.

"Don't eat garlic or onions, so that they don't take you for a peasant by your smell."

HEARTY VEGETABLE SOUP *with* BEANS *and* SAUSAGE

Olleta

Adapted from a recipe in Lorenzo Diaz's *La Cocina del Quijote,* this soup, says the author, should be cooked in an earthenware pot over a fire of grapevines or oakwood.

Use about 6 cups of vegetables. This rendition favors spring vegetables—fava beans, chard, and artichokes. But the soup is equally delicious with winter cabbage or summer zucchini. Serve the soup with bread and cheese for a hearty meal.

If you are using fresh artichokes, don't cut them up until the soup is bubbling. Then trim off the outer leaves, slice off the tops, and trim the artichokes to the hearts.

SERVES 6

1 tablespoon olive oil

6 ounces pork link sausage or Spanish soft chorizo, sliced or crumbled

1 cup chopped onion

4 garlic cloves, chopped

1 teaspoon sweet pimentón

1 cup canned crushed tomato

2 quarts water or light broth

1 cup shelled fava beans (1 pound in shells)

1½ cups green beans in 1-inch pieces (6 ounces)

1 cup diced turnip

2 cups chopped chard (2 to 3 stalks; 5 ounces)

1 cup diced carrot (2 to 3 carrots)

2 artichoke hearts, quartered (from 2 small artichokes; ½ pound)

1½ teaspoons salt

Freshly ground black pepper

2 cups cooked or drained canned cannellini beans (one 15-ounce can)

½ cup Spanish round-grain rice

Heat the oil in a soup pot over medium heat. Add the sausage and sauté until it begins to brown, 2 minutes. Add the onion and garlic and sauté for 3 minutes. Remove the pot from the heat and stir in the pimentón. Add the tomatoes and water and bring to a boil.

When the broth is boiling, add the vegetables, salt, and pepper to taste. Bring back to a boil, then cover and simmer until the vegetables are just tender, 20 minutes.

Add the cannellini beans to the soup. Uncover and cook for 5 minutes. Add the rice and cook for 12 minutes. Remove from the heat, cover, and allow to stand for 5 minutes before serving.

CHICKPEA PUREE *with* CRISP CROUTONS

Puré de Garbanzos con Pan Frito

This puree, with chickpeas, carrots, and potatoes, can be made with the leftovers of a grand *cocido* (page 120). If you are starting with uncooked ingredients, you will need about 1¼ cups dried chickpeas to make 3 cups cooked. Soak them in water for 12 hours. Add them to boiling water and simmer until tender, about 2 hours. Straining the soup after it is pureed eliminates the chickpea hulls and makes for a smoother soup. Use a conical chinois sieve, pushing on the solids.

SERVES 6

2 tablespoons plus 1½ tablespoons olive oil

¼ cup diced salt pork or bacon

1 cup sliced carrot

1 cup chopped onion

1 garlic clove, chopped

1 medium potato (½ pound), cut into pieces

3 cups cooked chickpeas

¼ cup tomato sauce, homemade (page 26) or canned (not concentrate)

2 quarts water, broth, or chickpea-cooking liquid

Pinch of cayenne

Salt and freshly ground black pepper

Pinch of dried thyme

1 bay leaf

1 cup bread in ½-inch dice

½ teaspoon coarsely chopped garlic

¼ teaspoon smoked hot pimentón

Heat 2 tablespoons of the oil in a soup pot over medium heat. Fry the salt pork until the fat is rendered and the pork is crisp, 2 minutes. Remove the pot from heat and tip it so the fat drains to one side. Skim out the salt pork and reserve.

Return the pot to the heat and add the carrot, onion, and chopped garlic. Sauté over medium heat until softened, 4 minutes. Add the potato and cook for 1 minute. Add the chickpeas, tomato sauce, and water. Season with cayenne, salt and pepper to taste, thyme, and bay leaf. Bring to a boil, cover, and simmer until the potatoes and carrots are tender, 20 minutes. Discard the bay leaf.

Puree the soup in batches in a blender. If desired, strain the puree.

Shortly before serving, reheat the pureed soup. In a small skillet, heat the remaining 1½ table-spoons oil over medium-high heat. Toss the diced bread in the oil until lightly toasted, 2 minutes. Add the ½ teaspoon garlic and reserved salt pork. Fry for 1 minute.

Serve the soup in shallow bowls. Scatter the croutons, garlic, and salt pork over the soup. Top each serving with a pinch of pimentón.

LENTILS *with* SAUSAGE

Lentejas con Chorizo

In Spanish homes, this is served as a first course for the *comida de mediodia,* midday dinner, the principal meal of the day, served at about 2:00 in the afternoon. The main course that follows would be a small piece of meat, chicken, or fish, perhaps with a side of vegetables, followed by fresh fruit for dessert. Nevertheless, this lusty lentil stew easily makes a full meal. Just add salad and good bread to round out the menu.

The most common variety of lentil in Castilla–La Mancha is the *rubia castellana,* big, flat disks of a pale greenish brown color. They cook up ever so soft, without turning to mush. The tiny, dark brown *pardina* lentils, which always stay al dente, can be substituted. Castilla–La Mancha grows 90 percent of the lentils produced in Spain, but, as this is insufficient to meet demand, much is imported. At my local store in southern Spain, the castellana lentils come from Canada!

Be sure to use soft water (bottled or filtered if your water is naturally hard) for cooking lentils. This helps the legume skins soften.

Pork belly, consisting of ribbons of lean and fat, is pancetta or bacon before it is salted and cured. Any fatty bits of fresh pork or even spareribs could be used. Soft chorizo is a fattier version of the hard chorizo. Morcilla, blood sausage, if available, is especially good with lentils. Any sausage, preferably unsmoked, could be substituted for the chorizo.

꙰ SERVES 4

1 pound dried green castellana lentils (about 2½ cups)

¼ pound pork belly (uncured pancetta)

¼ pound Spanish soft chorizo

¼ pound morcilla (optional)

1 teaspoon olive oil

2 whole cloves

1 small onion, peeled

1 head of garlic

2 carrots, sliced

1 whole tomato or 2 sun-dried tomatoes, cut up

1 bay leaf

1 teaspoon salt

Freshly ground black pepper

1 teaspoon pimentón, smoked or unsmoked

Hot red pepper flakes (optional)

½ pound potato (1 medium), peeled and cut into 1-inch cubes

Scarlet-Pickled Onions (page 282) and hot peppers, such as peperoncini, for serving

Place the lentils in a cazuela or soup pot and add 6 cups water.

Cut the pork belly into ½-inch strips. Slice the chorizo and morcilla, if you're using it, cross-wise. Heat the oil in a small skillet over medium heat and fry the pork and chorizo until lightly browned, about 4 minutes. Tip the skillet to drain the fat to one side, skim the pork and chorizo out, and add them to the lentils. Discard the fat.

Stick the cloves into the onion and tuck it into the lentils. Slice the top off the head of garlic and remove the outer, papery skin. Add the whole head of garlic to the lentils with the carrots, tomato, bay leaf, salt, and pepper to taste. Stir the pimentón into 1 tablespoon water until smooth, then stir it into the lentils. Add the red pepper flakes, if you're using them.

Bring to a boil, lower the heat to a simmer, and cover the lentils. Cook gently for 15 minutes. Add the potatoes and cook for 30 minutes more.

Remove and discard the onion and bay leaf. Remove the tomato, cut out the core, and discard the skin. Use the edge of a spoon to break the tomato into pieces and return them to the lentils. Squeeze the soft-cooked garlic cloves from their skins into the lentils. Let stand, covered, for 15 minutes before serving. Each person adds pickled onions and peppers to taste.

DON QUIXOTE'S FRIDAY LENTILS

Lentejas Para Viernes

On Fridays Don Quixote ate lentils. Or so Cervantes tells us in the first paragraph of the novel. Because it was Friday—a day of abstinence from meat in the Catholic Church—they were certainly lentils *viudas,* "widowed," bereft of meat or sausage. Nevertheless, well flavored with the olive oil of the region, garlic, onions, and spices such as cumin and pepper, they were probably a substantial and tasty meal. Potatoes—a plant from the New World—were not widely known in Don Quixote's day. In their place, *castañas pilongas,* dried chestnuts, were cooked with the lentils. If you choose to use them, soak the chestnuts in water to cover for 12 hours.

Use the tiny dark brown *pardina* lentils for this dish, which is served "dry," not soupy. Small le Puy green lentils could be used as well. With a salad, bread, and cheese, lentils make a fine vegetarian meal. They are also a good side dish with duck, ham, or pork.

SERVES 4 AS A MAIN DISH OR 6 TO 8 AS A SIDE DISH

1 pound dried small brown lentils (about 2½ cups)

One 1-inch piece lemon zest, slivered

2 bay leaves

1 teaspoon salt

¼ teaspoon saffron threads, crushed (optional)

3 tablespoons olive oil

1½ cups diced carrot

1 cup chopped onion

⅓ cup diced celery

3 garlic cloves, chopped

¼ teaspoon cumin seeds

Pinch of ground cloves

½ teaspoon freshly ground black pepper

1 hard-cooked egg, chopped (optional)

Lemon wedges for serving

Place the lentils in a pot or cazuela and add 6 cups water, the slivered zest, bay leaves, and salt. Bring to a boil and cook, covered, for 8 minutes. Drain the lentils, saving the liquid. Discard the bay leaves.

If you're using saffron, soak it in 2 tablespoons hot water for 15 minutes.

Heat the oil in a pot or cazuela over medium heat and sauté the carrot, onion, and celery for 5 minutes. Add the garlic and sauté for 3 minutes. Add the cumin seeds and sauté for 1 minute.

Stir in the lentils and 2 cups of the reserved liquid. Add the cloves, pepper, saffron, and additional salt, if necessary. Bring to a boil, then lower the heat and simmer, covered, for 20 minutes, or until the lentils and carrot are tender. Allow to stand for 10 minutes before serving.

If desired, serve garnished with chopped egg. Serve with lemon wedges to squeeze into the lentils.

BLACK-EYED PEAS *with* TOMATO SOFRITO

Potaje de Carillas con Sofrito

Black-eyed peas are especially delicious cooked with fatty sausage, pancetta, or ham hocks. But, if you prefer a vegetarian version, simply omit the pancetta. The sofrito of fried onion, peppers, and tomatoes provides lots of flavor.

SERVES 4

2 cups dried black-eyed peas (14 ounces), soaked for 8 to 12 hours

½ cup sliced leek

1 cup sliced carrot

2 bay leaves

2 tablespoons olive oil

½ cup diced pancetta, bacon, or fatty ham (3 ounces)

1 cup chopped onion

1 cup chopped green bell pepper

3 garlic cloves, chopped

Hot red pepper flakes

½ teaspoon smoked pimentón

1 cup peeled, seeded, and chopped tomato

1 teaspoon salt

¼ teaspoon ground cumin

¼ teaspoon dried oregano

1 tablespoon chopped fresh parsley

Pinch of ground cloves

Freshly ground black pepper

1 tablespoon wine vinegar

Drain the soaked black-eyed peas and place them in a pot with 6 cups fresh water. Bring to a boil and skim off the froth. Add the leek, carrot, and bay leaves. Cover and simmer the peas for 30 minutes.

Meanwhile, heat the oil in a skillet over medium heat and sauté the pancetta, onion, bell pepper, and garlic for 5 minutes. Stir in hot red pepper flakes to taste and the pimentón and immediately add the tomato. Season with salt, cumin, oregano, parsley, cloves, and pepper to taste. Cook for 8 minutes.

Add ½ cup cold water to the black-eyed peas. Bring back to a boil and stir in the mixture from the skillet. Cover and simmer until the peas are very tender, 1 to 1½ hours. Stir in the vinegar and cook for 5 minutes longer.

BEANS with GARLIC SAUCE

Bolos con Ajiaceite

This garlic sauce, known elsewhere in Spain as *alioli,* adds a sumptuous touch to ordinary beans. Spoon it over the cooked beans and let each person stir the sauce in. The sauce is also delicious as a dressing with other cooked vegetables.

SERVES 4

1 pound dried pinto beans (2¼ cups), soaked for 12 hours	2½ teaspoons salt
1 pound meaty ham bone or pork hock	2 carrots, sliced
½ onion, peeled	2 medium potatoes, peeled and quartered
1 celery stalk, sliced	1 egg
2 bay leaves	2 garlic cloves, peeled
Pinch of dried thyme	½ cup olive oil
	1 tablespoon wine vinegar

Drain the beans and place them in a soup pot with 6 cups water. Bring the beans to a boil and skim off all the foam that rises to the surface. Add the ham bone, onion, celery, bay leaves, and thyme. Bring back to a boil, reduce the heat, cover, and simmer the beans for 1½ hours.

Add 1 cup cold water to the beans and bring them back to a boil. Add 2 teaspoons of the salt along with the carrots. Reduce the heat to simmer and cook the beans until very tender, 1 hour. Add the potatoes to the beans. Cover and cook until the potatoes are tender, 30 minutes. Skim out 2 chunks of potatoes. Keep the beans warm over low heat.

Place the egg and garlic in a blender and blend until smooth. Add the 2 chunks of potatoes and blend. Blend in the oil to make a thick sauce. Blend in the remaining ½ teaspoon salt and the vinegar.

Place the beans in a large serving bowl. Separate the meat from the ham bone and add to the beans. Spoon half of the garlic sauce over the beans. Serve the remaining sauce separately.

CHICKPEAS *and* SPINACH *with* COD DUMPLINGS

Potaje de Garbanzos y Espinacas con Rellenos

This potage is typical for *Viernes Santo,* Good Friday, when observant Catholics don't eat meat. The chickpeas are so nicely flavored that you won't miss the sausage. *Rellenos,* a cross between fritters and dumplings, are first fried, then simmered. They are typical of the province of Cuenca.

Fresh cod can be used in place of the dry salt cod and, if it's not Holy Week, chopped, cooked ham can replace the fish. A sweet version of rellenos—without the cod, of course— is poached in milk and dusted with cinnamon and sugar.

SERVES 6

FOR THE DUMPLINGS

½ pound salt cod, soaked in several changes of water for 24 hours, or 1 cup chopped fresh cod

¼ cup sliced scallion

¼ cup coarsely chopped fresh parsley

1 cup fresh bread crumbs

1 egg

Freshly ground black pepper

Pinch of ground cloves

3 tablespoons olive oil

Squeeze out the soaked salt cod, place it in a pan, and cover with fresh water. Bring to a simmer and remove from the heat. Drain, saving 2 tablespoons of the liquid. Cool.

Remove and discard all skin and bones from the cod. Chop or flake the fish coarsely and reserve.

Mince the scallion and parsley in a food processor. Add the bread crumbs and cod and process until minced. Add the egg, pepper to taste, and cloves. Add 1 to 2 tablespoons of the reserved cooking liquid to make a paste that holds together.

Heat the oil in a heavy skillet over medium heat. With hands or 2 tablespoons, lightly shape the cod mixture into 1½-inch patties. Fry them until golden on both sides, 3 to 5 minutes. Set aside until the chickpeas and spinach are cooked.

FOR THE CHICKPEAS AND SPINACH

2 cups dried chickpeas (about 13 ounces), soaked for 12 hours

2 bay leaves

2 teaspoons salt

2 tablespoons olive oil

1 cup chopped onion

1 teaspoon sweet pimentón

½ teaspoon hot smoked pimentón or cayenne

½ cup peeled and chopped tomato

½ pound fresh spinach, chopped

1 pound potatoes (2 medium), peeled and cut into 1-inch pieces

1 hard-cooked egg

1 garlic clove, crushed

2 tablespoons toasted pine nuts

Put the chickpeas in an olla or soup pot and cover with water (about 7 cups). Bring to a boil and skim off the froth that rises to the surface. Add the bay leaves. Cover and simmer for 30 minutes.

Add the salt to the chickpeas and cook for 30 minutes more.

Heat the oil in a skillet over medium heat and sauté the onion for 5 minutes. Remove the skillet from the heat and stir in the sweet and hot pimentón. Add the tomato and continue sautéing for 3 minutes. Add the onion-tomato mixture to the chickpeas along with the spinach and potatoes. Bring to a boil, cover, lower the heat, and simmer until the potatoes are tender, about 20 minutes.

Mash the egg yolk with the garlic. Dilute with some of the liquid from the olla and stir into the chickpeas.

Add the fried cod dumplings to the chickpeas and cook gently for 5 minutes, until they are thoroughly heated.

Serve the chickpeas, spinach, and dumplings in deep soup bowls. Chop the egg white finely and scatter over the chickpeas along with a few pine nuts.

OLLA PODRIDA, ROTTEN STEW—AND THE MORE ROTTEN, THE BETTER

In the second part of the tale of Don Quixote, Sancho Panza finally gets his wish to govern an island, which he manages with some craft, aplomb, and adroitness. At the dinner table, however, he runs into problems. Don Quixote already has counseled Sancho to lay off onions and garlic, to keep his breath sweet (so no one would know he was a peasant). He also suggests moderation in eating and drinking.

Come poco, y cena más poco; que la salud de todo el cuerpo se fragua en la oficina del estómago. Sé templado en el beber, considerando que el vino demasiado, ni guarda secreto, ni cumple palabra.

"Eat little at dinner and less for supper, for good health is forged in the workshop of the stomach. Be temperate in drinking, for too much wine won't keep a secret nor fulfill a promise."

But it is a presumptuous doctor who keeps whisking away Sancho's food, supposedly to keep him from doing himself harm by eating the wrong victuals, who really gets him riled up.

When, finally, Sancho is allowed a supper of beef and onion hash and slow-cooked calves' feet, he digs in with as much relish as if it were fine pheasant from Rome, veal from Sorrento, quail from Seville, or goose from Lavajos. Sancho declares to the doctor who has been keeping him on restricted rations:

"Look, Doc, from now on, don't even think about feeding me dainties, nor fancy foods, because you'll just upset my stomach."

He declares he's got a finicky digestion, used to goat meat, fatty salt pork, beef jerky, turnips, and onions. Any of that hoity-toity palace food will just turn his stomach.

Lo que el maestresala puede hacer es traerme estas que llaman ollas podridas, que mientras más podridas son, mejor huelen.

"What the headwaiter can do is bring me some of what's called *ollas podridas*—rotten stews, which the more rotten they are the better they smell."

Rotten stew? Oh, yummy.

Olla podrida, considered the "mother of all stews," once was a dish fit for kings, containing all manner of game and meat—chicken, beef, mutton, salt pork, squab, partridge, thrush, pork loin, sausages, hare, salt beef, beef tongues, pigs' ears and trotters. The poor folks' version contained rancid ham bone, salt pork, chickpeas, and turnips. Very slowly cooked until the meat was falling off the bones, the stew acquired the descriptive name "rotten," just as overripe fruit gets mushy and falls away from the pit.

Another explanation for the name is that the olla usually incorporates salted meats, salt pork fat (*tocino*), and chunks of serrano ham and ham bone. The old ham bone, called *añejo*, meaning "well-cured, aged," imparts a pronounced rancid aroma to the potage which, tongue-in-cheek, could be called "rotten."

Or perhaps Sancho Panza, famous for fractured phrases and twisted refrains, was making a little pun. Perhaps by *podrida*—rotten—he actually meant *poderida*, powerful, meaning a stew pot filled with rich meat, an aristocrat's stew pot, not a rotten one. As the governor of an island, surely he deserved no less!

ONE-POT FEAST

Cocido Relleno para Días de Fiesta

Holiday means feast, a celebration. Whether a saint's day, Christmas Day, a wedding, or Sunday dinner with the family, there is no more festive dish than the *cocido,* a meal-in-a-pot cooked in the great *olla,* soup pot. Containing beef, ham, stewing hen, vegetables, sausages, and chickpeas, it provides a soup for a first course, then a main course, side dishes, and sauces. This version has a meat dumpling as well, *relleno,* that can be served with the soup or as a separate course.

The chickpeas need to soak for eight to twelve hours, so start them a day before you plan to serve. The cocido requires almost three hours of slow cooking. As you are not likely to have stewing hen, which needs long cooking, remove the chicken when it is very tender (about 1½ hours of cooking) so that it doesn't fall apart in the soup.

Both red chorizo and black morcilla sausages go into the cocido, although they are usually cooked in a separate pot so they do not color the cocido broth. Soft, or cooking, chorizo is fully cured but is softer than chorizo for cold cuts, as it has a higher fat content. If chorizo and morcilla are not available, you could substitute pork link sausage, bratwurst, andouille, or Polish sausage.

You will need three pots for this preparation. Use your largest (6-quart capacity) to cook the meats and vegetables. While the cocido is simmering in the big pot, prepare the meatball mixture. About an hour before serving time, start a second pot of water to cook the pumpkin, potatoes, and sausages. Have ready a third pot and a fine-mesh sieve to strain the broth for the soup.

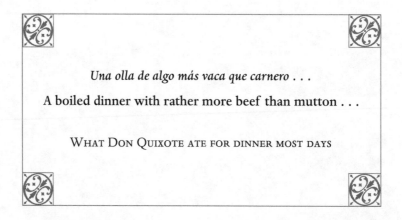

Una olla de algo más vaca que carnero . . .

A boiled dinner with rather more beef than mutton . . .

WHAT DON QUIXOTE ATE FOR DINNER MOST DAYS

Serve the broth with noodles and meatballs as the first course. Cut the meats and sausages into serving-size pieces and present them on a big platter. Put the vegetables and potatoes in another serving dish; the chickpeas in a bowl with some of the pumpkin sauce spooned over them; and the cabbage with its garlic-pimentón sauce in another bowl. Pass the pumpkin sauce separately. Each person spoons it over meat and vegetables to taste. Accompany the platters of food with Scarlet-Pickled Onions (page 282), gherkins, or peppers. Feast!

✕ SERVES 6

FOR THE BIG POT

1 cup dried chickpeas (about 7 ounces)

2 pounds ham hock or shank, preferably unsmoked

1 pound boneless shin or stewing beef

½ large chicken (2 pounds)

Giblets and liver from 1 chicken (optional)

6 peppercorns

1 celery stalk

1 small onion, halved

3 fresh parsley sprigs with stems

3 large carrots

1 large turnip, quartered

3 leeks

1½ teaspoons salt

Place the chickpeas in a large bowl and add water to 3 times their depth. Soak the chickpeas overnight or for at least 8 hours. Drain the chickpeas and discard the soaking liquid.

Place the ham hock, beef, chicken, and giblets, if you're using them, in a large stew pot. Add 3 quarts water and bring to a boil. Skim off and discard the foam that rises to the top. Keep skimming the pot for 5 to 10 minutes, until no more foam rises.

Add the drained chickpeas to the boiling liquid. Skim again when the liquid boils. Reduce the heat so the liquid bubbles very gently. Add the peppercorns, celery, onion, and parsley. Cover the pot and cook for 1½ hours. The chicken will be fully cooked. Lift it out and place it on a platter. Tent with foil to keep it warm. Remove the giblets and liver and cut into small dice. Reserve for the soup.

While the main pot is cooking, prepare first the mixture for the *relleno*, meatballs, and next the second pot for cooking the sausages and potatoes.

Add the carrots, turnip, leeks, and salt to the big pot. Bring back to a boil, then reduce the heat and simmer for 30 minutes.

Add the prepared meatballs (recipe follows) to the pot and poach them for 30 minutes.

Use a skimmer or slotted spoon to transfer the meats to a large serving platter. Separate the chicken into serving pieces. Slice the beef across the grain. Remove the skin and bone from the ham hock and slice the meat. Keep the meats warm.

Place the vegetables on a separate serving dish and keep warm.

Strain the soup through a fine-mesh sieve into a clean pot. Place the chickpeas in a serving bowl. Discard the cooked onion, celery, and parsley.

FOR THE RELLENOS

4 country bread slices (¼ pound), crusts removed

¾ cup milk

1 egg, beaten

1 garlic clove, minced

1 teaspoon grated lemon zest

½ teaspoon salt

¼ teaspoon freshly ground black pepper

2 tablespoons finely chopped fresh parsley

Pinch of ground cinnamon

Pinch of ground cloves

Pinch of freshly grated nutmeg

¾ pound ground pork, veal, chicken, or turkey

While the cocido is cooking, prepare the meatballs. Crumble the bread into a bowl. Toss with the milk and allow to stand for 15 minutes, until the bread softens. Break it up with a fork. Add the beaten egg, garlic, lemon zest, salt, pepper, parsley, cinnamon, cloves, and nutmeg. Stir to combine well.

Add the ground meat and mix very well. Wet your hands and shape the mixture into 12 golf-ball-sized balls.

Poach the meatballs in the strained soup broth. Serve 2 per person with the broth and noodles as a first course (instructions follow). (The meatballs also can be cooked in the cocido pot. Add them to the soup before serving.)

FOR THE PUMPKIN SAUCE AND SAUSAGES

2½ teaspoons salt

½ pound peeled pumpkin

1 large tomato

¼ pound Spanish soft chorizo (2 links)

½ pound morcilla (blood sausage)

1½ pounds potatoes (3 medium)

1 garlic clove

1 tablespoon wine vinegar

½ teaspoon ground cumin

About 1 hour before serving, bring 2 quarts water to a boil in a pot with 1½ teaspoons of the salt. Add the pumpkin, whole tomato, chorizo, morcilla, and potatoes. Cover and cook until the pumpkin and potatoes are tender, about 30 minutes.

Lift out the pumpkin and tomato and reserve, saving the cooking liquid. Skim out the chorizo and morcilla and add to the platter of meats from the big pot, cutting them into serving-size pieces. Place the potatoes with the carrots and turnips.

When cool enough to handle, remove the skin from the tomato. Combine the tomato, pumpkin, garlic, vinegar, remaining ½ teaspoon salt, and cumin in a blender with ½ cup of the broth from the main pot. Blend until smooth. Serve some of this sauce spooned over the chickpeas and the rest in a sauceboat to accompany the vegetables.

FOR THE CABBAGE

1 pound cabbage, shredded

1 teaspoon olive oil

1 garlic clove, minced

Hot red pepper flakes

1 teaspoon sweet pimentón

Bring the reserved cooking liquid to a boil and add the cabbage. Cook until very tender, 15 minutes. Drain, saving 3 tablespoons of the liquid. Place the cabbage in a serving bowl.

Heat the olive oil in a small skillet over medium heat. Add the garlic and red pepper flakes and sauté until the garlic begins to color, about 2 minutes. Remove from heat and stir in the pimentón. Stir in the reserved cabbage liquid. Pour over the cabbage.

FOR THE SOUP

9 cups strained cocido broth

12 rellenos (meatballs; recipe page 122)

Chopped cooked giblets and liver (optional)

½ pound (1½ cups) vermicelli noodles

1 tablespoon finely chopped fresh mint

Bring the strained broth to a boil. Add the meatballs and simmer, covered, for 15 minutes. Add the chopped giblets reserved from the cocido pot if you're using them. Bring the broth to a boil and add the noodles. Cook until done, 6 to 12 minutes, depending on whether they are fine or thick. Serve the soup in shallow bowls. Garnish with chopped mint.

ACCOMPANIMENTS

Scarlet-Pickled Onions (page 282)

Pickled peppers (*guindillas*), such as peperoncini

Serve the broth with noodles and meatballs as a first course. Serve a platter of carrots, turnips, leeks, and potatoes. Serve a bowl of chickpeas with accompanying pumpkin sauce. Serve the bowl of cabbage. Serve the platter of cut-up chicken, ham hock, beef, chorizo, and morcilla. Accompany with pickled onions and peppers.

Fish *and* Shellfish

I was having an early-morning coffee at a café in a small La Mancha town. A delivery van pulled up at the door. *Pescados Juanito,* Johnny's Fish. I supposed a crate of frozen fish was being delivered to the freezer in the restaurant's kitchen. The guy got out with a tray heaped with absolutely fresh sardines, still glistening and rigid. This was a place about as far away from the sea as you can get.

La Mancha is full of surprises. One of the biggest was discovering impeccably fresh fish in the markets and at very good prices. Every bit as good as what I can buy at the fish market near where I live in southern Spain, only about two blocks from a fishing port on the Mediterranean.

That's because Madrid, in the geographic center of the Spanish peninsula and a long way from the ocean, is a distribution hub for seafood. Fresh fish and shellfish arriving at major ports on the Bay of Biscay, Atlantic, or Mediterranean are packed on ice and shipped in refrigerated trucks to Madrid. From Madrid, one of the biggest wholesale fish markets in the world, fish is moved out to the provinces.

Of course, it wasn't always that way. Before refrigeration and automotive transport, the only fresh fish came from streams, rivers, and lagoons. From far-off oceans came salt fish of various sorts, carried overland by muledrivers. To this day La Mancha has a variety of preparations for *bacalao,* dry salt cod.

Freshwater trout gets top billing in this chapter. Wild trout once was abundant in the rivers and streams of Castilla–La Mancha, but nowadays farmed fish is marketed. Some of these recipes would work equally well with ocean fish such as small bass. From the ocean are hake in a luscious saffron sauce, sea bass with pine nuts, roasted red bream for Christmas, and sole in wine sauce.

TROUT STUFFED with HAM and MUSHROOMS

Truchas Rellenas con Jamón y Setas

Fresh trout doesn't need much gussying up. But if you have a good source and can enjoy it frequently, it's great to have a few variations on the tried and true. This recipe also works nicely with serving-sized sea bass.

SERVES 4

---

4 trout, each about ¾ pound, filleted (8 fillets)

Salt

1 tablespoon olive oil, plus olive oil for frying

½ cup chopped shallot

1 cup chopped mushrooms (about 3 ounces)

Pinch of dried thyme

1 cup dry white wine

¼ cup fresh bread crumbs

2 ounces serrano or cooked ham, thinly sliced

Flour for dredging

1 tablespoon fresh lemon juice

1 tablespoon chopped fresh parsley

Sprinkle the fillets with salt and let stand while you prepare the stuffing.

Heat 1 tablespoon oil in a small skillet over medium heat. Add the shallot and sauté for 2 minutes. Add the mushrooms and sauté for 5 minutes. Add the thyme and ¼ cup of the wine and cook until the liquid is evaporated. Stir in the bread crumbs. Remove from the heat and let cool slightly.

Spread the mushroom mixture on each of 4 trout fillets. Top with sliced ham. Top with another fillet, pressing gently to close. (The fillets will hold together without being tied.)

Dredge the trout in flour, patting off the excess. Heat olive oil to a depth of ¼ inch in a heavy skillet over medium heat. Fry the trout, in 2 batches, if necessary, until browned, about 4 minutes. Turn them and cook for about 4 minutes more. Transfer to a serving platter and keep warm.

Pour off all but 2 tablespoons of the oil from the skillet. Add the lemon juice and remaining wine. Boil for 3 minutes, until reduced by half. Add the parsley to the sauce and pour over the fish.

TROUT and MUSHROOMS in CAZUELA, GUADALAJARA STYLE

Trucha con Setas en Cazuela, al Estilo de Guadalajara

Guadalajara, a province in Spain (not Mexico) east of Madrid, at the top of the Castilla–La Mancha region, is famed for its trout.

Over the years I have become dedicated to cazuela cooking. A cazuela is an earthenware casserole that can go from top of the stove to oven to table. Once you become used to cooking in a cazuela, you can sauté foods and brown them nicely, then add liquid for a slow braise. Earthenware takes a long time to heat up, but then it maintains a steady and even cooking temperature.

❧ SERVES 4

---

4 trout fillets, 5 to 6 ounces each

Salt and freshly ground black pepper

1 pound oyster or other mushrooms, sliced

2 ounces serrano ham, cut into julienne strips

2 garlic cloves, chopped

¼ cup olive oil

⅓ cup dry white wine

Pinch of dried thyme

Chopped fresh parsley for garnish

Sprinkle the trout fillets with salt and pepper to taste and set aside for 20 minutes. Preheat the oven to 400°F.

Place the sliced mushrooms in a 9-inch cazuela. Scatter the ham and garlic on top. Drizzle with half of the oil.

Heat the cazuela over medium heat until the mushrooms begin to sizzle, about 3 minutes.

Place the trout fillets on top, skin side up, overlapping them slightly. Drizzle with the remaining oil, wine, and thyme. When the liquid begins to simmer, after about 2 minutes, place the cazuela in the oven. Bake until the trout flakes easily, about 15 minutes.

Transfer the fillets with a slotted spoon to serving plates, skin side down. Spoon the mushrooms and juice over them. Sprinkle with parsley and serve.

TROUT, JEWISH STYLE

Trucha a la Judía

The original version of this delectable dish probably consisted of no more than fish, olive oil, and onions, while the modern version is a sweet-sour confit with tomatoes, a nice counterpoint to trout. This dish can also be made with fillets of sea bass or mackerel.

SERVES 4

4 trout fillets, each about ¾ pound

Salt and freshly ground black pepper

2 tablespoons olive oil

1 cup sliced plum tomato, juice reserved

¼ cup fresh lemon juice

1½ teaspoons sugar

½ cup chopped fresh flat-leaf parsley

Sprinkle the trout with salt and pepper to taste and let stand for 30 minutes.

Heat the oil in a skillet over high heat and add the tomato. Cook for 2 minutes. Add the lemon juice, sugar, and parsley. Reduce heat to medium and cook until thickened, about 10 minutes.

Place the trout fillets on top of the tomato mixture, skin side down. Cook for 4 minutes. Turn skin side up and cook for 4 minutes longer.

Serve the trout with the tomato sauce spooned over the fillets.

A TROUT FISHERMAN IN CUENCA

North of the provincial capital of Cuenca, heading toward the high sierra, is an idyllic region of fast-moving trout streams, mountain retreats, forested valleys, tumbling waterfalls, and an "enchanted city," where wind and rain over several millennia have carved karstic limestone into phantasmal shapes. Hugging the rocky cliffs above the River Júcar is the village of Villalba de la Sierra. Across the bridge and nestled in a wooded area next to the river is El Tablazo, a hotel in a converted flour mill on a small lake. Javi Alegría, fisherman and outdoorsman, runs a trout fishing concession on the lake. Here I caught my first-ever fish.

"Grip the reel here and hold the line down with your finger, then swing the line out beyond those reeds, letting go of the line at the same time." Javi Alegría gives me some basic instructions and hands me the fishing rod. The hook on the end is baited with three kernels of corn.

I cast, and the line gets snagged. I do it again. And wait. Willows ring the small lake, dribbling branches in the shimmery water. I can hear the sound of the nearby river bouncing over stones. I pull the line in just a little. The float bobs, I feel a tug. Oh my goodness! I slowly reel in the line until, dangling before me, is a lovely rainbow trout. I am so excited that my shouts disturb the peaceful scene.

Javi laughs. *"Pescador que pesca un pez, pescador es."* Catch one fish, fisherman is he. Or fisherwoman. I was hooked. I landed two more of the beautiful fish and proudly delivered them to the hotel kitchen. My friends and I dined on our catch that evening.

Javi stocks the lake at El Tablazo with farmed rainbow trout and opens the fishing concession to guests. He weighs the catch on the way out and charges accordingly. Javi says even fly fishermen come to the lake because they can fish year-round. But when I ask to take his picture with a string of trout, he gets embarrassed and refuses. He doesn't really want to be seen with dead trout.

Javi fly-fishes *sin muerte,* catch and release. He showed me his selection of nymphs and dry flies. After the thrill of landing the trout, with no barb on the hook, it is released unscathed. Not dinner. If his mother wants to cook trout for dinner, he pulls them from the stocked lake. He fly-fishes on the Júcar, just a few yards from the lake, and in rivers higher into the sierra.

Javi grew up in Cuenca. His father was a *guardamonte*—forest ranger and game warden. Javi worked in government reforestation projects but got out because he didn't like the politics of land management. He and his brother took over El Tablazo in the 1990s.

"Environment is delicate," he says. And people have abused it. People of all sorts—hunters, fishermen, farmers, city people. "I love fishing. The beautiful part is landing a trout. But, in good conscience, I don't want to kill it."

When I met Javi, in the autumn after early rains, he was off on a mushroom-hunting expedition. In the winter, when the hills are dusted with snow, he hunts partridge and rabbit. In April the season for trout opens.

In bygone days trout was everyday fare in the cooking of Castilla–La Mancha. Every mill-stream was a source of trout. The River Tajo in Toledo was so abundant that it was pickled in escabeche. Now trout that appears at the market or in restaurants is always farmed rainbow trout. Castilla–La Mancha has more than two hundred miles of trout streams, mainly in Cuenca, Guadalajara, and Albacete provinces. With management of fishing and watercourses, stocks of wild trout are slowly recovering.

Here's a recipe for stuffing and baking trout that Javi shared with me. You need a really big trout—about 2¾ pounds. Clean it and pat dry with a clean cloth. Season it with salt, white pepper, and oregano. For the stuffing, chop pine nuts, bacon, and smoked salmon. Stuff the trout with this. Fry the trout in very hot oil until browned on both sides. Then place it in an earthenware cazuela with oil, white wine, water, chopped shallot, and any of the stuffing mixture left over. Bake in a preheated 350°F oven until the trout flakes easily.

FISH in A TANGY MARINADE

Pescado en Escabeche

In addition to trout, other freshwater fish, such as pike, tench, barbel, and carp, are found in the streams and lakes of La Mancha. Before the days of refrigeration *escabeche*, a strong vinegar marinade, was used to preserve cooked fish. Made with farmed catfish, this is a delicious cold dish.

SERVES 6

3 catfish or lake perch fillets, 10 to 12 ounces each

¼ cup olive oil

1 cup julienned onion

¼ cup julienned red bell pepper

2 garlic cloves, slivered

1 carrot, sliced

¾ cup white wine vinegar

¼ teaspoon peppercorns

Pinch of ground cloves

⅛ teaspoon celery seeds

¼ teaspoon dried oregano

¼ cup chopped fresh parsley, plus parsley for garnish

2 teaspoons salt

1 bay leaf

Hot red pepper flakes

1 large potato (12 ounces)

Leafy greens for serving

1 hard-cooked egg, quartered, for garnish

Extra virgin olive oil for serving

Cut each fillet into 4 pieces of similar size. Heat ¼ cup oil in a nonstick skillet or cazuela over medium heat and fry the fish until lightly browned, about 2 minutes per side. Remove the pieces and place them in one layer in a shallow nonreactive bowl or cazuela.

Add the onion, pepper, garlic, and carrot to the oil and sauté for 5 minutes, until the onion is softened. Add the vinegar and 2¾ cups water, the peppercorns, cloves, celery seeds, oregano, parsley, salt, bay leaf, and red pepper flakes to taste. Bring to a boil and cook for 5 minutes.

Ladle the vinegar marinade with the vegetables and spices carefully over the fish. Allow to stand until cool.

Cook the whole potato in boiling water until tender when pierced with a skewer, about 25 minutes. Drain and cool. When completely cool, peel the potato, cut it in half lengthwise, then cut it crosswise into ½-inch slices. Tuck the slices into the marinade with the fish.

Cover and refrigerate for at least 12 and up to 36 hours.

To serve, lift the fish, potatoes, and vegetables out of the marinade and arrange them atop leafy greens. Garnish the plate with egg and parsley. Drizzle with a little extra virgin olive oil and serve.

POACHED HAKE *with* SAFFRON SAUCE

Merluza al Azafrán

Saffron, grown in La Mancha, contributes subtle flavor to this sauce, which would enhance any poached or grilled fish. It goes especially well with delicate hake, a favorite fish in Spain. Fresh cod, halibut, or grouper could be used in its place. For best results, use very fresh fish, not frozen fillets. Leaving the skin on helps to keep a delicate fish from falling apart.

SERVES 4

Salt

4 pieces hake fillet, about 6 ounces each, skin on

½ teaspoon saffron threads

3 tablespoons extra virgin olive oil

½ cup chopped onion

2 garlic cloves, chopped

1 cup peeled, seeded, and diced tomato

1½ cups Simple Fish Broth (page 135) or ¾ cup clam juice and ¾ cup water

1 bay leaf

3 tablespoons chopped fresh flat-leaf parsley

Salt the fish fillets and allow to stand for 30 minutes.

Crush the saffron in a mortar and dissolve in 2 tablespoons warm water. Let it infuse for 15 minutes.

Heat the oil in a large skillet or flameproof casserole over medium heat. Sauté the onion and garlic until softened, 5 minutes. Add the tomato and cook for 5 minutes. Add the fish broth and simmer for 15 minutes. Add the saffron water.

Puree the sauce in a blender and strain, discarding the solids.

Pour the sauce into a deep skillet or flameproof casserole. Add the fish fillets, skin side down, and turn them to coat. Add the bay leaf. Bring the sauce to a simmer and cook, covered, until the fish flakes easily, 8 to 10 minutes.

Discard the bay leaf. Serve sprinkled with parsley.

✺ SIMPLE FISH BROTH *Caldo de Pescado*

At markets where you can purchase whole fish, you will be able to buy heads, bones, and trimmings to make a basic broth or stock, essential for fish soups and some sauces. Use trimmings from only white fish (such as snapper or halibut), never those from fatty fish such as salmon. Shrimp shells and clam or mussel liquid can be added to the broth. Freeze the broth in 2- or 3-cup quantities for use in sauces and soups.

✺ Makes 2 quarts

1 pound small white fish or fish heads, bones, and trimmings

Shrimp shells (optional)

2 teaspoons salt

1 leek

1 strip lemon zest

1 celery stalk

1 small carrot

Parsley stems

Pinch of dried thyme

1 bay leaf

½ cup dry white wine

Combine all the ingredients in a large pot with 10 cups water. Bring to a boil. Cover and simmer for 1 hour. Strain the broth and discard the solids.

SEA BASS *with* GARLIC, PINE NUTS, *and* CHILE

Lubina con Ajillo de Piñones

A classic way of preparing fish in Spain is *a la espalda*, fish grilled "on its back." Basically, a whole fish (with the head too) is butterflied and grilled. The spine is lifted out after cooking. Drizzled with a "sauce" of oil, garlic, and hot chile, it is simple but ever so tasty. This variation includes toasty pine nuts and can be prepared with fish fillets instead of a whole fish.

SERVES 4

Four 6-ounce sea bass or striped bass fillets, skin on

Salt

3 tablespoons plus 1 teaspoon olive oil

3 tablespoons pine nuts

½ cup dry white wine

¼ teaspoon hot red pepper flakes

1 tablespoon sliced garlic (2 to 3 cloves)

1 tablespoon fresh lemon juice

1 tablespoon chopped fresh parsley

Pinch of dried thyme

Sprinkle the fish fillets with salt and allow to stand at room temperature for 30 minutes.

Heat 1 teaspoon oil in a small skillet over medium-high heat and fry the pine nuts until golden, about 30 seconds. Tip the skillet so the oil drains to one side and skim out the pine nuts. Reserve the pine nuts and oil.

Preheat the oven to 375°F.

Use the oil remaining in the small skillet to brush a griddle or heavy skillet. Heat the griddle until very hot. Sear the fillets, skin side down, until lightly crisped, 1½ minutes. Place the fillets in a single layer, skin side down, in a baking pan.

Drizzle the fish with 2 tablespoons of the remaining oil and the wine. Bake, uncovered, until the fish just barely flakes, 6 to 8 minutes.

While the fish is in the oven, add the remaining tablespoon of oil to the small skillet and fry the red pepper flakes and garlic over medium heat until the garlic is golden, 20 seconds. Remove from the pan immediately so the mixture doesn't burn.

When the fish is cooked, lift the fillets out of the baking pan and place them on heated plates. Pour all the cooking liquid from the baking pan into the small skillet. Bring to a boil and cook for 1 minute. Add the lemon juice. Remove from the heat and add the pine nuts, garlic, red pepper flakes, parsley, and thyme.

Spoon this sauce over the fish fillets and serve immediately.

ROASTED BREAM *on* A BED OF POTATOES

Besugo al Horno con Patatas

Besugo is red bream, a much-appreciated fish throughout Spain. It's a reddish pink color, with white firm but delicate flesh. It's said that besugo doesn't acquire its full virtue until it arrives in (inland) Madrid, where it is considered an essential part of the family Christmas Eve dinner. Prices for this fish skyrocket the week before the holiday.

While it's customary to roast a whole fish, including the head, the recipe works fine even if the head has been removed. A 2-pound fish (without the head) will serve four if this is a main course. As part of a much larger meal, it will serve six. Bream may not be easy to come by in American markets. Try this recipe with red snapper, grouper, or large bass if you can't find it.

乄 SERVES 4 TO 6

1 whole fish, gutted and scaled (2 to 2½ pounds)	2 bay leaves
Salt	¼ cup chopped fresh parsley
1½ pounds potatoes (3 medium), peeled and sliced ¼ inch thick	2 teaspoons chopped garlic
	1 cup fresh bread crumbs
½ cup sliced onion	1 slice lemon
¼ cup olive oil	½ cup dry white wine

Sprinkle the fish inside and out with salt and allow to stand for 30 minutes.

Preheat the oven to 375°F.

Place the potatoes and onion in a bowl and drizzle with 1 tablespoon of the oil and ½ teaspoon salt. Toss to coat the potatoes. Spread them in an oven pan large enough to hold the fish. Tuck the bay leaves into the potatoes. Cover with foil and bake for 10 minutes.

Combine the parsley, garlic, bread crumbs, and 1 tablespoon of the remaining oil in a small bowl.

Pat the fish dry. Cut 2 slashes on the top side of the fish. Cut the lemon slice in half and insert a slice in each slash.

Remove the potatoes from the oven and discard the foil. Use a spatula to turn the potatoes. Place the fish on top of the potatoes. Spread the bread crumb mixture on top of the fish, patting it into place.

Return the pan to the oven and bake for 10 minutes. Combine the wine with the remaining 2 tablespoons oil. Drizzle a little over the fish and the rest around the fish. Return to the oven until the flesh just barely pulls away from the bone, about 20 minutes longer. (If the fish needs more roasting time, it may be necessary to add water to the pan so that the potatoes don't scorch on the bottom.)

Use 2 spatulas to transfer the fish to a heated serving platter. Place the potatoes around it and serve immediately. Or divide the fish into 4 fillets in the kitchen. Arrange them on individual plates, adding some of the bread crumbs and potatoes to each serving.

FILLETS OF SOLE with WHITE WINE SAUCE and GRAPES

Filetes de Lenguado con Uvas

On New Year's Eve, friends go out for a gala supper with *cava,* sparkling wine, then, at midnight everybody gathers in the town plaza to await the twelve bells, swallowing one grape at every bell—assuring good luck for the coming year. Then it's dancing till dawn. These fillets of sole with grapes are a perfect addition to an elegant and festive menu. Use good dry white wine or cava in the sauce.

Sole fillets are long and fairly thin, so they can be folded in thirds. Fillets of turbot, flounder, or John Dory can be substituted.

SERVES 4

Four 6-ounce sole fillets

Salt

2 ounces serrano ham, thinly sliced

2 tablespoons olive oil

⅓ cup chopped shallot

1 tablespoon all-purpose flour

½ cup dry white wine

1 cup Simple Fish Broth (page 135) or ½ cup clam juice and ½ cup water

Pinch of saffron threads, crushed

1 cup red or white seedless grapes, peeled or halved

1 tablespoon cold butter, cut into pieces

Spread the fillets out flat. Sprinkle with salt. Top with sliced ham. Fold the fillets over the ham into thirds (like a letter). Cut bands of foil 2½ inches wide. Wrap the bands like a belt around the center of the folded fillets. Pinch the ends of the foil together to prevent the fillets from unrolling. Place them in an oven pan just large enough to hold them in one layer.

Heat the oil in a small skillet over low heat. Sauté the shallot until softened but not browned, 4 minutes. Stir in the flour. Add the wine and fish broth and stir. Raise the heat to medium and cook, stirring frequently, for 10 minutes.

Place the crushed saffron in a blender. Add the sauce from the skillet. Blend to make a smooth sauce.

Preheat the oven to 350°F.

Pour the blended sauce around the fish fillets. Cover the baking pan with foil and bake until the fish just flakes, 12 to 14 minutes.

Transfer the fillets to a warm platter and snip off the foil bands. Keep warm.

Pour all of the sauce and liquid from the baking pan into the skillet. Bring to a boil and add the grapes. Simmer for 2 minutes. Add the butter, a bit at a time, swirling or stirring to blend it into the sauce. Do not boil.

Serve the sole fillets with the sauce and grapes.

FARMHOUSE RICE with FISH and GREENS

Arroz a la Quintería

A *quintería* is a traditional Manchegan farmstead, where this dish would be made with salt cod. However, nowadays frozen fish is a viable alternative. The greens could be wild spring greens, such as *collejas,* a kind of catchfly. Here I have used spinach.

Use round-grain Spanish rice for this dish. If you can get it, the Bomba variety is best, because it doesn't "flower" and open up when cooked. Please avoid the temptation to stir the rice! Let it bubble gently until just al dente.

SERVES 4 TO 5

¾ pound fish fillet, such as cod, snapper, or monkfish

¼ cup olive oil

1½ cups diced tomato

1 small head of garlic

1 medium potato (½ pound), cut into 1-inch pieces

Hot red pepper flakes

4 cups shredded spinach (½ pound)

⅛ teaspoon saffron threads, crushed, or 1 teaspoon pimentón

2 teaspoons salt

Freshly ground black pepper

2 cups Spanish round-grain rice

Cut the fish fillet into 8 to 10 slices or chunks. Heat the oil in a cazuela or sauté pan over medium heat and quickly fry the fish, about 1 minute per side. It does not need to brown. Remove the fish and reserve. Add the tomato to the oil and cook over high heat for 2 minutes. Slice the top off the head of garlic and add to the pan with the potato and pepper flakes. Cook for 5 minutes. Add the spinach and cook for 5 minutes more.

Combine the saffron with 2 tablespoons warm water and allow to stand.

Add 5 cups water to the pan along with the salt and pepper to taste. Bring to a boil. Cook, uncovered, over medium heat for 10 minutes. Add the saffron water. Bring the liquid to a boil and add the rice. Return the pieces of fish to the pan.

Let the rice cook over high heat for 3 minutes. Lower the heat so that it bubbles gently and cook for 10 minutes longer. This rice dish is not "dry" like paella but a little juicy. Remove from the heat, cover the pan, and allow to stand for 5 minutes before serving.

OLIVE PICKERS' COD *and* POTATO STEW

Pote Aceitunero

This one-pot stew comes from the Montes de Toledo, an area famous for its olive oil. January, when groups of pickers gather in the olive groves, can be bitter cold. The pickers make a roaring fire to warm the hands and cook the midday meal. The traditional version is made with *bacalao,* dry salt cod that has been soaked for twenty-four hours to desalt it. In this recipe I have used fresh cod, which needs only minutes to cook. If you use salt cod, cook it very gently with the potatoes. I like the addition of something green—in this case asparagus.

SERVES 4

1 pound cod fillets, cut into ¾-inch cubes

Salt

2 pounds potatoes, peeled and cut into ¾-inch cubes

¼ cup olive oil

1 bay leaf

1 small dried chile, such as cayenne

2 garlic cloves, 1 peeled

1 medium tomato

1 cup coarsely chopped onion

¼ teaspoon ground cumin

½ teaspoon sweet pimentón, preferably smoked

½ teaspoon hot pimentón or a pinch of cayenne

1 cup sliced cooked asparagus (optional)

1 egg

Sprinkle the cod with salt and let stand at room temperature.

Place the potatoes in a soup pot or deep skillet with the oil and sauté over high heat for 2 minutes. Tuck the bay leaf and chile into the potatoes and add 2 teaspoons salt and 2 cups water. Bring to a boil.

Cut a small slit in one unpeeled garlic clove and add it to the potatoes with the whole tomato and chopped onion. Cover and simmer the potatoes until almost tender, 15 to 20 minutes. Remove and discard the bay leaf and chile. Skim out the garlic clove and tomato.

Remove the skin from the cooked garlic and tomato and place them in a blender with the peeled garlic clove, cumin, sweet pimentón, hot pimentón, and ½ cup of liquid from the potatoes. Blend until smooth. Add this sauce to the potatoes and cook for 5 minutes.

Add the cod to the pot and cook until it just flakes, about 3 minutes. Stir in the asparagus if you're using it. Raise the heat so the liquid bubbles. Break the egg into the pot. Use a fork to stir it into the cod and potatoes, about 1 minute. Remove from the heat and allow the stew to rest 5 minutes. Serve in shallow soup bowls.

CODFISH BALLS *with* WALNUTS

Albóndigas de Bacalao

Salt cod (*bacalao*) was once a staple in the Manchegan kitchen, so housewives learned to prepare it in dozens of appetizing ways. These codfish balls, nicely flavored with cinnamon, nutmeg, and pepper, can be made with small pieces of cod left over after cutting up a large piece for another recipe. Use this recipe to make fish balls with scraps of any cooked fish. If the fish balls are to be served as a main course, accompany them with rice and a vegetable such as sautéed chard (page 251).

MAKES ABOUT 16 FISH BALLS, SERVING 8 AS A TAPA OR 4 AS A MAIN COURSE

1 pound salt cod, soaked in several changes of water for 24 hours

1 bay leaf

2 slices bread

¼ cup milk

1 egg

1 tablespoon chopped fresh parsley

⅛ teaspoon ground cinnamon

Grating of fresh nutmeg

Freshly ground black pepper

Fresh lemon juice

2 tablespoons all-purpose flour

3 tablespoons olive oil

¼ cup dry Sherry or white wine

⅛ teaspoon saffron threads, crushed

Pinch of ground cloves

Salt if necessary

¼ cup chopped walnuts

Drain the soaked cod. Put it in a pan with the bay leaf and cover with fresh water. Bring to just under a boil, then lower the heat to a bare simmer and cook for 5 minutes. Drain, reserving the liquid.

Remove all the skin and bone from the cod. Flake the fish and place it in a blender or food processor.

Place 1 slice of the bread in a saucer and pour the milk over it. When softened, break it up and add to the cod with the egg, parsley, cinnamon, nutmeg, and pepper. Process briefly to make a stiff paste.

Moisten your hands with lemon juice and roll the paste into 1-inch balls. Roll them in flour. Heat 2 tablespoons of the oil in a skillet over medium heat and fry the balls until browned on all sides. Remove.

Add the remaining tablespoon of oil to the skillet and fry the remaining slice of bread. Place it in the blender or processor with the wine, saffron, cloves, and ½ cup of the reserved liquid. Blend to make a smooth sauce.

Place the sauce in a cazuela with ½ cup more of the reserved liquid. Cook, stirring, for 10 minutes.

Place the codfish balls in the cazuela and cook for 10 minutes more. Taste for salt. Scatter the walnuts over the top.

SALT COD *with* ROASTED PEPPERS, MANCHEGAN STYLE

Bacalao a la Manchega

See the instructions on page 10 for how to soak the salt cod. If you can purchase *lomo de bacalao,* cod "loins," or center cut, you will have nice meaty chunks of fish. If buying a whole split (half a salt cod), the skinny tail and bony gill sections yield smaller pieces. Scraps and trimmings can be saved for another dish, such as codfish balls (page 145).

A favorite dish for meatless meals during the Lenten season preceding Easter, this would be served with an egg per person poached on top of the cod, peppers, and potatoes.

SERVES 4

1¼ pounds salt cod, soaked in several changes of water for 24 hours, or 1 pound fresh cod fillets

1 tablespoon anisette or brandy

4 red bell peppers

3 tablespoons olive oil

1 cup chopped onion

1½ cups diced tomato

1½ pounds baking potatoes (3 medium), peeled and cut into 1-inch chunks

3 garlic cloves, peeled

¼ cup fresh parsley leaves

1 teaspoon sweet pimentón

½ teaspoon ground cumin

Pinch of saffron threads, crushed (optional)

Freshly ground black pepper

½ teaspoon salt

1 egg per person or 1 hard-cooked egg, quartered

Fresh parsley for garnish

Drain the soaked cod and squeeze it out gently. Remove and discard all skin and bone. Cut the cod into 2½-inch pieces. Place them in a bowl and drizzle with the anisette. Allow to marinate for 1 hour, turning occasionally.

Roast the peppers over a flame or under a broiler, turning them until charred on all sides. Remove and cover the peppers with a lid. When cool enough to handle, peel off the blackened skin, removing the stems and seeds. Cut or tear the peppers into short strips.

Heat the oil in a cazuela or deep skillet over medium heat. Sauté the onion until softened, 5 minutes. Add the peppers and tomato and cook until the tomato has sweated out some of its liquid, 5 minutes. Add the potatoes.

In a blender, combine the garlic, parsley, pimentón, cumin, saffron if you're using it, pepper, and salt with ½ cup water. Blend until smooth. Pour over the potatoes along with ½ cup water. Bring to a boil, then simmer, covered, for 15 minutes.

Add the pieces of cod to the cazuela. (If you're using fresh cod, add it during the last 10 minutes of cooking.) Simmer over low heat until the potatoes are tender, 15 minutes more. Do not allow the liquid to boil, or it will toughen the cod.

If using poached eggs, break the eggs on top of the potatoes and cod. Cover and simmer until the whites begin to set, 3 to 4 minutes. Remove the cazuela from the heat and allow to stand, covered, for 5 minutes.

Lift the egg, cod, potatoes, and some liquid from the cazuela with a skimmer or large spoon. Serve in shallow soup bowls with a sprinkling of chopped parsley. If you haven't poached eggs with the cod, top each serving with a quarter of hard-cooked egg.

CLAMS, MARINER'S STYLE

Almejas a la Marinera

Mariner's style in land-locked La Mancha? Well, yes. This recipe points up a double Manchegan paradox. For one thing, seafood is super-fresh, distributed from coastal waters to inland markets in twenty-four hours. And, second, weird as it may seem, Spain's national naval museum and archives are situated in El Viso del Marqués, a town in the province of Ciudad Real, far from the sea, in the renaissance *palacio* (mansion) of Don Alvaro de Bazán, an admiral in the Spanish navy in the sixteenth century. Go figure.

SERVES 4

4 dozen Manila or littleneck clams (about 2 pounds)

3 tablespoons olive oil

½ cup chopped onion

3 garlic cloves, chopped

1 teaspoon sweet pimentón

Pinch of hot red pepper flakes

2 tablespoons fine dry bread crumbs

⅓ cup dry white wine

¼ cup chopped fresh flat-leaf parsley

Wash the clams and place them in a basin of water for 2 hours before cooking.

Heat the oil in a deep skillet or flameproof casserole over medium heat and sauté the onion and garlic until softened, about 4 minutes. Stir in the pimentón, red pepper flakes, and bread crumbs. Add the wine and ⅓ cup water. Bring to a boil.

Lift the clams out of the soaking water and add to the skillet. Cover and cook over high heat until the clam shells open, 3 to 4 minutes. Discard any clams that do not open. Sprinkle with parsley and serve the clams and their broth in soup bowls.

SHRIMP in CAZUELA

Cazuela de Gambas

A cazuela is an earthenware casserole that goes from stovetop to oven to table. It is slow to heat, but then holds its temperature even after being removed from the stove. In tapa bars, shrimp are sizzled to order in small, individual cazuelitas. Incidentally, it is customary to peel the tails too, so the whole shrimp is edible. Serve the shrimp with bread for sopping up the juices or spoon it over steamed rice.

SERVES 4

2 tablespoons olive oil	2 garlic cloves, crushed
¼ cup diced bacon or serrano ham	2 tablespoons dry white wine
1 cup chopped leek	Salt
Pinch of hot red pepper flakes	⅓ cup chopped fresh flat-leaf parsley
1¼ pounds peeled medium shrimp	¼ teaspoon smoked pimentón

Heat the oil in a 10-inch cazuela or heavy skillet over medium-low heat. Add the bacon and leek and sauté until the leek is soft but not browned, 10 minutes. Add the pepper flakes.

Turn up the heat until the leeks are sizzling. Stir in the shrimp and sauté for 3 minutes. Add the garlic and wine and cook until the shrimp are pink, about 2 minutes. Add salt to taste.

Remove the cazuela from the heat and stir in the parsley. Sprinkle with the pimentón and serve immediately.

Poultry and Small Game

La Mancha is still a very rural region, where *quinterías,* small farms, dot the landscape. A cluster of whitewashed buildings house granary, barn, stables, chicken and rabbit coops, living quarters, kitchen and pantry, bake house, well house, wine press. While four-wheel-drive vehicles and tractors have replaced the mules and old-fashioned plows of yore, the chickens clucking and scratching in the dirt in the farmyard are as timeless as the land. Producing eggs for daily consumption and the occasional fowl for the stew pot, chickens are a source of culinary wealth.

La Mancha also has chicken farms, sending cheap, battery-raised birds to supermarkets at astonishingly low cost. Nevertheless, there is nothing so delicious as free-range, preferably organically raised, birds.

The *corral,* or farmyard, on a quintería also typically has rabbit hutches and dovecotes. Young rabbits and pigeons make an admirable addition to the stew pot—as Don Quixote himself enjoyed for Sunday dinner.

Hunting is much a part of the rural life of La Mancha. A small landowner—one man, one gun, one dog—typically hunts both feathered and furred small game on his lands, partridge, quail, wild rabbit, and hare being the most abundant. There are also fancy hunts, *cacerías,* on huge estates owned by aristocrats.

I realize that most American cooks seldom find wild partridge or hare available. For that reason, I have grouped chicken recipes with those for small game because most are interchangeable. That means if you find a partridge recipe that sounds enticing, you can probably prepare it with chicken or turkey. You will find suggestions for substitutes in each recipe. Additionally, as farm-raised rabbit, a lean and flavorful meat, becomes more widely available in supermarkets, I suggest you experiment by substituting it for chicken.

CHICKEN *with* PEPPERS *and* TOMATOES, TOLEDO STYLE

Pisto con Pollo Toledano

Pisto is the emblematic dish of La Mancha. It derives from the Moorish *alboronía,* originally meat braised with onions and eggplant. As other vegetables appeared on the scene, such as peppers, squash, and tomatoes from the New World, they were incorporated into the dish. This version with chicken calls only for onions, tomatoes, and peppers, which become both sauce and vegetable side dish. Serve it with bread, rice, or noodles to soak up the delicious juices.

SERVES 4 TO 5

1 frying chicken, cut up, or about 2½ pounds chicken pieces

Salt and freshly ground black pepper

5 large green bell peppers

1 tablespoon olive oil

1½ cups chopped onion

2 garlic cloves, chopped

2½ pounds tomatoes (6 to 7 medium), peeled, seeded, and chopped

½ teaspoon salt

⅛ teaspoon cumin seeds

1 tablespoon wine vinegar

Pitted olives such as arbequinas (optional)

Season the chicken pieces with salt and pepper and set aside.

Roast the peppers over a flame or under the broiler, turning them until charred on all sides. Transfer them to a bowl and cover them. When cool enough to handle, peel off the charred skin, using your fingers or scraping with a knife. Discard the stems and seeds. Rinse the peppers under running water. Tear or cut into bite-sized pieces.

Heat the oil in a large cazuela or deep sauté pan over medium heat. Brown the chicken pieces, about 15 minutes. Remove them and reserve. Drain off all but 1 tablespoon of the fat.

Add the onion and garlic to the pan and sauté for 5 minutes. Raise the heat, add the peppers, and sauté for a few minutes longer. Then add the chopped tomatoes and cook over high heat for 5 minutes. Stir in the salt, cumin seeds, and vinegar. Return the chicken pieces to the pan. Cook, uncovered, over medium heat, turning the chicken once, until the vegetables and chicken are very tender, 40 to 60 minutes. Serve garnished with a few pitted olives.

NOTE: *If desired, the chicken pieces can be skinned, in which case let them brown very briefly before adding the onion.*

MANCHEGO CHICKEN *with* ANISETTE

Pollo Manchego con Aguardiente

Aguardiente de anís is a clear anise-flavored brandy, sweet or dry, much appreciated throughout Spain. It makes a pleasant digestive after a meal, served neat in a snifter or over ice. Hardy peasants might sip it for breakfast, when it's said to *matar el gusanillo,* kill the little "worm" of hunger. For this recipe, use dry aguardiente. If not available, substitute anisette. This chicken is good served over rice.

SERVES 4 TO 6

2½ to 3 pounds chicken pieces	½ teaspoon ground cinnamon
Salt and freshly ground black pepper	Pinch of ground cloves
3 tablespoons olive oil	Grating of fresh nutmeg
2 garlic cloves, chopped	2 tablespoons aguardiente de anís or dry anisette
Pinch of dried thyme	¼ cup dry white wine

Sprinkle the chicken pieces with salt and pepper and set aside for 15 minutes. Heat the oil in a large skillet or sauté pan over medium heat. Add the chicken and brown it, about 5 minutes. Turn the chicken and add the garlic. Sauté until the chicken is lightly browned on the other side, about 5 minutes longer.

Sprinkle the thyme, cinnamon, cloves, and nutmeg over the chicken. Add the anisette, wine, and ¼ cup water. Cover and simmer until the chicken is very tender, 35 to 50 minutes, depending on the size of the pieces.

CRISPY, CHEESY CHICKEN BREAST
with QUINCE SAUCE

Pechuga de Pollo Empanada con Salsa de Membrillo

A classic combination is Manchego cheese and *membrillo,* sweet quince jelly. Quince is a fruit so rich in pectin that, when cooked with sugar, it sets up solid and can be cut into cubes. Paired with cheese, it makes a tantalizing appetizer or dessert. You can buy membrillo imported from Spain at specialty food stores (or see the recipe on page 329).

Here the quince points up the cheese in breaded chicken breasts. If membrillo is not available, substitute sweetened applesauce for the quince jelly, with the vinegar, but without the addition of water.

I like to use small breast halves (5 to 6 ounces), allowing one per person. If you can get only larger pieces, cook two or three and cut them in half to serve. Garlicky spinach (page 252) is a good side with the crispy chicken.

SERVES 4

¼ pound *membrillo* (about a 2-inch cube), cut into pieces

2 teaspoons Sherry vinegar

4 small boneless, skinless chicken breast halves (1¼ pounds)

Salt

¼ teaspoon dried basil

1 cup grated Manchego (3 ounces), preferably cured

1 cup fine dry bread crumbs

2 eggs, beaten with 2 teaspoons water

About 6 tablespoons olive oil for frying

To make the sauce, combine the membrillo, vinegar, and ⅓ cup hot water in a blender. Blend until smooth. Set the sauce aside.

Remove the chicken tenders and reserve for another use. Place the chicken breasts between layers of plastic wrap and pound to equal thickness, about ½ inch. Sprinkle with salt and basil.

Combine the grated cheese and bread crumbs in a shallow pan. Place the beaten eggs in another pan. Dip each chicken breast first into beaten egg, then into the cheese-crumb mixture, again into egg, and again into the crumbs. Set them on a baking sheet and allow to dry for 30 minutes.

Heat the oil in a heavy skillet over medium heat until hot but not smoking. Fry the chicken breasts (in 2 batches, if necessary) until browned on both sides and cooked through, about 4 minutes per side. Drain briefly on paper towels.

Heat the quince sauce in a small saucepan. Serve it alongside the chicken breasts.

CHICKEN BREAST *with* CRUNCHY VEGETABLES *and* RICE

Pechuga de Pollo con Arroz y Verduras Frescas

In the shadow of Toledo's grand cathedral is the eponymous restaurant of Adolfo Muñoz, passionate proponent of everything gustatory. Adolfo has one of the finest wine cellars in the country, situated below street level in an excavated house dating from medieval times. He's a television chef and an enthusiastic promoter of La Mancha's great products, such as saffron and olive oil.

This recipe is adapted from a dish I savored at Restaurante Adolfo, where it was prepared with squab breast cooked very rare and rice that was slightly crunchy. I have substituted chicken breasts, which should be thoroughly cooked but not overcooked. The vegetables should be slightly crunchy and the rice al dente.

SERVES 6

FOR THE BROTH	
1 tablespoon olive oil	1 carrot
1 pound chicken carcass or wings	1 celery stalk
½ onion, sliced	Pinch of dried thyme
¼ cup dry white wine	1 bay leaf
1 tomato, quartered	1 fresh parsley sprig
	1 teaspoon salt

Heat the oil in a heavy pot over medium-high heat and brown the chicken carcass or wings with the onion until flecked with dark brown, 8 to 10 minutes.

Add the wine, tomato, carrot, celery, thyme, bay leaf, parsley, salt, and 6 cups water. Bring to a boil, cover, and simmer for 1 hour.

Strain the broth, pressing hard on the solids. Discard the solids. Let the broth stand for 20 minutes. Skim off and discard the fat that rises to the top. Set aside 3 cups of the broth to cook the rice. Reserve the remainder for another use (it can be frozen).

FOR THE CHICKEN BREASTS, VEGETABLES, AND RICE

4 boneless chicken breast halves with skin (about 2 pounds)

Salt and freshly ground black pepper

2 tablespoons olive oil, plus oil for the grill

1½ cups long-grain rice

⅓ cup diced carrot

⅓ cup diced leek

⅓ cup diced red bell pepper

⅓ cup diced mushrooms

½ cup diced asparagus

¼ teaspoon saffron threads, crushed

¼ cup dry white wine

Pinch of dried thyme

Pinch of dried rosemary

Season the chicken breasts with salt and pepper. Heat a ridged grill pan and brush with oil. Sear the chicken breasts, skin side down, over high heat, about 1½ minutes. Turn them crosswise and grill for 1 minute more. Turn them over and repeat the turns. Transfer the breasts to a skillet big enough to hold them in one layer.

In a dry heavy skillet over medium heat, cook the rice, stirring constantly, until golden and toasted, about 8 minutes. Reserve.

Heat 2 tablespoons oil in a saucepan. Add the carrot and leek and sauté for 3 minutes. Add the bell pepper and sauté for 2 minutes. Add the mushrooms and sauté for 2 minutes. Add the asparagus and sauté for 1 minute. The vegetables should be crunchy.

Add 2 tablespoons hot water to the saffron and allow to infuse.

Add the reserved 3 cups broth to the vegetables. Add salt to taste. Bring to a boil. Add the toasted rice and saffron infusion and boil for 3 minutes. Remove from the heat, cover tightly, and let the rice set for 10 minutes. The rice will be al dente.

Add the wine, thyme, and rosemary to the chicken breasts. Bring to a boil, cover, and simmer, turning once, until they are cooked through, about 12 minutes.

Slice the chicken breasts on the diagonal. Serve alongside the rice and vegetables. Bring the remaining wine in the skillet to a boil and spoon it over the chicken, rice, and vegetables.

SAFFRON, FROM FIELD TO KITCHEN

The locals say you can never predict the day of the *manto*, when the saffron fields are blanketed in blooms. It could come as early as October 25 or as late as November 5. It depends on the weather, the fall rains, and the temperature. The picking begins from the time the first few saffron flowers (*Crocus sativus*) begin poking up through red dirt and continues daily for a week to ten days.

As it happens, this year the day of the manto falls on November 1, and at dawn a dense fog covers the low-lying saffron fields on the outskirts of the village of Campillo de Altobuey on the eastern edge of Cuenca province.

The pickers are already at work, men and women, young and not so young, ghostly figures in the gray mist. Bending from the waist, they move down the rows, plucking the tiny mauve-colored crocuses and piling them in esparto baskets.

Beyond the saffron fields, the countryside stretches across the stubble of wheat and lentil fields, bent sunflower stalks, and coppery leaves of vineyards. In the distance olive groves spread across the flanks of a low rise, not quite a hill.

"*Hay que madrugar mucho,*" says Antonio, the foreman on the picking operation. You have to get up really early to pick saffron.

The saffron flowers—they are called *rosas*, roses—must be picked early in the morning, when the petals are barely opened and still glossy. Once warmed by the sun, the flowers open and become limp, making the picking difficult because it's easy to break the flower and damage the stigmas. Besides, as the sun burns off the fog, bees start working the saffron fields. Paca, one of the pickers, reaches for a flower and gets stung by a bee. Within minutes, her arm starts swelling and she retires to pop an antihistamine.

Done so close to the earth, picking crocuses is backbreaking work.

"It's an easy job to learn," says María, "but, I'll tell you, your back always hurts."

The saffron from these fields belongs to a small family business, Bealar, which wins prizes for the quality of its saffron.

All morning long Antonio hauls crates filled with saffron crocuses to town in his little van. He delivers them to the *roseras*, the "ladies of the rose," or *mondaderas*, the women who perform *mondeo*, extracting the three threads of the stigma from each crocus. The stigmas must be removed the same day that the flowers are picked or the flowers become pulpy and the precious stigmas are lost.

The stigmas, once dried, become the spice known as *saffron,* which imparts a bittersweet aroma—somewhat reminiscent of fresh hay—and glorious golden color to foods with which it cooks. It takes the stigmas of approximately seventy thousand crocuses to make one pound of spice.

The women sit in groups of six to eight around a table. Heaped in the center are saffron flowers. Swiftly, deftly, the women open the petals of the crocus with the fingers of one hand and, with the other, pull out the three stigmas. They discard the purple flowers in a heap on the floor. The wisps of orange-red saffron stigmas slowly accumulate on plates. Each woman will be paid by the weight of saffron she has prepared. Vicenta holds the record, with 7½ ounces of saffron in a single day.

During the first few hours of the *mondeo,* the ladies chatter, joke, gossip, and exchange recipes around the table. They argue about what to include in the *cocido,* the midday meal-in-a-pot. Amparo insists on beef bone, lean pork, pig's foot, salt pork, stewing hen, chorizo and morcilla sausages, chickpeas, plus potato, celery, leek, carrot, turnip, parsnip, and cardoon. But Concha snorts that that was a "garden without flowers." She uses only beef and ham bone, chickpeas, and potatoes. Many of the local women say they add a pinch of saffron to the *caldo,* the broth from the cocido, but only on very special occasions. Saffron is too highly valued for everyday flavoring.

Campillo is closer to Valencia than to Madrid, so paella is made here in the true Valencia manner, with rabbit, chicken, rosemary, snails, green beans, butter beans, and, of course, saffron to color the rice golden. In the old style, saffron also was added to lentil stew.

All agree that saffron is essential for *gallina en pepitoria,* chicken braised in an almond-saffron sauce. Sometimes embellished with dumplings, the dish is called *guiso de boda,* wedding stew.

After a couple of hours, the ladies fall silent. A transistor radio plays in the background. Their fingers are stained from the flowers and their feet are awash in the discarded blossoms. Antonio sweeps them into a crate to return to the fields for composting.

Once the wisps of saffron are separated from the flowers they must be toasted lightly to reduce their humidity and to fix their color and aroma. Antonio spreads the saffron on trays to dry over electric heating elements.

Traditionally, saffron production was a small family enterprise, with each family planting no more than what its members could pick and process in a day—the morning in the fields, the afternoon at the mondeo, the night tending the braziers for the drying operation. The proceeds from saffron, called "poor folks' gold," hidden beneath the linens at the bottom of a hope chest (saffron-scented sheets are reputed to have aphrodisiac qualities), were a girl's dowry, a family's payment for a piece of land, a new tractor. In the old days, members of the extended family who helped with the picking and extracting were paid not in money but in quantities of the spice.

Saffron doesn't grow just anywhere. Since the Moors introduced its cultivation in the ninth century, saffron has found compatible terroir in very few places in La Mancha, where well-drained sandy soil or light clay provides ideal growing conditions. Supposedly, saffron bulbs planted twenty miles away do not flourish.

Bulbs are set out in the summer. They will produce flowers the second year. The third and fourth years are best. By the fifth year, production diminishes. Then the bulbs are lifted and the fields are planted in wheat or lentils (Campillo is famed for its lentils). The bulbs can be planted in new fields, but it takes fifteen to twenty years before they will flower again in the same plot.

The gathering and processing is seasonal work, so it always has been a sideline to farming. Unfortunately nowadays, young people are more likely to find steady jobs in a nearby plant manufacturing auto parts, or in computer technology, so are not available for the saffron harvest.

Spain once was the world's largest producer of saffron, but it has been surpassed in recent years by Iran, which is flooding the market with cheap saffron, some of which is falsely labeled "mancha quality." To protect their reputation (and price), growers and packagers of authentic La Mancha saffron have set standards and labeling requirements. La Mancha saffron has the seal of the Denominación de Origen Azafrán de La Mancha. Every label is numbered and has a mauve saffron flower and a Quixote emblem to prove its authenticity.

The saffron of La Mancha is said to be the best in the world—the most intense (and enduring) golden color, the headiest aroma, and the most complex taste. Some of these attributes can actually be quantified in a laboratory, but it is in the kitchen where the real gold shines.

WEDDING STEW with CHICKEN and MEATBALLS

Guiso de Bodas de Camacho

The most memorable meal in the story of Don Quixote is certainly that of the *bodas de Camacho*, the wedding feast of a rich man named Camacho (who doesn't, by the way, get the girl). Don Quixote and Sancho Panza encounter some fifty cooks at work preparing the meal. A whole young steer stuffed with a dozen suckling pigs is roasting on a huge spit. Lamb, hare, and chickens are stewing in enormous earthenware ollas. Loaves of bread are piled into a mountain, and whole cheeses, stacked like bricks, form a wall. A treasure chest of spices is at hand. Cooks are frying sweet pastries in great cauldrons of oil, then dipping them into boiling honey syrup.

Sancho cannot contain himself. He begs permission to dip a crust of bread into one of the cook pots and is bidden to skim off what he likes—and take the ladle too! Happy, he scores three chickens and a couple geese for breakfast.

This chicken stew, rich with ground almonds, might well have been stewing in the earthenware pot at that wedding feast. The addition of meatballs (or chicken balls) turns it into rather a grand version of chicken *pepitoria*, a favorite fiesta dish in Spain.

The meatballs can be prepared up to a day in advance, poached, then refrigerated. Reheat them in the stew during the last fifteen minutes of cooking. While chicken breast makes a delightfully light dumpling, veal, pork, or a combination can be used instead.

Steamed white rice makes the perfect accompaniment to this sensuous chicken dish with its "gravy" perfumed with golden saffron and ground almonds.

SERVES 6, WITH 18 MEATBALLS

FOR THE MEATBALLS

⅓ cup fresh flat-leaf parsley leaves

2 tablespoons chopped onion

½ cup fine fresh bread crumbs

1 boneless, skinless chicken breast half (12 to 14 ounces), cut into 1-inch pieces

1 egg, separated

⅛ teaspoon freshly grated nutmeg

⅛ teaspoon freshly ground black pepper

½ teaspoon salt

1½ tablespoons fresh lemon juice

1 quart chicken broth, homemade (page 94) or low-sodium canned, or water

---

Use a food processor to finely chop the parsley. Add the onion, bread crumbs, chicken breast, and egg yolk. Process until the chicken is uniformly minced. Add the nutmeg, pepper, salt, and 1 tablespoon of the lemon juice.

Beat the egg white on high speed in a small bowl until it holds stiff peaks. Beat in the remaining lemon juice. Fold the egg white thoroughly into the ground chicken.

Dip your hands in water and lightly roll the mixture into walnut-sized balls.

Bring the broth to a boil. (The broth can be used in the chicken stew.) Reduce the heat to simmer and poach the meatballs for 4 minutes. They may not be completely cooked through but will finish cooking in the stew. Remove and reserve.

FOR THE CHICKEN STEW

2¾ to 3 pounds chicken legs and thighs (about 8 pieces)

Salt and freshly ground black pepper

Flour for dredging

¼ cup olive oil

4 garlic cloves, peeled

1 cup blanched almonds

½ teaspoon saffron threads

1 cup dry white wine

1/16 teaspoon ground cloves

1 tablespoon chopped fresh flat-leaf parsley, plus chopped parsley for garnish

1¼ cups chicken broth, homemade (page 94) or low-sodium canned

2 hard-cooked egg yolks

A few toasted almonds for garnish

Sprinkle the chicken pieces with salt and pepper and let them stand for 20 minutes. Then dredge them in flour, patting off the excess. Place on a tray.

Heat the oil in a large skillet over medium heat. Add 2 of the garlic cloves and the almonds. Fry until golden, about 1 minute. Remove with a slotted spoon and reserve.

In the same oil, fry the chicken pieces over medium heat until nicely browned on all sides, 5 to 10 minutes. Transfer the pieces as they are browned to a large cazuela or deep sauté pan.

Crush the saffron in a mortar. Add 2 tablespoons hot water and let it steep for 15 minutes.

Place the fried garlic plus the remaining 2 cloves and the fried almonds in a blender with the wine. Blend until the almonds are smoothly pureed. Add the saffron infusion, cloves, ¼ teaspoon black pepper, parsley, and 1 teaspoon salt. Add 1 cup of the chicken broth.

Pour the sauce over the chicken pieces. Raise the heat until the sauce begins to bubble. Cover the casserole and cook very gently for 30 minutes.

Turn the chicken pieces and stir the sauce. Cover and cook until the chicken is very tender, about 30 minutes more.

When the chicken is tender, mash the hard-cooked egg yolks until smooth. Blend the remaining ¼ cup broth into the yolks. Stir into the stew. Add the cooked meatballs to the stew and cook for 15 minutes more.

Serve the stew in the cazuela, sprinkled with chopped parsley and a few toasted almonds.

CHICKEN BRAISED in SPICED VERJUICE

Pollo al Agraz

Where there are vineyards, there will be food cooked in the juice of the grape. Juice from unripe grapes, known as *verjuice*, adds tartness to this chicken dish, which is adapted from a renaissance recipe in *Carlos V a la mesa*, by L. Jacinto García, describing culinary trends in the 1500s.

If you have access to grapevines, try pressing your own verjuice from underripe grapes. The grapes should be juicy but very tart—two to four weeks before harvest. Use a food mill to crush grapes that have seeds (or a blender for seedless grapes). Strain the pulp, saving the juice and discarding pips and skins. Four cups of grapes will make approximately 1½ cups verjuice.

Bottled verjuice can be purchased at specialty stores.

SERVES 6

4 pounds chicken pieces or 1 large chicken, cut up

Salt and freshly ground black pepper

1 tablespoon olive oil

½ cup diced pork belly (uncured pancetta) (3 ounces)

1 cup chopped leek

¼ teaspoon saffron threads, crushed

1½ teaspoons ground ginger

1 teaspoon freshly grated nutmeg

¼ teaspoon ground cinnamon

¼ teaspoon ground coriander

Pinch of ground cloves

1 cup verjuice

2 tablespoons fresh lemon juice

¼ cup chicken broth, homemade (page 94) or low-sodium canned, or water

2 egg yolks

Sprinkle the chicken pieces with salt and pepper to taste and allow to stand for 30 minutes.

Heat the oil in a large skillet or sauté pan over medium heat and fry the diced pork belly until the fat is rendered and the meat is browned. Skim out the pieces of pork and reserve.

Brown the chicken pieces in the fat over medium-high heat, about 5 minutes per side. Remove the chicken and reserve.

Pour off all but 1 tablespoon of the fat from the skillet. Add the leek and sauté until softened, 3 minutes.

Combine the crushed saffron with ¼ cup warm water and allow to steep for 15 minutes. In a small bowl, combine the ginger, nutmeg, cinnamon, coriander, cloves, ¼ teaspoon black pepper, and ½ teaspoon salt.

Return the chicken and pork bits to the pan with the leek. Add ¾ cup of the verjuice, lemon juice, the broth, saffron water, and spices. Bring to a boil, then cover and simmer the chicken for 20 minutes. Turn the chicken pieces and cook until very tender, 20 to 30 minutes longer.

Beat the egg yolks in a bowl with the remaining ¼ cup verjuice. Stir into the chicken and cook without boiling, uncovered, until the sauce is slightly thickened, 10 minutes.

CHICKEN with WILD MUSHROOMS and POSSIBLY TRUFFLES

Pollo con Setas y Trufas Cuando Hayan

Pepe Expósito in Albacete makes gorgeous artisanal knives. The day I visited him in his workshop, he was packing a favorite, a bowie knife (he explained that this was originally a European knife that the English brought to the United States) of heavy steel with a horn handle. He told me he was going hunting—truffle hunting. From January to February he finds black truffles. In the spring, March to April, he hunts white ones. Pepe told me he brings back truffles ranging in size from a small nut to a fist. He finds them in "determined places," near watercourses. One site is only minutes away from an industrial estate. Pepe says his wife does the cooking at his house, but when he brings home wild mushrooms or truffles, he prepares them. He cooks truffles very simply, *revueltos*, scrambled with eggs. Or, surprisingly, for forty seconds in the microwave with olive oil and salt.

This chicken recipe works beautifully with any wild mushroom and the addition of truffles, should you happen to find some.

SERVES 6

1 chicken, cut into serving pieces (3½ to 4 pounds)

Salt and freshly ground black pepper

1 tablespoon olive oil

1 cup chopped onion

2 garlic cloves, chopped

¼ cup chopped fresh parsley, plus chopped parsley for garnish

Freshly grated nutmeg

½ cup dry white wine

1½ cups chicken broth, homemade (page 94) or low-sodium canned, or water

1 pound mushrooms, such as portobello, shiitake, oyster

Truffles as desired

3 tablespoons all-purpose flour

Sprinkle the chicken pieces with salt and pepper to taste and let them stand for 30 minutes.

Heat the oil in a large sauté pan over medium heat and brown the chicken pieces on all sides, 5 to 10 minutes. Pour off most of the accumulated fat. Add the onion and garlic to the pan and sauté until lightly browned, 5 minutes.

Season the chicken with ¼ cup chopped parsley, the nutmeg, wine, and ½ cup of the broth. Cover and cook until the chicken is fork-tender, 40 to 60 minutes.

Clean the mushrooms and truffles with a dampened cloth and trim. Slice big ones into quarters. Place them in a saucepan with the remaining 1 cup broth. Bring to a boil and simmer, covered, for 10 minutes.

Toast the flour in a small dry skillet over medium heat until nutty brown, about 2 minutes. Place the flour in a bowl and whisk in about 1 cup of the liquid from the chicken. Stir to blend thoroughly.

Add the flour mixture to the chicken with the mushrooms. Bring to a boil, stirring. Cook, uncovered, for 10 minutes.

Serve the chicken and mushrooms garnished with chopped parsley.

CHICKEN WINGS in ESCABECHE

Escabeche de Alitas de Pollo

Escabeche is an ancient way of preserving foods in a spiced vinegar marinade. During the hunting season, partridge, quail, and wild rabbit would be roasted or boiled, packed in crocks, and pickled in escabeche to be kept during cold months. Partridge in escabeche is a canned gourmet product. Escabeche gives a new lease on life to leftover roast turkey and turns ordinary chicken wings into something a little different. These are not a true conserve, so keep them refrigerated and use within two or three days.

Serve the chicken wings at room temperature or reheated. Place on a bed of greens and garnish with cherry tomatoes and sliced eggs. To serve as finger food, reheat the wings to liquefy the sauce and skim them out of the liquid. If desired, wrap the ends in foil and serve with paper napkins, as wings are a bit messy. They can also be used in the recipe for Salad of Pickled Partridge or Chicken (page 43).

Dusting the wings with flour before frying keeps them from splattering in the hot oil and allows them to brown nicely. If you're using leftover roast turkey, simply add it to the marinade and bring to a boil. It does not need to cook further.

❧ MAKES 24 PIECES, SERVING 12 AS A TAPA, 6 AS A SALAD, OR 4 AS AN ENTREE

12 chicken wings, tips discarded and wings separated at the joint (4½ to 5 pounds)

Flour for dredging

½ cup olive oil

1 medium onion, halved and sliced

1 carrot, halved lengthwise and sliced

1 leek, white part only, sliced crosswise

2 garlic cloves, quartered lengthwise

1 small dried red chile or hot red pepper flakes to taste

2 bay leaves

2 teaspoons dried oregano

2 teaspoons sweet pimentón

1 tablespoon salt

3 cloves

¼ teaspoon black peppercorns

3 slices orange

1 cup dry white wine

1 cup wine vinegar

Dredge the wing pieces in flour and pat off the excess. Heat the oil in a deep skillet over medium heat. Fry the wings in 2 batches until browned on all sides, about 4 minutes. Remove.

Skim off 1 tablespoon of the oil and place in a clean pan. Add the sliced onion, carrot, leek, garlic, chile, bay leaves, oregano, pimentón, salt, cloves, peppercorns, and orange slices. Place the wings on top. Pour on the wine, vinegar, and 2½ cups water. Bring to a boil, then reduce the heat and simmer, covered, until the wings are tender but not falling off the bone, about 30 minutes.

Remove the pan from the heat and allow the wings to cool in the cooking liquid. Place the wings and liquid in a nonreactive bowl or jar, cover tightly, and refrigerate for at least 24 and up to 48 hours.

Serve at room temperature or warmed.

CHICKEN *with* PINTO BEANS *and* PASTA RAGS

Pollo con Andrajos

In the villages of the rugged sierra in the south of Albacete province, this dish is prepared with wild hare. I've substituted chicken thighs. The "rags" are made from a simple flour and water paste, rolled out thinly and cut or torn into irregular pieces. Won ton wrappers, cut into strips, could be used instead of the pasta.

SERVES 4

1½ cups all-purpose flour, plus flour for rolling out the dough

Salt

⅓ cup plus 1 tablespoon hot-to-the-touch water (110°F)

1½ pounds boneless, skinless chicken thighs

Freshly ground black pepper

3 tablespoons olive oil

1 cup chopped onion

½ cup chopped green bell pepper

2 garlic cloves, chopped

1 tablespoon sweet pimentón

1½ cups peeled, seeded, and chopped tomato

Hot red pepper flakes

Dash of ground cloves

1 bay leaf

2 cups chicken broth, homemade (page 94) or low-sodium canned, or water

2 cups drained cooked pinto beans (one 15-ounce can)

Chopped fresh mint for garnish

Combine the flour and salt in a mixing bowl. Make a well in the center and pour in the hot water. Stir the flour into the water to make a soft dough. Turn out on a board and knead until smooth and satiny, 5 minutes. Add only enough flour to prevent the dough from sticking to the board. Gather the dough into a ball, cover with a clean towel, and leave to rest at room temperature for 30 minutes.

If the chicken thighs are large, cut them in half. Sprinkle with salt and pepper.

Heat the oil in a deep sauté pan or cazuela over medium high-heat. Sauté the chicken pieces until lightly colored, about 1 minute per side. Remove them from the pan. Add the onion and green pepper and sauté over fairly high heat for 3 minutes. Add the garlic and sauté until the onion begins to brown, 2 minutes more.

Remove the pan from the heat and stir in the pimentón. Add the tomato, return to fairly high heat, and cook for 5 minutes more. Add the red pepper flakes, cloves, bay leaf, and broth. Add salt if needed. Return the chicken to the pan with any accumulated juices. Simmer, covered, until the chicken is tender, 30 to 45 minutes.

While the chicken is cooking, roll out the pasta dough very thinly (1/16 inch). Use a knife to cut it into strips about 3/4 inch wide. Cut the strips into 3-inch lengths. Line a baking sheet with nonstick baking parchment. Lift the strips of pasta dough off the board and place them in a single layer on the parchment.

When the chicken is cooked, uncover the pan and raise the heat so the liquid bubbles. Add the pasta gradually, stirring it into the liquid. Cook for 5 minutes.

Add the beans and cook for 5 minutes more. Allow to stand for 10 minutes before serving. Serve in deep bowls garnished with chopped mint.

ROAST CHICKEN STUFFED with LIVER and SPRING HERBS

Pollo Asado Relleno con Hierbas

The stuffing is like an herby, chicken-liver terrine that cooks inside the chicken. Use your favorite herbs in this poultry stuffing. I like thyme, mint, celery leaves, and a little fennel. But rosemary, oregano, basil, and tarragon also make a good combination. If possible, choose a free-range or organic chicken for this dish.

❧ SERVES 6, INCLUDING 3 CUPS STUFFING

FOR THE STUFFING

1 tablespoon olive oil

½ pound chicken livers, chopped

¼ cup chopped onion

1 cup fresh bread crumbs

1 tablespoon raisins

1 cup chopped fresh flat-leaf parsley

2 to 4 tablespoons chopped fresh herbs or 1 to 2 tablespoons dried

1 teaspoon salt

¼ teaspoon grated lemon zest

Freshly ground black pepper

¼ cup chicken broth, homemade (page 94) or low-sodium canned, or dry white wine

Heat the oil in a skillet over medium-high heat and sauté the chopped chicken livers and onion until the livers lose their pink color, about 3 minutes.

Combine the bread crumbs, raisins, parsley, herbs, salt, lemon zest, pepper to taste, chicken broth, and sautéed livers and onion.

FOR THE CHICKEN

1 roasting chicken, 3½ to 4½ pounds

Salt and freshly ground black pepper

3 slices salt pork or bacon

½ cup chopped leek

½ cup chopped onion

2 bay leaves

1 fresh rosemary sprig

½ cup dry white wine

1½ cups chicken broth, homemade (page 94) or low-sodium canned

Preheat the oven to 375°F.

Rub the chicken inside and out with salt and pepper. Let stand at room temperature for 1 hour. Stuff the chicken with the herb and liver stuffing. Use poultry skewers and kitchen twine to close the cavity. Cover the chicken breast with salt pork or bacon.

Place the leek and onion in a roasting pan with the bay leaves and rosemary. Place the chicken on top.

Roast the stuffed chicken for 20 minutes.

Reduce the oven temperature to 325°F. Pour the wine and chicken broth over the chicken. Continue roasting the chicken, basting frequently. The chicken is done when an instant-read thermometer inserted in the thigh registers 165°F, 60 to 90 minutes. Transfer to a serving platter and allow to stand for 15 minutes before carving.

Skim the fat from the drippings in the roasting pan. Strain the drippings, pressing on the solids. Discard the solids. Serve the sauce with the chicken and stuffing.

COUNTRY CHICKEN CASSEROLE *with* RICE

Cazuela de Pollo con Arroz a la Campesina

Serve this for an informal supper. Everything cooks in one casserole, so it's an easy dish for entertaining. Not everyone has a cazuela large enough to hold all the ingredients, so I suggest making it in a Dutch oven or extra-large sauté pan.

I use a large chicken, cut into joints (legs, thighs, wings, and breasts split into 4 pieces), for this tasty chicken and rice dish. I separate the bony backs and use them to make a light broth that adds flavor to the rice. But you could use legs and thighs or legs and breasts and substitute store-bought broth.

Use Spanish round-grain paella rice for this recipe. If you can get it, the Bomba variety is best, because it does not "flower" when cooked with lots of liquid. If Spanish rice is not available, use Arborio rice.

SERVES 8

3 pounds chicken pieces

Salt and freshly ground black pepper

3 tablespoons olive oil

3 garlic cloves

1 bay leaf

1 cup chopped green bell pepper

1 cup chopped onion

1 cup peeled and diced tomato

1 cup fresh or frozen peas

1 cup fresh or frozen shelled fava or lima beans

1 cup fresh or frozen green beans, preferably romano, cut into short lengths

5 cups chicken broth, homemade (page 94) or low-sodium canned

¼ teaspoon saffron threads

10 peppercorns

2 cloves

⅛ teaspoon cumin seeds

1 teaspoon sweet pimentón

Pinch of cayenne

1 cup peeled diced potato

2 cups Spanish round-grain rice

Sprinkle the chicken pieces with salt and pepper and allow to stand for 30 minutes.

Heat the oil in a very large cazuela or stew pot over medium-high heat. Fry 2 of the garlic cloves and the bay leaf until the garlic is golden and the bay leaf crisped, about 50 seconds. Skim them out and reserve.

Brown the chicken pieces in the same oil, turning to brown all sides, 8 to 10 minutes. (Use high heat for an earthenware cazuela, medium heat for a Dutch oven or sauté pan.) Remove the chicken as it is browned.

Sauté the green pepper and onion for 3 minutes. Add the tomato and sauté over high heat for 2 minutes. If you're using fresh peas, fava beans, and green beans, add them now. Add 1 cup of the broth and 1 teaspoon salt. Return the chicken pieces to the pan. Bring to a boil, then reduce the heat so the liquid bubbles gently. Cover the pan and cook for 8 minutes.

In a mortar, crush the saffron to a powder. Put the peppercorns, cloves, and cumin seeds in the mortar and grind them coarsely. Add the fried garlic, remaining garlic clove, and reserved bay leaf and mash to a paste. Add the pimentón and cayenne. Mix with ¼ cup water.

Stir the spice mixture into the chicken. Add the potato. Cover and cook for 5 minutes more. Add the remaining quart of broth. Bring to a boil and stir in the rice. (If you're using frozen peas, fava beans, and green beans, add them now.) Taste for salt and add more if necessary. Reduce the heat so the liquid bubbles gently. Cover the pot and cook for 15 minutes, stirring only once during this time.

Remove the pot from the heat and let stand for 10 minutes before serving.

DUCK BRAISED in RED WINE

Pato al Vino Tinto

La Mancha is a region of surprises. You expect the flatness—and much of it is flat—and the arid landscape. Yet areas of steep hills, rocky mountains, and canyons astonish the traveler. Even more surprising, perhaps, are vast wetlands, where marshes shelter waterfowl of many sorts.

Such is Tablas de Daimiel, a national park in the province of Ciudad Real, where two rivers, the Cigüela and Guadiana, encountering terrain so flat they have nowhere to flow, spread out into marshlands. Today it is protected, with paths and blinds for birdwatching. But in former times the wetlands were a rich source of food for those who lived in the region. Crayfish, carp, wild dove, and wild duck (mallard) were free for the taking.

Wild duck is not appreciated for its flavor. Feeding on fish and crustaceans, it acquires a "fishy" flavor. From that derives the custom of cooking it with assertive flavors, such as sour oranges, tangy olives, or strong wine and brandy. This recipe, adapted for farm-raised duck, such as Pekin, derives from a traditional one.

I start out with whole ducks and cut them up, using the legs for a slow braise, the breasts for a fast sauté to be served rare, and the rest of the carcass to make a deep-flavored stock to add substance to the sauce. (You will not need all of the stock for the sauce. Use it to embellish duck and rice paella.) If you don't want to bother with the duck stock, substitute Simple Chicken Broth (page 94).

However, if you prefer, use whole ducks, simply quartered, or cut-up legs and breasts.

Duck is fatty, so, happily, it doesn't dry out in reheating. If you make this dish a day in advance, you can skim off all the fat that rises to the surface before finishing the sauce, which is thickened with the pureed carrots, onions, and leeks. Red wine makes a sauce that's not quite brown, so leave some of the chopped vegetables unpureed to give the sauce a little color.

I choose one of the "new style" La Mancha wines, made with a *coupage* (blend) of traditional Tempranillo grape, plus Cabernet Sauvignon and Syrah, for both cooking and serving with this duck dish.

Spanish polenta (page 279) makes a good side dish. Quince jelly, *membrillo,* is a classic accompaniment.

FOR THE DUCK BROTH

3 farm-raised ducks, each about 4½ pounds

2 celery stalks

1 orange, quartered

1 onion, quartered

1 teaspoon salt

2 cloves

8 peppercorns

1 bay leaf

1 fresh rosemary sprig

6 parsley stems

Remove the legs (thigh and drumstick in one piece) of the ducks. Use a sharp boning knife to remove each breast half, keeping the skin intact. Split the remaining carcasses in half. Set aside the duck pieces and put the carcasses in a deep pot. Add the celery, orange, onion, salt, cloves, peppercorns, bay leaf, rosemary, parsley, and 10 cups water. Bring to a boil, cover, and simmer for 2 hours.

Strain the stock, discarding all the solids. You should have about 8 cups stock. Cool, then refrigerate for at least 6 hours. When chilled, skim off and discard the fat that congeals on top. Set aside 2 cups for this recipe and refrigerate or freeze the rest. It will last for 2 to 3 days in the refrigerator, 8 weeks in the freezer.

FOR THE BRAISED DUCK

1 tablespoon olive oil

3 cups chopped onion

3 carrots, halved lengthwise and sliced

1½ cups chopped leek

¼ teaspoon dried thyme

Pinch of ground cloves

1 celery stalk

2 strips orange zest

¼ cup brandy

2 cups full-bodied red wine

1 tablespoon honey

Prick the skin of the duck legs all over with a skewer or sharp-tined fork. Use a small sharp knife to score the skin of the breasts.

Heat the oil in a heavy skillet over medium heat. Brown the legs on both sides, a few at a time, and remove. Put the pieces of breast in the skillet, skin side down, and cook over medium heat until the fat is rendered and the skin crisped, 8 minutes. Turn and brown the flesh side, 2 minutes. Remove and reserve.

Pour off and discard all but 1 tablespoon of the fat from the skillet. Add the onion, carrots, and leek and sauté over medium heat until the onion begins to brown, 8 minutes.

Place the duck legs in a pot or heatproof casserole. Add the contents of the skillet to the duck. Add the thyme, cloves, celery, and orange zest. Pour on the brandy, wine, and 2 cups duck broth. Bring to a boil, then cover and simmer for 40 minutes. Turn the duck legs and simmer until tender, 30 minutes longer.

Add the reserved breasts to the pot and cook for 10 minutes longer.

Remove all the pieces of duck from the pot and set aside (or refrigerate). Discard the celery and orange zest. Allow the liquid to stand for at least 1 hour, then skim off all the fat that rises to the top. (Or refrigerate for at least 6 hours and remove the fat once it has congealed.)

Puree all but 1 cup of the liquid in a blender. Return the puree to the pot with the vegetables. Stir in the honey. Heat the sauce. Return all of the duck to the pot and heat it in the sauce.

PARTRIDGE, START TO FINISH

In early February winter spreads across the highlands of the Montes de Toledo, in western Castilla–La Mancha. It is the last day of the open season for hunting partridge. At a hunting lodge on a large country estate not too distant from the little town of Los Yébenes, a center for hunting of both large and small game, a group of hunters gathers over steaming coffee to draw lots for the *puestos,* blinds, that they will occupy on the hunt. Some of the hunters come from abroad and are staying at the manor house, whose twin spires are visible through the branches of bare trees. Others, like Teodoro, a well-to-do businessman, have driven down from Toledo, bringing dogs, guns, and gear.

The hunters (a few women among them) move out in SUVs, bumping along rutted dirt tracks and fording a small stream. Leaving the vehicles, they hike cross-country to the first shooting site. Sun breaks through the cloud cover, glinting on flat outcroppings of shiny granite. The rough terrain is dotted with thickets of chaparral and carved by ravines. Tramping boots release the powerful scents of wild thyme, marjoram, and red lavender.

Teodoro, dressed in cropped pants with gaiters and loden green jacket, is flanked by a loader, who will keep his guns ready to fire, and a *secretario*, who spots the downed birds and later recovers them. Some friends of Teodoro and an observer also occupy his blind. They must stay crouched on a tarp on the ground, because, as the hunter swings around to shoot, raised heads are in danger. Teodoro tethers his one-year-old Labrador-cross retriever, Popi, to a stake.

The hunters with their entourages spread along the ridge, taking up ten blinds. The *ojeadores,* beaters, announce the start of the hunt with a blast on a conch shell. They move along the ravine's embankment, thrashing the bushes, banging, and yelling *"Vamos, vamos"* (Let's move, come on, let's go).

The first shots ring out, but it is too distant to see the birds fall. The beaters continue toward Teodoro's position, flushing birds before them. Suddenly, with a rush of wings, a covey of partridge lofts skyward. They seem to scatter in the air, some soaring high, others dipping toward the next ridge. Teodoro shoots in rapid succession. One bird falls very near the blind, causing Popi to snap to attention.

When the beaters reach the end of the line, they signal the end of the shoot with a horn, and everyone scrambles to find the downed birds. Popi excitedly works the hillside, retrieving partridge one after another to Teodoro. The secretario strings them on leather thongs and hitches them to his belt. The whole hunting party treks overland to another line. A light snow is falling.

At the end of the second shoot (typically there are four or five lines in a day of hunting) the secretarios spread all the birds taken in a clearing on the ground, arranging them in braces. There are 126 partridge. Teodoro, the best shot, claims 28. Some he will take home with him. He says his mother prepares them en conserva, packed in jars in a mild escabeche.

Behind the hunters comes the pollero, poultryman. He buys the birds from the organizer of the hunt and hauls them to a processing plant, where they are cleaned and plucked, ready for sale to restaurants and specialty meat stores.

A day later, in the restaurant kitchen at Casa Apelio in Los Yébenes, three women are processing six hundred partridge from several different shoots. The birds are singed, one by one, over a gas flame, chilled, and packed for freezing. According to Apelio García, the third generation to run Casa Apelio, his restaurant is one of the few in Spain that serves wild native red partridge. (Most buy farm-raised birds.) His aunt Valentina prepares them in a salad, stewed with beans, and braised in an onion-wine sauce.

In the restaurant a roaring fire in the hearth warms the dining room, which is hung with deer heads and racks of antlers (Los Yébenes has four working taxidermists). Caged partridge (they are used for hunting al reclamo, with decoys) cackle and call from a shelf on one side of the dining room.

To start, there is partridge pâté with toast. The creamy pâté, produced in Los Yébenes by Taller Gastronómico, comes from a can. The partridge salad features tender boned partridge in a mild escabeche heaped on top of sliced tomatoes, sprinkled with oregano, and generously dribbled with the local extra virgin olive oil with denomination Montes de Toledo. The beans, nicely flavored with garlic and pimentón, stretch one partridge into two or more servings. Partridge braised in a winey onion sauce, a Toledo classic, calls for a smooth reserva La Mancha red wine.

Partridge, start to finish.

BRAISED PARTRIDGE, TOLEDO STYLE

Perdiz Estofada a la Toledana

Autumn brings the opening of the season for game birds. This manner of preparing partridge, braised with lots of onions, is traditional in the Montes de Toledo, the mountainous region in the south part of Toledo province. If partridge is not available, try the dish with Cornish game hen or plump little poussin. Tucking sprigs of thyme and rosemary in the bird's cavity adds a "wild" taste. The partridge go nicely with pan-sautéed cabbage (page 253) and, of course, a red *reserva,* aged wine, from one of the many wineries in Toledo province.

SERVES 4

4 partridge, small chickens, or Cornish game hens (12 to 18 ounces each)

Salt and freshly ground black pepper

4 fresh rosemary sprigs (optional)

¼ cup olive oil

2 onions, halved and sliced

1 carrot, diced

¼ cup diced serrano ham (optional; about 1½ ounces)

6 garlic cloves, chopped

2 tablespoons chopped fresh parsley

½ teaspoon dried thyme

2 bay leaves

1 tablespoon brandy (optional)

1½ cups dry white wine

Sprinkle the birds inside and out with salt and pepper. If desired, tuck a small sprig of rosemary in the cavity of each. Tie the birds with kitchen twine to keep legs and wings close to the bodies. Allow them to stand for 30 minutes at room temperature.

Heat the oil in a deep sauté pan or cazuela over medium-high heat. Brown the partridge on all sides, 10 minutes. Remove them.

Add the onions and carrot to the remaining oil. Sauté over medium-high heat until the onions begin to brown, 10 minutes. Add the ham, if you're using it, and the garlic. Place the partridge on top of the onions. Sprinkle with the parsley and thyme. Tuck the bay leaves between the birds. Pour on the brandy, if you're using it, and the wine. Bring to a boil, cover, and reduce the heat so the liquid just simmers. Cook the partridge for 25 minutes, then turn them and cook, covered, until very tender, 35 to 45 minutes longer.

Transfer the partridge to a platter. Cook the onions and liquid left in the pan, uncovered, until slightly reduced. Discard the bay leaves and remove the strings from the partridge. Serve with the onion sauce.

PARTRIDGE *with* BEANS

Judías con Perdiz

Y vivieron felices, comieron perdices y a mí no me dieron. And they ate partridge and lived happily ever after. Thus ends many a Spanish fairy tale.

In this dish, beans stretch the servings of partridge, so a single bird, split in half, might serve two. (If you choose to serve half a partridge, split the birds after cooking.) If partridge is not available, use Cornish game hens or turkey thighs. I prefer to cook the beans separately from the partridge, as beans can take well over an hour to cook. You could use canned cannellini beans (two 15-ounce cans). If you're using dried beans, soak them for at least 6 hours before cooking.

SERVES 4

2 cups dried cannellini beans, soaked for 6 to 24 hours

1 head of garlic

2 bay leaves

1 fresh rosemary sprig

¼ onion

1 fresh or 2 sun-dried tomatoes

2 teaspoons salt, plus salt for the partridge

2 to 4 partridges, about ¾ pound each

Freshly ground black pepper

¼ cup olive oil

2 cups chopped onion

2 garlic cloves, chopped

1 teaspoon sweet pimentón

2 tablespoons wine vinegar

1 cup dry white wine

10 peppercorns

Drain the beans and place them in a pot with water to cover. Bring to a boil and skim off the froth.

Slice the top off the head of garlic and place the whole head in the pot with the beans. Add the bay leaves, rosemary, onion, tomato, and 1 teaspoon of the salt. Cover and simmer the beans for 30 minutes. Add ½ cup cold water, bring again to a boil, and simmer until the beans are very tender, 30 to 60 minutes more.

Meanwhile, sprinkle the partridge with salt and pepper. Heat the oil in a large cazuela or deep skillet over low heat. Brown the partridge very slowly, about 10 minutes on the first side. Turn them, then add the chopped onion and garlic. Continue sautéing until the partridge and onions are golden, about 10 minutes.

In a small bowl, mix the pimentón with the vinegar. Add to the partridge with the wine and 1 cup water. Add the peppercorns and remaining teaspoon of salt. Cook at a gentle bubble for 30 minutes. Turn the partridge and simmer for 30 minutes more.

Drain the beans, reserving the liquid. Discard the bay leaves and rosemary. Add the beans to the cazuela with the partridge. Slip the skin from the tomato and break it up into the cazuela. Squeeze the cloves of garlic into the partridge. Add 2 cups of the bean liquid. Simmer all together for 30 minutes and serve.

SQUABS STUFFED *with* RAISINS, APRICOTS, *and* WALNUTS

Pichones Rellenos

Once every farmyard had a dovecote. Besides providing an excellent source of guano fertilizer, it yielded tender young squabs for the stew pot. This squab, stuffed with dried fruit and nuts, is elegant enough for a special dinner party. If squabs are not attainable, substitute Cornish game hens.

SERVES 6

¼ cup seedless raisins

½ cup chopped dried apricots

½ cup medium-dry Sherry, such as amontillado or oloroso seco

3 tablespoons olive oil

½ cup chopped shallot

¼ cup diced serrano ham or bacon (about 1½ ounces)

1 cup fresh bread crumbs

⅓ cup coarsely chopped walnuts

¼ cup chopped fresh parsley

Salt and freshly ground black pepper

Pinch of dried thyme

6 squabs or game hens, each about 10 ounces

½ cup dry white wine

1 cup chicken broth, homemade (page 94) or low-sodium canned

3 tablespoons cream

Combine the raisins and apricots in a mixing bowl and add 3 tablespoons of the Sherry. Macerate for 30 minutes.

Heat 1 tablespoon of the oil in a small skillet over low heat and sauté half of the shallot until softened, 5 minutes. Add the diced ham and sauté for 1 minute.

Add the shallot and ham to the raisins and apricots. Add the bread crumbs, walnuts, parsley, ¼ teaspoon of salt, pepper to taste, and the thyme. Combine well.

Clean out the cavities of the squabs. Rinse and pat them dry. Fill the cavities with the stuffing mixture. Skewer the openings closed. Tie the legs together with kitchen twine.

Heat the remaining 2 tablespoons oil in a large skillet over medium heat. Slowly brown the squabs on all sides, 8 to 10 minutes. (Brown them in 2 batches if necessary.) Remove when browned and place in a shallow roasting pan just large enough to hold them.

Preheat the oven to 375°F.

Pour the white wine over the squabs and place them in the oven, uncovered, until they reach an internal temperature of 160°F, 30 to 40 minutes.

While the squabs are roasting, add the remaining shallot to the oil remaining in the large skillet and sauté for 3 minutes. Add the broth and remaining Sherry. Bring to a boil, then simmer for 10 minutes.

When the squabs are roasted, transfer them to a serving platter. Remove the skewers and twine. Tent the squabs with foil and keep them warm. Add ¼ cup water to the roasting pan and scrape up any drippings. Add to the skillet with broth and Sherry. Bring to a boil, reduce the heat, and add the cream. Cook gently for 3 minutes.

Serve the squabs accompanied by the sauce.

. . . y algún palomino de añadidura los domingos . . .

. . . and on Sundays, the addition of some squab
for good measure . . .

WHAT DON QUIXOTE HAD FOR DINNER

QUAIL in "SLIPCOVERS" OF RED PEPPERS

Codornices con Fundas

Red bell peppers flavor the quail and keep them moist. A sausage stuffing bastes them from the inside out. A single quail does not a dinner make, so serve this as a starter or light supper dish. If you cannot get morcilla sausage, add a spoonful of pimentón and a pinch of ground cloves and cinnamon to the pork sausage.

❧ SERVES 6

6 quail, about 6 ounces each

Coarse salt

2 tablespoons plus 1 teaspoon olive oil

¼ cup minced shallot or onion

6 ounces morcilla or pork link sausage, casing removed and sausage chopped

1 cup fresh bread crumbs

6 large red bell peppers

½ cup dry white wine

1 cup boiling water

Rinse the quail in running water. Drain and pat them dry. Sprinkle with salt to taste.

Heat 1 teaspoon of the oil in a small skillet over medium heat and sauté the shallot until softened, 1 minute. Add the chopped morcilla and fry for 3 minutes, breaking up the pieces of sausage with a wooden spatula.

Remove the skillet from the heat and stir in the bread crumbs. Stuff the quail with the sausage-crumb mixture, using about ¼ cup for each.

Heat the remaining 2 tablespoons oil in a skillet over medium heat and brown the quail on all sides, about 3 minutes. Remove and reserve.

Preheat the oven to 375°F.

Cut off the tops of the peppers. Scoop out and discard the seeds and membranes.

Working with one quail at a time, tuck the legs against the body and insert each quail, legs first, into a pepper. Place in a baking dish.

Pour the wine and boiling water over the quail-stuffed peppers. Bake them, uncovered, until the peppers are completely softened and the quail tender, about 1½ hours. If the pan liquid cooks away, add ½ cup boiling water.

Allow the peppers to stand for 15 minutes. If desired, peel the peppers. Serve them hot, with the pan juices spooned over them.

HUNTERS' RICE with RABBIT

Arroz al Cazador

When is a paella not a paella? When it's cooked in a *perol,* a deep two-handled frying pan with flared sides, instead of in a shallow paella pan. A flat-bottomed wok makes a perfect perol. Hunters in the field cook the rice and wild rabbit over a campfire. As farm-raised rabbit from the butcher's shop is more likely to be available, I suggest adding mountain herbs for a subtle "wild" flavor. A hunter's version might include wild asparagus and wild cardoons or artichokes. In this recipe I have used cultivated asparagus and artichokes.

Rabbit is naturally very lean, so it profits from cooking with juicy chorizo sausage. If not available, you could use pork link sausage plus a heaping teaspoon of pimentón. A tender, young farm-raised rabbit will cook in the time the rice cooks, but, should you have wild rabbit or a substantially larger rabbit, you will need to simmer it for 15 to 20 minutes in the liquid before adding the rice.

Please resist the urge to stir the rice! Once rice and pieces of rabbit are distributed in the pan, let them cook undisturbed. Stirring breaks up the rice grains and makes them gummy. It is permissible, though, to shake the pan to keep the contents from sticking to the bottom.

Trim the artichokes immediately before adding them to the frying pan so they don't darken. They do not need to be rubbed with lemon.

SERVES 5 TO 6

1 rabbit (about 2½ pounds), cut into 6 pieces

Salt and freshly ground black pepper

¼ cup olive oil

1 cup chopped green bell pepper

6 garlic cloves, chopped

2 Spanish chorizo links (5 ounces), preferably soft, casing removed and sausage chopped

1 cup diced tomato

¼ teaspoon saffron threads

6 peppercorns

4 baby artichokes or 1 medium artichoke

1 cup chopped green asparagus (½ pound thin spears)

2 bay leaves

1 fresh rosemary sprig

1 fresh thyme sprig

2 cups Spanish round-grain rice

Sprinkle the pieces of rabbit generously with salt and pepper and allow to come to room temperature, 1 hour.

Heat the oil in a deep skillet or sauté pan over medium heat and brown the rabbit, turning the pieces to brown lightly on both sides, about 8 minutes. Remove the rabbit.

Add the green pepper, garlic, and chorizo to the pan and sauté for 3 minutes. Raise the heat and add the tomato. Fry for 3 minutes more.

Crush the saffron in a mortar with the peppercorns. Stir in ¼ cup water and allow to infuse.

Snap off the outer leaves of the artichokes and trim away the top two-thirds of the leaves. Cut baby artichokes in half; cut a medium artichoke into eighths. Add the artichoke to the pan with the asparagus, bay leaves, rosemary, and thyme. Add 1 quart water and bring to a boil. Return the rabbit to the pan. Add 1 teaspoon salt and the saffron-pepper water. Stir in the rice.

Cook over fairly high heat for 10 minutes. Reduce the heat to medium-low and cook until the rice is al dente, 8 to 10 minutes longer. Cover the pan with a lid or foil and allow to rest for 10 minutes before serving. If convenient, remove the bay leaves and rosemary and thyme sprigs before serving.

RABBIT *with* FIGS *and* MUDÉJAR SPICES

Conejo con Higos al Estilo Mudéjar

Toledo, evocative, a little mysterious, sits on a hill over the River Tajo (Tagus). Still enclosed by ancient walls and monumental gates, the old town of narrow cobbled streets preserves much of its medieval character. Inhabited over the centuries by Romans (the ruins of a Roman circus, one of the largest of the empire, lies just outside the walls), Visigoths (at least one church originally was Visigothic), Sephardic Jews (two synagogues remain in the old Jewish quarter), Arabs and Berbers (a tenth-century mosque is preserved), and Christians, who built an astonishing cathedral and dozens of convents and monasteries, Toledo is at once monumental and intimate.

The Muslim Moors took Toledo in 712. When King Alfonso VI wrested control of the city from them in 1085, many of the Moors opted to stay under Christian dominion. Called *Mudéjars*—meaning "permitted to remain"—they had an enormous influence on architecture, building churches, synagogues, and civic buildings in the graceful Mudéjar style, with its low towers, horseshoe arches, plaster, tile, and wood decorations. The Toledo School of Translators flourished, bringing together Arab, Hebrew, and Latin scholars who translated Greek philosophy, Persian literature, and Arabic medicine into Latin and Spanish.

The Mudéjar influence permeated the style of cooking as well, bringing exotic spices from Eastern lands into Spanish cooking. This rabbit dish, subtly sweet and sour, perfumed with cinnamon, clove, anise, and saffron, is a delicious example. If rabbit is not an option, make it with bone-in half chicken breasts.

Serve the rabbit with rice or couscous and Minted Carrots (page 256). A Syrah wine from Dominio de Valdepusa would complement the spices in the rabbit dish.

SERVES 4

¼ cup honey (preferably rosemary honey)

¼ cup Sherry vinegar

One 1-inch piece fresh ginger, cut in half

5 peppercorns

5 coriander seeds

¼ teaspoon mustard seeds

⅛ teaspoon aniseeds

One 1-inch cinnamon stick

1 clove

12 dried figs, stems removed

⅛ teaspoon saffron threads, crushed

¼ cup olive oil

¼ cup blanched almonds

3 garlic cloves, peeled

1 rabbit, 2 to 2½ pounds, cut into 8 pieces

½ cup chopped onion

½ cup dry white wine

Salt and freshly ground black pepper

Combine the honey, vinegar, ginger, peppercorns, coriander, mustard seeds, aniseeds, cinnamon, and clove in a saucepan with 1½ cups water. Bring to a boil, then simmer for 5 minutes. Remove from the heat and add the figs. Cover and let them macerate for at least 2 and up to 24 hours.

Add ¼ cup warm water to the saffron and let it steep for at least 15 minutes.

Heat the oil in a cazuela or sauté pan over medium heat, and fry the almonds and garlic until light golden, about 1 minute. Skim them out and reserve.

Add the rabbit pieces to the hot oil and sauté over medium heat until lightly browned on all sides, about 8 minutes. Add the chopped onion and continue sautéing.

Put the fried almonds and garlic in a blender with the wine and process to make a smooth paste.

With a slotted spoon, remove the figs from the spiced liquid and reserve them. (Don't worry if some spices cling to the figs.) Strain the liquid and reserve it. Discard the spices. Add the liquid to the rabbit with the saffron. Stir in the almond paste. Season with salt and pepper to taste. Cover and simmer for 30 minutes. Add the figs to the rabbit and cook until the rabbit is tender, another 15 to 20 minutes.

HUNTER'S STEW *with* HARE

Liebre a la Cazadora

While rabbit is "white meat," hare is definitely red meat. Wild mushrooms, thyme, and brandy add to the "wild" flavor. You could make this recipe with beef chuck roast, increasing the cooking time to 2½ hours.

Serve the braised hare with noodles and a side of Chard Sauté (page 251). Accompany with a red *reserva* wine from Valdepeñas.

SERVES 4

1 hare, 2½ to 3 pounds, cut into 6 to 8 serving pieces

Salt and freshly ground black pepper

3 tablespoons olive oil

1½ cups chopped onion

6 garlic cloves, chopped

½ cup diced bacon (3 ounces)

¼ teaspoon ground allspice

½ teaspoon dried thyme

¼ cup brandy

½ cup dry red wine

2 tablespoons chopped fresh parsley

3 cups sliced fresh mushrooms, such as porcini (cèpes) or oyster

Sprinkle the pieces of hare with salt and pepper to taste and allow to stand at room temperature for 30 minutes.

Heat the oil in a heavy skillet over medium heat. Add the pieces of meat and brown them slowly on all sides, 10 minutes. Add the onion, garlic, and bacon and continue frying for 5 minutes.

Sprinkle with the allspice, thyme, brandy, wine, and parsley. Add ½ cup water. When the liquid begins to bubble, cover, lower the heat, and cook slowly for 30 minutes.

Turn the pieces of hare. Add the mushrooms and cook for 45 minutes more, or until the meat is fork-tender.

SHEPHERD'S STEW *with* GAME *or* TURKEY

Gazpachos de Pastor

If you're wondering what turkey is doing in gazpacho, take note that this stew is gazpachos—plural—not to be confused with Andalusian cold soup (though the origin of the name is the same, as *gazpacho* refers to fragments of bread). Gazpachos is an ancient dish, with its roots in the pastoral life of La Mancha. Shepherds tending their flocks far from villages cooked whatever wild game they could shoot or bring down with a slingshot, sometimes with foraged greens and wild mushrooms. It was stewed over a wood fire and embellished with *torta*, an unleavened campfire bread that thickened the stew and served as a dinner plate.

Over the years, gazpachos has been domesticated, prepared in home kitchens with chicken and farm-raised rabbit, as well as game. A commercial version of the torta is sold in La Mancha today. It's a crisp flatbread, about fifteen inches in diameter, that looks for all the world like matzo on steroids.

Homemade torta is soft and pliable when fresh off the griddle. It's delicious dipped in olive oil as a breakfast bread. But it quickly dries into hardtack. Break it into pieces before adding to the stew, where it cooks up like pasta. If you don't want to prepare the homemade version, substitute matzo or water biscuits.

I prefer dark-meat turkey to game. But you could use chicken or rabbit as well. I've added chard in place of wild greens and oyster mushrooms to impart a woodsy taste. If you're using bone-in turkey, cooking time will be 2 hours or more. Chicken, partridge, or rabbit will cook much faster.

❦ SERVES 6

FOR THE TORTAS

2 cups all-purpose flour, plus flour for rolling out the dough

½ teaspoon salt

½ cup plus 2 tablespoons hot water (140°F)

Olive oil for the griddle

Combine the flour and salt in a mixing bowl. Make a well in the center and pour in the hot water, 2 tablespoons at a time, gradually stirring the flour into the water to make a soft dough. Gather the dough into a ball.

Divide the dough into 4 equal pieces and roll each into a ball. Knead each ball on a lightly floured board until smooth and stretchy, about 1 minute. Place the balls in a bowl, cover with plastic wrap and a dampened towel, and allow to stand at room temperature for 1 hour and up to 4 hours.

Roll out each ball on a floured surface to an 8-inch circle, about ⅛ inch thick. Place the circles on a lightly floured baking sheet. Prick them all over with a fork.

Heat a griddle or large cast-iron skillet over medium heat and brush lightly with oil. Place a torta on the griddle and cook until it is blistered and lightly browned on the bottom, about 1½ minutes. Turn and cook the other side for 1 minute. Transfer to a pan and cover with a dry cloth. Cook the remaining tortas in the same manner.

Cool the tortas, covered with a cloth. They can be eaten fresh or be allowed to dry and broken into pieces to cook with the stew.

FOR THE STEW

3 tablespoons olive oil	1 fresh rosemary sprig
3 to 4 pounds turkey drumsticks and thighs	10 peppercorns
1 head of garlic	3 cloves
½ cup sliced onion	1½ cups sliced oyster mushrooms
2 teaspoons salt	1½ cups peeled, seeded, and chopped tomatoes
¼ teaspoon dried thyme, crumbled	1 teaspoon sweet pimentón
2 bay leaves	1 cup chopped chard (optional)
	6 sheets matzo or 4 tortas, broken into pieces

Heat the oil in a large deep skillet or a flat-bottomed wok over medium heat. Brown the turkey pieces, turning them to brown all sides, 8 to 10 minutes. Transfer the turkey to a large stew pot.

Peel off the papery outer layers from the head of garlic. Slice off the top of the head, leaving the cloves attached at the root. Add the head of garlic and the onion to the oil remaining in the skillet and sauté them for 3 minutes. Tip the pan so the oil drains to one side, skim out the garlic and onion, and add them to the stew pot. Reserve the oil in the skillet.

Add 2 quarts water to the stew pot with the turkey. Add the salt, thyme, bay leaves, rosemary, peppercorns, cloves, and mushrooms. Bring to a boil, cover, and cook slowly until the turkey is very tender, turning the pieces occasionally, about 2 hours.

Lift the turkey out of the broth and reserve. Discard the bay leaves and cloves. Reserve the broth with the mushrooms.

Heat the oil reserved in the skillet. Add the tomatoes and fry over high heat for 5 minutes. Stir in the pimentón, chard if you're using it, and 5 cups of the reserved broth and mushrooms. Bring to a boil and simmer for 15 minutes.

Strip the turkey from the bones, discarding the skin, bones, and tendons. Use kitchen scissors to cut the chunks of meat across the grain into pieces. Reserve.

Add the pieces of matzo to the skillet and cook until soft (10 minutes for matzo, 15 to 18 minutes for homemade torta).

Add the cut-up turkey to the stew. Stir to combine and heat thoroughly, 10 minutes.

Meat

In La Mancha you can drive for miles on secondary highways and never pass another car. On these back roads you will frequently see the standard signpost for a livestock crossing—a sign with a cow. Except rarely will you actually see a cow. Livestock in La Mancha means sheep. Sheep, sometimes goats, and more sheep. They graze on stubbled fields on the plains; they spread across hillsides; they huddle in the shade of a solitary tree. Accompanied by a shepherd and his dogs, the herds of sheep are a timeless symbol of La Mancha life.

Sheep are raised both for meat and to produce milk for cheesemaking. In an age of synthetic textiles, the wool is no longer valued as it was in bygone days. Several breeds of sheep are raised in La Mancha, but the Manchega breed is especially valued, both for its meat and for milk production. It is the only milk allowed in the production of authentic Manchego cheese. Lamb from this breed that has the special label Denominación Específica Cordero Manchego is finished in feedlots on natural feeds and slaughtered before age three months. It is wonderfully tender meat, whether roasted or braised. Also much appreciated is baby suckling lamb, slaughtered at thirty-five days. Where this is available, a whole shoulder or leg of the tiny lamb makes one serving. In Spain, lamb is the most favored choice for the festive family dinner on Christmas Eve.

There are, indeed, cattle in La Mancha and some very fine veal and young beef. There are pigs too, both of the porker variety and of the famed Iberico breed that makes especially succulent ham. La Mancha has a long tradition of customs and recipes associated with the *matanza*, annual pig slaughter, when families get together to make sausages and hams. One such dish is *sopa de cachuela*, a heavy-duty stew with tripe and pork liver, which might be served to the helpers at a matanza. I haven't included the recipe for cachuela because, if you haven't slaughtered a hog, a whole pig liver may not be easy to come by. But here are many recipes for slow-cooked stews and braises, quick-cooking cutlets, and nicely flavored roasts. Recipes for small game, both furred and feathered, appear in the poultry chapter. But I've placed a recipe for venison here, because it works equally well with beef.

BRAISED VEAL LARDED *with* OLIVES *and* SALT PORK

Ternera Mechada con Aceitunas y Tocino

According to the dictionary, *ternera* means "veal." However, in Spain *ternera* means young beef from a yearling steer, unless the word is followed by a qualifier such as *lechal,* "milk-fed." The meat has very little marbling, so it benefits by this method of cooking, threaded with lardoons—strips of fat—and slow-braised in aromatic wine sauce.

A special tool exists for larding meat. It's a pointy tube that inserts the strip of fat through the length of meat. I don't own one, so I do what most home cooks do: use a knife to cut slits in the meat and fingers to insert the lardoons. Freezing the strips of fat makes it easier to poke them into the slits.

A shoulder roast is best for this slow-cooked pot roast. (However, see the variation, in which a rump roast is roasted medium-rare.) If the shoulder roast comes already rolled and tied, do not untie it. This manner of larding and braising is also used for large cuts of boned pork such as a butt roast.

The meat can be braised several hours to one day in advance. Cool, then refrigerate it, covered. Refrigerate the strained sauce separately. Before serving, remove and discard the congealed fat from the surface of the sauce. Thinly slice the meat and reheat in a little of the sauce.

※ SERVES 8

3 ounces salt pork or bacon in one piece	3½ pounds boneless veal shoulder roast
⅓ cup pimiento-stuffed olives, finely chopped	1 tablespoon olive oil
2 garlic cloves, crushed	1 large onion, quartered and sliced
2 tablespoons chopped fresh flat-leaf parsley, plus chopped parsley for garnish	1 carrot, chopped
Salt and freshly ground black pepper	1½ cups dry white wine
Pinch of dried thyme	1 bay leaf

Cut 1 ounce of the salt pork into ¼-inch strips. Place them in one layer on a sheet of plastic wrap and freeze them for at least 30 minutes.

Finely chop the remaining salt pork. Combine it with the chopped olives, half of the garlic, 1 tablespoon of the chopped parsley, salt and pepper to taste, and the thyme.

Place the meat on a work surface. With a sharp knife, cut deep slits lengthwise through the meat, spacing the gashes regularly on the meat's surface. With the tip of a knife or fingers, push as much of the olive paste as possible into the slits.

Removing 3 or 4 frozen "sticks" of salt pork from the freezer at a time, insert one into each slit. Continue, filling all of the slits. Use any remaining pieces of salt pork to plug the gashes.

If the meat is not already tied, tie it with butcher's string to hold the larding in place and shape the roast. Wipe off any of the olive paste clinging to the meat's surface and sprinkle the meat with salt and pepper. Let it stand at room temperature for 30 minutes.

Preheat the oven to 325°F.

Heat the oil in a lidded cazuela or heavy braising pot over medium heat. Brown the roast, turning it to brown all sides. On the last turn, add the onion and carrot to the pan and let it brown.

Add the wine and ½ cup water, the remaining garlic, remaining tablespoon of parsley, bay leaf, and any unused olive paste. Bring to a boil, then reduce the heat so the liquid just simmers. Turn the roast to moisten both sides. Cover tightly and place in the oven.

After 45 minutes, turn the roast and continue braising until the meat is very tender when tested with a fork, about 1 hour and 15 minutes more.

Transfer the meat to a cutting board and let it rest for at least 15 minutes. Pour the cooking liquid through a strainer into a saucepan, pressing hard on the solids. Discard the solids. Skim off the fat.

Thinly slice the meat with a sharp knife and place on a heated serving platter or individual plates. Heat the sauce until it begins to boil. Spoon some of it over the sliced beef and pass the rest separately. Garnish the meat with a little chopped parsley.

VARIATION: *Use a boned rump roast, bottom round, eye round roast, or round tip roast, all of which are quite fine-grained, instead of the shoulder roast. Insert the olive paste and salt pork as directed. After browning the meat, place the meat and liquid, uncovered, in a preheated 350°F oven. Roast until medium-rare, to an internal temperature of 140°F, about 1 hour, depending on the shape and thickness of the meat. Remove and allow to rest before slicing very thinly. Boil the remaining liquid to reduce slightly, then defat it and strain.*

STUFFED VEAL ROLL

Aleta de Ternera Rellena

Brisket or breast is a cut of veal that benefits from slow braising. For this pot roast the brisket is opened up, spread with ground meat, carrots, eggs, and olives, then rolled. When sliced, the meat shows nuggets of orange, white, green, and red.

Have the butcher remove visible fat and membrane from the brisket and then cut it open horizontally through the middle so the slab of meat opens like a book. Trim the meat to make an approximate rectangle.

SERVES 12

4½ to 5 pounds boneless beef or veal brisket
1 pound ground pork
1 ounce salt pork or fatty bacon, chopped
2 garlic cloves, minced
1 shallot, chopped
¼ freshly teaspoon grated nutmeg
Pinch of ground cloves
½ teaspoon freshly ground black pepper
1 teaspoon salt
¼ cup chopped fresh parsley
¼ cup dry white wine
3 carrots
2 hard-cooked eggs
12 pimiento-stuffed olives
2 tablespoons olive oil
½ onion, sliced
1 tomato, quartered
2 bay leaves
1 cup dry Sherry
1½ pounds turnips, peeled and halved (optional)

Open the meat and pound it with a meat mallet to an even thickness.

Combine the ground pork, salt pork, garlic, shallot, nutmeg, cloves, pepper, salt, parsley, and white wine in a bowl. Mix thoroughly and allow the mixture to stand for 30 minutes.

Cook 2 of the carrots in water to cover until tender. Drain, saving the water. Cut the cooked carrots in half lengthwise. Cut the eggs in half lengthwise.

Spread the pork mixture in a thin layer to within 2 inches of the edges of the open brisket. Lay the carrots in 2 rows parallel to the short sides of the meat and press them into the ground pork. Place the eggs, cut side down, in a row down the middle. Make a line of olives on either side of the eggs.

Starting on a short side, roll up the brisket, enclosing the stuffing. Tie at intervals with kitchen string.

Preheat the oven to 350°F.

Heat the oil in a cazuela or heavy braising pot over medium heat. Brown the brisket on all sides. Slice the remaining carrot and add to the meat with the onion, tomato, bay leaves, Sherry, and ¾ cup of the reserved carrot water. Heat on top of the stove until the liquid begins to simmer. Cover with foil or a lid and place in the oven.

Pot-roast the meat for 1 hour. Remove from the oven and carefully turn the meat. If you're using turnips, add them to the cazuela with the meat. Cover and return to the oven until the meat is fork-tender, about 1½ hours. If necessary, add water or broth so that there is always at least 2 inches of liquid in the bottom of the roasting pan.

Transfer the meat to a platter. Tent it with foil and allow to stand 30 minutes. Transfer the turnips to a serving bowl.

Skim the fat from the liquid remaining in the pot. Discard the bay leaves. Puree the remaining liquid and vegetables in a blender, then pass it through a strainer, pressing hard on the solids. Reheat the sauce in a small saucepan.

Remove the strings from the meat. Slice the meat into ½-inch slices and arrange on a serving platter. Drizzle with some of the sauce and pass the rest separately. Serve the turnips alongside the meat.

BEEF or VENISON CUTLETS in ADOBO

Filetes de Ciervo en Adobo

In Los Yébenes, a hunting area south of Toledo, I enjoyed the way venison was prepared by Taller Gastronómico, a company that distributes gourmet game products. First marinated in an adobo, it was thinly sliced and quickly pan-grilled so the meat was just cooked through and still juicy. I have exchanged the venison for beef in this recipe. If possible, use some smoky pimentón de la Vera in the adobo mixture (see Sources). While not essential, it adds a wonderful smoky dimension to the meat. Use this adobo spice rub also with pork butt or pork loin. The piece of meat also can be roasted instead of sliced and pan-grilled. Roast to an internal temperature of 140°F for medium-rare, 60 to 70 minutes. Allow to stand for 10 minutes before slicing the meat as thinly as possible.

SERVES 6

2 pounds boneless beef or venison, such as eye of round, rump roast, round tip roast, or sirloin butt

5 garlic cloves, peeled

2 tablespoons smoked pimentón

2 teaspoons dried oregano

½ teaspoon dried thyme

½ teaspoon ground cumin

½ teaspoon ground coriander

2 tablespoons coarse salt

2 tablespoons chopped fresh parsley

¼ cup wine vinegar

1 tablespoon olive oil, plus oil for the skillet

¼ teaspoon black peppercorns

2 bay leaves

Place the piece of beef or venison in a nonreactive container. Puree the garlic in a blender with the pimentón, oregano, thyme, cumin, coriander, salt, parsley, vinegar, and oil to make a smooth paste. Coat the meat with the paste. Sprinkle with the peppercorns and tuck the bay leaves under the meat. Cover tightly and refrigerate. Marinate the meat for at least 24 and up to 72 hours, turning it twice a day.

Slice the meat across the grain ⅜ inch thick. Brush a griddle or heavy skillet with oil and heat it until very hot. Grill the cutlets in 2 or 3 batches until they are browned on one side, 1 minute. Turn them and brown the reverse side, 1 minute.

"ALTOGETHER" VEAL *or* BEEF STEW

Tojunto

This dish comes from Almagro, in the southern part of Castilla–La Mancha, and can be made with veal, beef, pork, chicken, or rabbit. All the ingredients are put to cook together—thus the name, *tojunto*, or *todo junto*, meaning "all together." Supposedly this allowed the women of Almagro to get on with their lacemaking (they make very pretty bobbin lace), the shepherd to keep the cheesemaking going, and the hunter in the fields to have a meal ready when he returned to camp. Flank steak is a good cut for this slow-cooked stew.

SERVES 4

1 onion, quartered and sliced

1 green bell pepper or 2 mild green chiles such as Anaheim, cut into 1-inch pieces

1 large tomato or 3 plum tomatoes, peeled and cut into eighths

2 garlic cloves, chopped

1 large carrot, peeled and quartered

4 medium potatoes, peeled

1½ pounds boneless veal or beef, cut into 1½-inch pieces

Pinch of ground cloves

Freshly ground black pepper

2 bay leaves

¼ teaspoon saffron threads, crushed

1 teaspoon sweet pimentón

1 cup green beans in 1-inch pieces (¼ pound)

2 teaspoons salt

¼ cup olive oil

½ cup dry white wine

Chopped fresh parsley for garnish

Place the onion, pepper, tomato, and garlic in a cazuela or stew pot. Add the carrot, potatoes, and meat. Sprinkle the meat with cloves and pepper to taste. Tuck the bay leaves around the meat.

Combine the crushed saffron and pimentón in a small bowl. Add ¼ cup water and stir to dissolve. Pour the liquid over the meat. Place the green beans on top. Sprinkle with salt. Pour on the oil and wine plus 1 cup water. Cover the cazuela or pot and bring to a boil. Reduce to a simmer and cook, without stirring, until the meat is very tender, 2 to 2½ hours. Allow to stand for 10 minutes before serving garnished with chopped parsley.

HEARTY BEEF STEW *with* SAUSAGE

Carcamusas

This hearty beef stew, a dish from Toledo, improves if prepared a day in advance and reheated. However, potatoes are best if cooked shortly before serving, so cook them separately and add to the stew when it is reheated.

⁂ SERVES 6

2¼ pounds boneless stewing beef, such as skirt, shin, or rib

¼ cup olive oil

1 cup chopped green bell pepper

1 cup chopped onion

6 garlic cloves, 3 chopped and 3 sliced

1½ cups peeled, seeded, and chopped tomato

1 cup dry white wine

¼ teaspoon black peppercorns

1 teaspoon salt

1 bay leaf

¼ cup diced serrano ham or bacon

6 ounces Spanish chorizo, preferably soft

6 ounces morcilla sausage (optional)

1 cup frozen peas

1 roasted and peeled red bell pepper, cut into strips (⅓ cup)

6 small potatoes (1¼ pounds), peeled and cooked

¼ teaspoon hot red pepper flakes

½ teaspoon dried oregano

1 teaspoon sweet pimentón

Cut the beef into 1-inch cubes. Heat 3 tablespoons of the oil in a heavy skillet over high heat. When the oil is smoking, add the beef. Allow it to brown on one side, 2 minutes, then turn the meat. Add the green pepper, onion, and chopped garlic. Fry for 3 minutes. Add the tomato and fry for 2 minutes.

Add the wine and 1 cup water. Season with peppercorns, salt, and bay leaf. Bring to a boil, cover, and reduce the heat so the stew just simmers. Cook for 1 hour.

Add the ham, chorizo, and morcilla if you're using it. Return to a boil, reduce the heat, and simmer until the beef is very tender, another hour.

Add the peas and strips of roasted pepper. Cook, uncovered, for 10 minutes. Add the cooked potatoes and heat.

Heat the remaining tablespoon of oil in a small skillet over medium heat. Add the sliced garlic, red pepper flakes, and oregano and fry until the garlic is golden, about 1 minute. Remove the skillet from the heat and stir in the pimentón plus 3 tablespoons of liquid from the stew.

Slice the sausages (kitchen shears work well). Serve the stew, sausage, and cooked potatoes with the fried garlic mixture drizzled on top.

BEEF-STUFFED PEPPERS *with* CHUNKY TOMATO SAUCE

Pimientos Rellenos con Salsa de Tomate

Stuffed peppers in a fresh tomato sauce deliciously celebrate summer. In Spain, the peppers might be thin-skinned green frying peppers (somewhat like a very mild Anaheim chile) or fat bell peppers. Green ones are preferred for stuffing, but red ones add a nice sweetness to the dish. If you are using bell peppers, don't slice off the tops, but cut around the pepper's stem, leaving a small opening for stuffing. You can use ground beef, as in this recipe, or a combination of beef and pork. I like to use ground chicken thighs in place of beef.

SERVES 4

4 large bell peppers, green and/or red

2½ pounds tomatoes (about 6)

2 slices bread

Milk or water for soaking the bread

1 egg, beaten

¼ cup minced onion, plus 1 cup chopped (about 1 large)

3 garlic cloves, 1 minced and 2 chopped

2 teaspoons salt

¼ teaspoon freshly grated nutmeg

Pinch of ground cloves

Freshly ground black pepper

¼ cup chopped fresh parsley

1 pound ground beef

¼ cup chopped serrano ham or pancetta

1 tablespoon all-purpose flour

¼ cup olive oil

¼ teaspoon ground cumin

Remove the stems and seeds from the peppers. Bring a large pot of water to a boil and blanch the tomatoes until the skins split, about 1 minute. Drain and let them cool, then peel the tomatoes. Cut them into wedges or small chunks.

Soak the bread in milk until softened. Squeeze out the liquid and discard. Crumble the bread into a mixing bowl.

Remove 1½ teaspoons of the beaten egg and reserve in a saucer. Add the remaining egg to the bread. Add the minced onion and minced garlic. Stir in 1 teaspoon of the salt, the nutmeg, cloves, pepper to taste, and parsley. Add the ground beef and chopped ham. Combine the mixture well. Stuff the peppers with the meat mixture.

Dip the open ends of the peppers in the reserved beaten egg, then into the flour.

Heat the oil in a deep skillet over medium heat. Fry the peppers, floured side down. Add the chopped onion and garlic and turn the peppers to let them fry slowly on all sides, about 8 minutes. Add the tomatoes, cumin, remaining teaspoon of salt, and pepper to taste. Bring to a boil, cover the skillet, and simmer for 45 minutes, turning the peppers occasionally. Remove the lid and cook for another 20 minutes, until the pepper skins are shriveled and the tomato sauce is reduced.

Cut the peppers in half lengthwise and arrange on a serving platter. Spoon the sauce over them.

MEAT-STUFFED EGGPLANTS SPICED *with* NUTMEG

Berenjenas Rellenas

Use ground beef, pork, lamb, or chicken for this tasty stuffed eggplant, spiced with freshly grated nutmeg. With a salad on the side, it makes a light luncheon or supper dish.

✻ **SERVES 6**

3 medium eggplants (about ¾ pound each)

3 tablespoons olive oil

¼ cup chopped bacon (3 slices)

1 cup chopped onion

4 garlic cloves, chopped

1 pound ground beef

1 teaspoon salt

Pinch of freshly grated nutmeg

Freshly ground black pepper

½ cup tomato sauce, homemade (page 26) or canned

2 ounces Manchego, grated (about 1 cup)

Preheat the oven to 375°F.

Remove and discard the stems and leaves from the eggplants, then cut them in half lengthwise. Slash the flesh at 1½-inch intervals. Place the eggplants in a single layer in a baking pan and brush with 2 tablespoons of the oil. Bake until fork-tender, about 20 minutes.

While the eggplants are baking, heat the remaining tablespoon of oil in a large skillet over medium heat and sauté the bacon for 1 minute. Add the onion and garlic and fry for 3 minutes. Add the ground beef and continue frying over high heat, breaking up the meat, until it loses its red color, 2 to 3 minutes. Add the salt, nutmeg, and pepper to taste, the tomato sauce, and ½ cup water. Bring to a boil, then reduce the heat and simmer, covered, for 20 minutes.

When the eggplants are tender, scoop out the flesh and reserve the shells. Add the flesh to the meat in the skillet. Uncover the skillet and cook for 5 minutes more, or until most of liquid has cooked away. Arrange the eggplant shells in a single layer in a baking pan. Spoon the meat filling into the shells. Top with the grated cheese. Add enough water to cover the bottom of the pan.

Bake, uncovered, until the cheese is melted and the filling bubbling, 15 minutes. Allow to stand for 10 minutes before serving.

THE CUTTING EDGE—AN ALBACETE TRADITION

The nine-inch chef's knife, made of forged molybdenum-vanadium stainless steel, feels just right in hand, light but balanced. It slices effortlessly through an onion. Roberto Arcos holds the knife with respect. He made it. Not personally. It is one of seventy thousand pieces of cutlery and kitchen utensils manufactured daily at his factory in Albacete. The plant produces high-quality professional and kitchen knives that are sold worldwide.

The company dates back to 1875, when Sr. Arcos's great-grandfather, Gregorio Arcos Aroca, set up a knife-making workshop in Albacete.

"My great-grandfather made *navajas* [folding pocket knives] and rustic knives for country and hunting," said Sr. Arcos. "They were all made artisanally. My grandfather later began to mechanize the workshop." By the 1950s and '60s, with massive movement of people to the cities, demand for hunting knives had decreased. "My father decided to change production to domestic knives. We're still expanding our range of both professional and home kitchen knives."

The line of cutlery includes specialty items, such as a ten-inch flexible blade designed especially for thinly slicing serrano ham from the bone.

"The thinner the slice, the more aromatic the ham," said Sr. Arcos. There are also thin and flexible ridged knives for thinly slicing salmon, Japanese-style knives, serrated knives for slicing tomatoes, fish scalers, filleting and boning knives.

Butchers and fish sellers use Arcos knives. Professional chefs use Arcos knives. Karlos Arguiñano, a well-known Spanish chef, uses them on his television cooking show. Home cooks use Arcos knives.

The Arcos plant, with cutting-edge technology—literally and figuratively—employs about three hundred persons and twenty-five robots.

Programmed machines cut the blades from strong forged steel. The molybdenum and vanadium alloy improves hardness, which is a measure of a knife's tensile strength, resistance to corrosion, and ability to hold an edge. The steel blades are next tempered in furnaces at high temperatures to harden and strengthen them. Two stones hone the edges. A white-cloaked robot looking like a witch wields the blades in a mesmerizing sequence of sharpening. Polishing follows before the blades are inserted into handles.

Knife handles are variously hard plastic, soft plastic, or different woods, depending on the knife design (and, ultimately, price). The top line of Arcos professional chefs' knives has handles of tough polyoxymethylene, making them exceedingly resistant to wear, but those destined for butchers, who use knives all day long, have soft handles for ease of use. The tang—the sheath of metal that extends the full length of the handle—is completely encased in the soft coating for a seamless handle, more comfortable for prolonged use in a butcher's shop or slaughterhouse.

The knives receive a final sharpening before passing quality control and moving to packaging. Here a line of women puts the final polish on the knives before they are packaged. Smoothing the blades with polishing cloths, they look at risk of slashing themselves. The plant foreman acknowledged that workers can never become overconfident in the handling of sharp instruments. Working with knives requires respect.

Albacete, whose name derives from the Arabic *al basit,* meaning "flat lands," lies on the extreme southeast of the La Mancha plain. Though not nearly as well known as the other provincial capitals of Castilla–La Mancha—Toledo, Cuenca, Ciudad Real, and Guadalajara—Albacete is, surprisingly, larger than any of them.

The city has a long and illustrious history of knife making. Archaeological digs have turned up iron knives and pincers from the Celtiberian and Phoenician eras from before the fourth century B.C. Arabs brought their honed skills to the region during their domination, dating from the eighth century. By the fifteenth century occasional mentions of Albacete's knife trade appeared in documents. By the second half of the sixteenth century records show a developing artisanal business in scissors, daggers, swords, and knives. A hundred years later, Albacete began to stand out, with most of the workshops located in a single street. By the eighteenth century, the city's craftsmen were considered the best cutlers in Spain, displaying a high level of quality and great artistry. Besides superior blades, artisans crafted beautiful handles of bone, horn, inlaid silver and gold. The nineteenth century saw a setback, as French products invaded the national market. This also was the beginning of a separation between the small, artisanal shop and the industrialized factory such as the Arcos family business. Albacete still has small workshops producing hand-made pocketknives and hunting knives.

PORK CHOPS in GARLICKY SAUCE

Chuletas de Cerdo al Ajo Manchego

This dish can be made with chops or pork stew meat. The chops are juiciest if browned, removed from the pan while the vegetables cook, and then returned to the pan to finish cooking. However, cubes of stew meat cut from a picnic shoulder can be braised with the vegetables. Garlic added at the end is pungent! I especially like the flavor of bittersweet (*agridulce*) pimentón de la Vera with the pork, though ordinary sweet pimentón can be used.

SERVES 4

4 thick bone-in pork chops (about 2 pounds)

Salt and freshly ground black pepper

3 tablespoons olive oil

1 cup chopped onion

1 cup chopped green bell pepper

1½ pounds baking potatoes, peeled and cut into 1-inch pieces

1 cup peeled, seeded, and chopped tomato

½ teaspoon pimentón, bittersweet if available

Pinch of ground cloves

Freshly grated nutmeg

Pinch of dried thyme

3 garlic cloves, peeled

⅓ cup chopped fresh flat-leaf parsley

Sprinkle the chops with salt and pepper and let them stand for 30 minutes. Heat the oil in a large skillet over high heat and fry the chops, turning to brown both sides, for 3 to 4 minutes. Remove them from the skillet.

Add the onion, green pepper, and potatoes and sauté for 5 minutes. Add the tomato and cook for 5 minutes. Add ½ cup water, ½ teaspoon salt, the pimentón, cloves, nutmeg, and thyme. Cover and cook, stirring occasionally, until the potatoes are tender, 30 minutes.

Return the pork chops and any juices to the pan and reheat gently until the chops are cooked through, 5 to 10 minutes.

Puree the garlic and parsley in a blender with ⅓ cup water. Stir into the skillet and combine with the pan juices. Cook for 5 minutes.

BAKED PORK CHOPS *with* LEMON MARINADE

Chuletas de Cerdo al Horno

Lemon marinade adds tang to both pork chops and potatoes. Cauliflower or Broccoli with Golden Garlic and Almonds (page 255) is a good side dish.

SERVES 4

6 garlic cloves, peeled

¼ cup fresh flat-leaf parsley

¼ teaspoon dried thyme

1 teaspoon salt

1 teaspoon smoked pimentón

¼ cup fresh lemon juice

¼ cup olive oil

Freshly ground black pepper

Four 1-inch-thick bone-in pork chops (about 2 pounds)

1½ pounds potatoes, peeled and thinly sliced

2 bay leaves

Combine the garlic, parsley, thyme, salt, pimentón, lemon juice, oil, pepper to taste, and ¼ cup water in a blender. Process to make a smooth marinade. Place the pork chops in a single layer in a nonreactive pan. Pour the marinade over them and turn the chops to coat both sides. Allow to stand at room temperature for 1 hour or refrigerate for up to 4 hours.

Preheat the oven to 375°.

Place the sliced potatoes in the bottom of an ovenproof pan or casserole. Place the chops on top with all of the marinade. Cover the pan with foil and bake for 45 minutes. Remove foil and bake for 15 minutes more. Allow the chops and potatoes to stand for 10 minutes before serving.

SPICED PORK LOIN *in* CONFIT

Lomo de la Orza

An *orza* is an earthenware jug or amphora in which, at a traditional *matanza*, hog slaughtering, whole pork loins are placed in a spiced, salty marinade. After the brining, the meat is cooked (whole or sliced), then packed in the orza, completely immersed in lard or olive oil, which seals the meat against bacteria. In cold winter months the pork, a sort of confit, keeps for several months. A few slices of the pork, fried with potatoes in some of the fat from the orza, made very tasty "fast food" in the traditional Manchegan kitchen.

In modern times, refrigerators and freezers make preserving unnecessary. But the special flavor is enjoyed nevertheless.

Pork loin cooked in this manner makes a great party entree, because it can be prepared well in advance and served hot or cold. If you're not feeding a crowd, after marinating and cooking the whole loin, cut it into smaller pieces and freeze them with some of the oil in which the loin was cooked.

SERVES **12 TO 18**

3½ to 4 pounds boneless pork loin

10 garlic cloves, peeled

¼ cup coarsely chopped fresh parsley

1 teaspoon ground cinnamon

2 teaspoons freshly ground black pepper

¼ teaspoon ground cloves

¼ teaspoon ground coriander

¼ teaspoon coarsely ground aniseeds

¼ teaspoon caraway seeds

1 teaspoon freshly grated nutmeg

¼ cup sweet pimentón

2 bay leaves, broken into pieces

½ teaspoon dried thyme

1 teaspoon dried oregano

1 cup dry white wine

¼ cup coarse kosher salt

3 cups olive oil

Pierce the pork loin with a skewer 10 to 12 times on both sides. Place it in a nonreactive container. If necessary to fit, cut the loin in half.

In a blender, combine the garlic, parsley, cinnamon, pepper, cloves, coriander, aniseeds, caraway, nutmeg, pimentón, bay leaves, thyme, oregano, and wine. Blend until smooth.

In a large saucepan, bring 1 quart water and the salt to a boil. Boil for 1 minute. Add the spice mixture and bring again to a boil. Remove the pan from the heat. Allow to cool, then refrigerate until chilled.

Pour the spiced brine over the pork loin. Cover tightly and refrigerate for 24 hours.

Turn the pork over in the brine and marinate for 24 hours more.

Remove the pork from the brine, drain well, and pat dry with paper towels. Discard the brine.

Place the oil in a pot deep enough to hold the pork. Heat until barely shimmering, about 250°F. Very carefully place the pork in the hot oil. (It will not be completely covered in oil.) Keep the oil just bubbling gently around the pork (oil temperature about 190°F). Cover the pot and poach the pork in the oil for 30 minutes.

Very carefully turn the pork over in the oil. Cover and continue cooking for 20 minutes more. Test the meat with an instant-read thermometer. Turn the pork and immediately test the internal temperature again. The pork is done when it reaches 150°F. If not, cover and cook for 10 minutes more, and test again.

Remove the pot from the heat and allow the pork to cool in the oil. Place it in a nonreactive container just large enough to hold it and pour the oil over it. The pork should be completely immersed in the oil. Cover and refrigerate for at least 1 day and up to 1 week.

To serve, slice the pork loin about ⅜ inch thick. It can be reheated in some of the oil or served at room temperature.

PORK TENDERLOINS *with* GLAZED ONIONS

Solomillos de Cerdo con Cebolletas Glaseadas

This is the sort of dish to serve for a special dinner party. Sweet "raisin" wine glazes the little onions that roast with the meat and makes a luscious sauce. The wine is made from Pedro Ximénez grapes, which are allowed to dry in the sun for several days before vinification, concentrating the sugar and aroma. If this is not to be found, use a muscatel or medium-dry Sherry.

SERVES 8

2 pork tenderloins, each about 1¼ pounds

Salt and freshly ground black pepper

1 teaspoon dried thyme

3 tablespoons olive oil

1 pound small onions (18 to 20)

1 cup sweet wine such as Pedro Ximénez

2 tablespoons Sherry vinegar

Sprinkle the tenderloins with salt, pepper, and thyme, then rub with 1 tablespoon of the oil. Allow them to sit at room temperature for 2 hours.

Peel the onions and cut a small slit in the root end. Cook them in boiling salted water to cover until just tender, about 15 minutes. Remove them with a slotted spoon. Reserve the cooking liquid.

Preheat the oven to 400°F.

Heat the remaining 2 tablespoons oil in a large, heavy skillet over medium-high heat and brown the tenderloins on all sides, 6 to 8 minutes. When browned, transfer them to a roasting pan just big enough to hold the tenderloins. Place the onions around the meat. Pour on ½ cup of the wine, the vinegar, and ½ cup of the reserved onion-cooking liquid.

Roast for 15 minutes. Turn the onions and baste the meat with some of the liquid in the pan. Roast until a meat thermometer inserted into the center of pork registers 150°F, about 10 minutes longer.

Transfer the meat to a platter and cover with foil. Swirl the onions in the syrupy glaze in the roasting pan, then transfer them to a serving platter and keep warm.

Add the remaining ½ cup wine and 1 cup of the remaining onion liquid to the roasting pan and cook over medium heat, stirring up the glaze on the bottom, until reduced by half.

Cut the pork into ½-inch slices. Accompany with the onions. Drizzle the sauce over and serve.

MACARONI *with* CHORIZO SAUSAGE

Macarrones con Chorizo

In Spain, just as in Italy, pasta is usually served as a starter, not a main course. Here is an everyday way to prepare pasta. Chorizo provides the flavor "package." Cheese on top is optional.

SERVES 4

3 tablespoons olive oil

1 cup chopped green bell pepper

1 cup chopped onion

1 cup diced zucchini (½ medium zucchini)

1 garlic clove, chopped

1½ cups diced Spanish chorizo, hard or soft (6 ounces)

2 cups chopped tomato

Pinch of dried oregano

Salt and freshly ground black pepper

½ pound penne pasta

Grated Manchego cheese for serving (optional)

Heat the oil in a deep skillet or cazuela over high heat and sauté the green pepper, onion, zucchini, garlic, and chorizo for 10 minutes. Add the tomato, oregano, and salt and pepper to taste. Cook until slightly reduced, about 20 minutes longer.

Cook the pasta in boiling water until al dente (according to package directions, but usually about 8 minutes). Drain the pasta and combine with the sauce. Serve with grated cheese if desired.

BLOODLESS BLOOD SAUSAGE

Morcilla Blanca

Morcilla, blood sausage or black pudding, is one of the most distinctive sausages in the Spanish repertoire of pork products. It adds spiciness to stews with lentils or chickpeas. Variations abound. Some morcilla contains rice and onions, others only onion. In La Mancha it is often made with mashed potato and pumpkin. One version exchanges the onions for apples. Clove, cinnamon, and sweet pimentón are the predominant spices.

As pig's blood is not easy to come by, I suggest making white morcilla, using rice and ground pork belly, which is about equal parts lean and fat. You needn't bother with sausage casings. Just wrap the sausages in cheesecloth. This is not a cured sausage, so store it, refrigerated, like any cooked meat. Use within two or three days. If you want to keep the sausage longer, wrap it tightly in plastic wrap, place in an airtight container, and freeze.

MAKES 6 SAUSAGE LINKS, WEIGHING ABOUT 2 POUNDS

---

2 bay leaves

2 teaspoons salt

⅓ cup Spanish round-grain rice

1 cup chopped onion

1½ pounds ground fresh pork belly (uncured pancetta)

2 garlic cloves, crushed

½ teaspoon freshly ground black pepper

1 teaspoon sweet pimentón

½ teaspoon bittersweet smoked pimentón

1 teaspoon dried oregano

½ teaspoon ground cinnamon

¼ teaspoon ground cloves

Grating of fresh nutmeg

⅛ teaspoon crushed aniseeds

1 tablespoon dry white wine

1 egg, beaten

Bring 1⅓ cups water to a boil with one of the bay leaves and 1 teaspoon of the salt. Add the rice, cover, and simmer until the water is absorbed, 15 minutes. Remove from the heat and allow to cool. Discard the bay leaf.

Cook the onion in boiling water for 5 minutes. Drain, saving the liquid.

Combine the onion, rice, and ground pork belly in a bowl. Add the crushed garlic. In a small bowl, mix the pepper, both kinds of pimentón, oregano, cinnamon, cloves, nutmeg, aniseeds, and remaining teaspoon of salt. Sprinkle half of the spice mixture over the pork. Turn the pork mixture over and sprinkle on the rest of the spices.

Add the wine and egg and knead the sausage mixture until thoroughly mixed. Make a 2-inch patty. Fry it on both sides in a small skillet. Cool slightly and taste the patty. Add salt or spices, if necessary.

Cut a double thickness of cheesecloth into 3 rectangles measuring 12 × 8 inches. Divide the sausage mixture into 3 parts. Spread a sheet of wax paper on the work surface. Roll and pat one part of the sausage into a log, about 10 inches long and 1 inch thick. Place it on one edge of a cheesecloth rectangle and roll the sausage log in the cheesecloth. Tie the ends with kitchen twine. Tie the middle of the roll, dividing it into 2 links of sausage. Continue with the remaining 2 pieces of sausage mix.

Place the reserved onion water, remaining bay leaf, and enough additional water in a pot deep enough to hold the sausages in one layer. Bring to a boil; add the sausages, and cook, covered, for 30 minutes.

Drain the sausages. Hang them in a cool place to dry for 3 hours. Refrigerate the sausages in a covered container and use them within 3 days.

Before serving, remove and discard the cheesecloth. The sausages can be sliced and eaten cold, added to stews and cocidos, or fried.

MORCILLA with RAISINS and PINE NUTS

Morcilla con Pasas y Piñones

I tasted this at a very old Madrid tapa bar, where it was served with a red wine from Valdepeñas in La Mancha. The morcilla should be one made with rice (such as the white morcilla in the preceding recipe). If you are substituting another type of blood sausage (such as *boudin noir*), add about ¾ cup of cooked rice to the skillet with the sausage. At the tapa bar, the morcilla was served heaped on a platter placed in the center of the table, accompanied by forks and chunks of bread. We all helped ourselves straight from the platter. At home I serve the morcilla atop salad greens.

SERVES 4 AS A MAIN DISH OR 6 TO 8 AS A TAPA

2 tablespoons olive oil

¼ cup pine nuts

1 pound morcilla, casings removed and sausage sliced

¼ cup raisins

¼ cup dry white wine

Salad greens for serving

Heat the oil in a skillet over medium-high heat and fry the pine nuts until golden, 30 seconds. Tip the skillet so the oil flows to one side and skim out the pine nuts.

Add the morcilla and raisins and fry for 3 minutes. Use a wooden spatula to break the morcilla into smaller pieces. Add the wine and simmer for 5 minutes, until the morcilla begins to sizzle again.

Spoon the hot morcilla onto salad greens and scatter the pine nuts on top.

SLOW-COOKED PIG'S FEET

Manos de Cerdo Estofadas

I finally "get it" about pig's feet, after various experiments in eating them and cooking them. They fall into the same category as snails—the sauce is so delicious that it makes preparing something a little oddball, with a weird texture to boot, worth all the trouble. Pig's feet have a lip-sticking, gelatinous texture that either you are crazy for or else you don't want to know.

I consulted various recipes for cooking pigs' feet. Invariably they instructed me to boil the trotters, remove the bones, and cut up the "meat."

Well, let me tell you, pig's feet don't have "meat." Meat is, really, muscle, and feet don't have muscle. They have thick skin and gelatinous cartilage. The broth they cook in, which sets up into a firm gelatin, makes a serious soup or sauce. The "meat," cut into bits and stewed in a flavorful sauce, is unctuous, a little slippery, and ever so delicious. (If you want a meatier version, add ¼ pound of pork shoulder meat to cook with the trotters.) Serve the pig's feet very hot with lots of fresh bread for sopping up the sauce.

SERVES 4

4 pig's feet (trotters), split in half (4 to 4½ pounds)

2 leeks, white part only

3 carrots

1 dried choricero pepper or 3 ñora peppers (optional)

2 bay leaves

½ teaspoon black peppercorns

3 cloves

1 tablespoon plus ½ teaspoon salt

3 tablespoons wine vinegar

2 tablespoons olive oil

1 cup chopped onion

3 garlic cloves, chopped

2 tablespoons all-purpose flour

½ teaspoon hot pimentón or pinch of cayenne

1 to 3 teaspoons sweet pimentón

2 tablespoons dry red wine

Chopped fresh parsley for garnish

Put the pig's feet in a large stew pot with water to cover. Bring to a boil, boil for 5 minutes, and drain.

Rinse out the pot and put the trotters in with fresh water to cover. Bring to a boil. Add the leeks, carrots, choricero pepper, bay leaves, peppercorns, cloves, 1 tablespoon of the salt, and the vinegar. When the pot boils, cover and reduce the heat to a simmer. Cook until the pig's feet are fork-tender, about 2 hours.

Lift the pig's feet out of the broth. When they are cool enough to handle, remove all the bones and thick parts of the skin and discard them. Cut the remaining meat, skin, and cartilage into bite-sized pieces. Skim out the carrots and choricero peppers and reserve. Discard the bay leaves.

If using the choricero or ñora peppers, split them open and scrape the pulp with the blunt edge of a knife. Save the pulp and discard the skins.

When the broth cools, skim off and discard the fat that rises to the surface.

Heat the oil in a deep skillet over medium heat and sauté the onion until it begins to brown, 5 minutes. Add the garlic and sauté for 2 minutes.

Remove the pan from the heat. Stir in the flour. Add the pulp of the choricero peppers plus the hot pimentón and 1 teaspoon of sweet pimentón. If not using the choricero peppers, stir in 1 tablespoon of sweet pimentón.

Gradually stir in 2 cups of the broth in which the trotters cooked. Add the remaining ½ teaspoon salt. Return the pan to the heat and cook, stirring, until the sauce thickens. Return the reserved meat to the sauce. Simmer, covered, for 30 minutes.

Slice the reserved carrots and add to the sauce. Heat. Serve the pig's feet with the sauce very hot, garnished with chopped parsley.

NOTE: *Choricero and ñora peppers are dried sweet peppers. The choricero is long and skinny; the ñora is round and plum sized. They are available at shops that specialize in products from Spain (see Sources). If not available, use additional pimentón in the recipe.*

LAMB ROASTED *with* SAFFRON POTATOES

Cordero en Rustidera con Patatas

A *rustidera* is a shallow roasting pan, big enough to hold a whole baby lamb that is cut into pieces and combined with potatoes, onions, and tomatoes. The giant casserole is carried to a large baker's oven to roast. This version uses leg of spring lamb and can be roasted in a regular oven. Choose a small leg, weighing 3½ to 4 pounds. Use a roasting pan, an oval cazuela, a tian, or an ovenproof casserole big enough to hold the lamb. Ideally you should be able to serve the lamb in the pan in which it roasts.

SERVES 6

One 4-pound leg of lamb, excess fat removed

Salt and freshly ground black pepper

⅓ cup olive oil

2 pounds baking potatoes, peeled and cut into ¼-inch slices

1 large onion, cut in half and thinly sliced

1 green bell pepper, cut into strips

3 tomatoes (about 1 pound), sliced

¼ cup chopped fresh parsley

½ teaspoon saffron threads

2 cloves

10 black peppercorns

½ teaspoon ground cinnamon

3 garlic cloves, crushed

3 bay leaves

2 cups dry white wine

Sprinkle the lamb with salt and pepper and allow to come to room temperature.

Preheat the oven to 400°F.

Pour half the oil into the bottom of roasting pan or cazuela. Layer the sliced potatoes, onion, green pepper, and tomatoes in the pan, sprinkling with salt and parsley.

In a mortar or spice grinder, grind together the saffron, cloves, and peppercorns. Add ¼ cup hot water and allow to stand for 10 minutes. Stir in the cinnamon and crushed garlic. Pour the spice mixture over the potatoes. Tuck the bay leaves into the layered vegetables. Pour on the wine. Place the leg of lamb on top. Pour the remaining oil over the lamb.

Reduce the oven temperature to 350°F and roast the lamb until the potatoes are fork-tender and an instant-read thermometer inserted in the thickest part of the lamb registers 140°F for medium, about 1 hour. (If you prefer rare, place the pan with potatoes, uncovered, in the oven for 30 minutes before placing the lamb on top of it. Roast the lamb for about 30 minutes, to an internal temperature of 125°F.)

Transfer the lamb to a cutting board. Allow to rest for 10 minutes, then carve the meat off the bone. If roasted in a cazuela that can be served at table, arrange the meat on top of the potatoes. Otherwise, use a wide spatula to transfer the potatoes and other vegetables to a serving platter, discarding the bay leaves, and place the meat on top.

VARIATION: *Substitute 3½ pounds lamb shanks for the leg of lamb. Place the lamb and vegetables in a preheated 400°F oven for 30 minutes. Reduce the heat to 350°F. Cover the roasting pan with a lid or heavy-duty foil and bake until the meat is well done and very tender, about 1½ hours.*

LEG OF LAMB ROASTED *with* MEDITERRANEAN HERBS

Pierna de Cordero Asado con Hierbas

One of the glory dishes of Castilian cooking is baby lamb roasted in a wood-fired oven. Rubbed with lard and a few herbs, placed in a cazuela on a bed of onions and laurel (bay) leaves, it emerges with crisp skin, succulent flesh. I heartily recommend a trip to Spain to sample roast lamb at its best. Should this not be possible, here is a way to roast spring lamb that recalls the flavors of Castile. Look for the smallest possible leg of lamb and trim it of excess fat.

Should you be able to obtain baby lamb (a whole lamb weighs 12 to 15 pounds), split it open lengthwise and prepare in the same manner as described here. Baby lamb is not served rare, so roast it to an internal temperature of 155°F.

I like crisp-fried Hot Potatoes (page 271) and Artichoke Sauté (page 247) with the lamb. A *crianza* wine with a Vinos de la Tierra de Castilla denomination (see page 350) would be a fine accompaniment.

SERVES 6

1 leg of lamb, about 4 pounds

Salt and freshly ground black pepper

1 teaspoon minced fresh rosemary

1 teaspoon minced fresh thyme

¼ cup chopped fresh flat-leaf parsley

2 garlic cloves, crushed

1 tablespoon olive oil or lard

1 tablespoon wine vinegar

1 onion, halved and sliced

3 bay leaves

1 cup dry white wine

Fresh rosemary sprigs for garnish (optional)

Trim the lamb of excess fat. Salt it generously and sprinkle with pepper. Combine the rosemary, thyme, parsley, garlic, oil, and vinegar. Spread this mixture on all sides of the meat. Allow to stand for 1 hour at room temperature or 4 to 6 hours refrigerated.

Preheat the oven to 400°F.

Spread the sliced onion and bay leaves in the bottom of a cazuela or roasting pan and place the leg of lamb on top. Roast it for 30 minutes.

Reduce the oven temperature to 350°F. Pour the wine and 1 cup water around the lamb. Roast until the internal temperature, tested with an instant-read thermometer, reaches 140°F for medium-rare meat, about 30 minutes longer. (A larger leg of lamb will take longer to reach this temperature and may require more water added to the roasting pan.)

Transfer the lamb to a carving board and let it rest for 10 minutes. Skim any fat from the pan juices. Discard the bay leaves. Puree the pan juices and onions in a blender.

Carve the meat and arrange on a heated serving platter. Add the juices that collect on the board to the pureed sauce. Serve the lamb with some of the sauce spooned over it and the rest in a sauce bowl. Garnish with sprigs of rosemary if desired.

ROAST LAMB with SPINACH and BREAD CRUMB STUFFING

Cordero Asado con Relleno

The spinach, pine nuts, and raisins in the stuffing make this an especially tasty way to prepare a boned leg of lamb. Don't worry that the slab of meat is somewhat ragged. Tie it at intervals to hold the stuffing in. Once roasted, the meat can be sliced thickly, showing a spiral of stuffing, and arranged onto a platter or individual plates.

SERVES 6

One boneless leg of lamb, 3½ to 4 pounds

Salt and freshly ground black pepper

10 to 12 spinach leaves, stems removed

2 tablespoons olive oil

¼ cup pine nuts

¼ cup finely chopped shallot

¼ cup chopped bacon or pancetta

¼ cup raisins

1 tablespoon chopped fresh mint

1 cup fine fresh bread crumbs

1 egg white, lightly beaten with 1 tablespoon water

½ cup dry white wine

Trim the lamb of excess fat. Lay the meat open on a work surface. With the knife parallel to the surface, slice partway through the 2 thickest humps of the meat in order to fold them open, creating a slab of more or less equal thickness. Sprinkle with salt and pepper.

Arrange a layer of spinach leaves, shiny side down, on top of the meat.

Heat the oil in a small skillet over medium-high heat. Toast the pine nuts until golden, 30 seconds. Skim them out and reserve. Add the shallot and bacon to the oil and sauté for 2 minutes. Remove from the heat and add the pine nuts, raisins, mint, bread crumbs, and egg white. Season with salt and pepper. Spread this mixture on top of the spinach leaves.

Starting at the narrowest end, roll the meat up, enclosing the stuffing. Fasten with poultry skewers, then tie with butcher's twine.

Place the meat in a nonreactive bowl just large enough to hold it. Pour on the wine. Marinate the lamb for 2 hours. Turn the meat and marinate for 2 hours more.

Preheat the oven to 400°F.

Place the lamb in a roasting pan. Pour on the marinating wine and 1 cup water. Roast the lamb, basting occasionally with pan juices, to an internal temperature of 140°F for medium-rare, about 70 minutes. Add water as needed so there is always liquid in the bottom of the pan.

Allow the meat to rest for 15 minutes. Remove the skewers and twine and slice thickly. Spoon the pan juices over the meat.

HERB-ROASTED KID

Cabrito Asado

This is a specialty of Guadalajara. The herbs and vinegar in the marinade give the meat a delicious flavor. It is best roasted in a large oval earthenware cazuela, but any roasting pan will work fine. If you parboil the unpeeled onions, you can peel them much easier, without tears.

SERVES 6

2 legs of kid (young goat), about 3 pounds 10 ounces total

¼ cup wine vinegar

12 garlic cloves, peeled

1 teaspoon fresh mint

½ teaspoon minced fresh rosemary

½ teaspoon dried thyme

¼ cup fresh flat-leaf parsley

1 teaspoon salt

Freshly ground black pepper

1 tablespoon olive oil

12 very small potatoes (about 1 pound 10 ounces)

12 small onions (¾ pound)

Place the legs in a nonreactive container large enough to hold them.

In a blender, combine the vinegar, garlic, mint, rosemary, thyme, parsley, salt, pepper to taste, oil, and ¼ cup water. Blend until smooth. Rub the herb blend on both sides of the legs. Cover with foil and refrigerate for at least 6 and up to 24 hours, turning the legs at least once.

Peel the potatoes and parboil in salted water for 10 minutes. Drain. Trim the tops and roots of the onions, but do not peel. Parboil them for 2 minutes and drain. When they are cool enough to handle, slip off the skins.

Preheat the oven to 400°F. Place the legs and all of the herb marinade in a large oval earthenware cazuela or roasting pan. Put the potatoes and onions around the meat. Add 1 cup boiling water and place the cazuela, uncovered, in the oven. Immediately lower the oven temperature to 300°F. Roast for 1 hour.

Add 1 cup boiling water. Roast until the meat registers 180°F when tested with an instant-read thermometer, about 30 minutes longer. Add water so that there is always liquid in the bottom of the pan.

Remove from the oven and allow the meat to stand for 10 minutes before carving. Carve the meat off the bones and place on a heated platter with the potatoes and onions. Reheat the pan drippings (adding water if necessary) and serve with the meat.

LAMB STEW in CAZUELA

Cazuela de Cordero

Almost any cut of lamb—neck, shoulder, shank, or leg—works for this stew. I prefer the shoulder. I ask the butcher to bone it and then use the bones to make a simple broth that adds so much flavor to the finished dish. If you don't have lamb broth, substitute chicken broth.

SERVES 4

2 tablespoons olive oil

3 cups julienned onion (2 medium onions)

1½ pounds boneless lamb, cut into 1½-inch pieces

¼ cup fresh flat-leaf parsley

1 teaspoon sweet pimentón

4 garlic cloves, peeled

¾ cup dry white wine

1 cup lamb or chicken broth

1 teaspoon salt

Freshly ground black pepper

2 bay leaves

2 carrots, quartered

1 pound potatoes, peeled and cut into 1-inch pieces

1½ cups fresh or frozen peas

1 tablespoon chopped fresh mint

Heat the oil in a cazuela or stew pot over medium-high heat and sauté the onion until softened, 5 minutes. Add the lamb and sauté for 3 minutes longer.

Place the parsley, pimentón, garlic, and wine in a blender and puree the mixture. Add to the lamb with the broth, salt, pepper to taste, bay leaves, and carrots. Bring to a boil, reduce the heat, and simmer, covered, until the meat is tender, about 50 minutes.

Add the potatoes. If you're using large fresh peas, add them now. If using frozen peas or tiny fresh ones, add them during the last 5 minutes of cooking. Simmer until the potatoes are tender, about 20 minutes.

Remove the cazuela from the heat and allow to stand for 10 minutes before serving. Sprinkle with the mint.

BRAISED LAMB *with* CHILES

Caldereta de Cordero

This rustic dish derives from the shepherds' *caldereta,* or iron stew pot, in which meals were cooked over embers. At its most basic, the stew was eaten straight from the pot, with bread for sopping up the gravy. Other versions use either the lamb liver, grilled and mashed, or ground almonds, pine nuts, or walnuts to thicken the sauce. A very similar lamb stew is called *cochifrito.*

Keep the lamb covered with liquid as it cooks and, if preparing it in advance, keep the cooked meat completely covered with liquid so that it doesn't darken and dry out.

Ñoras are plum-sized dried sweet chiles. After cooking, the soft flesh is scraped from the insides of the peppers. Mild California chili pods are a possible substitute, though they are not quite as fleshy as the ñora. Otherwise use a spoonful of sweet pimentón. Use only a little hot chile in addition to the mild. I like to add some smoky Pimentón de la Vera to make up for the shepherds' wood fire smoke.

I serve the lamb and gravy with Potatoes Mashed with Green Garlic (page 270), but rice or couscous would be equally good.

SERVES 6

2½ to 3 pounds lamb steaks cut from the leg, with or without bone

Salt and freshly ground black pepper

3 tablespoons olive oil

1 large onion, quartered and sliced

3 ñora peppers or 1 dried Anaheim chile pod, stem and seeds discarded

1 small hot dried chile, such as cayenne

4 sun-dried tomatoes, sliced

½ red bell pepper

¼ cup chopped fresh flat-leaf parsley

½ teaspoon dried thyme

2 bay leaves

2 heads of garlic, char-roasted (see note page 238) and peeled

1 cup dry white wine

¼ cup blanched almonds

1 teaspoon smoked pimentón (sweet, bittersweet, or hot)

Trim off as much fat as possible from the lamb. Sprinkle it liberally with salt and pepper and allow to stand at room temperature for 1 hour.

Heat the oil in a large stew pot or lidded cazuela over medium heat and sauté the sliced onion until lightly browned, 6 to 8 minutes. Put in the pieces of meat and turn them in the oil for a few minutes. They do not need to brown, only to lose their pink color. Add ñoras or the Anaheim chile pod with the whole dried chile, tomatoes, bell pepper, parsley, thyme, bay leaves, and peeled garlic cloves.

Add the wine and 3 cups water. Bring to a boil, then cover and simmer until the meat is very tender, 1 to 1½ hours.

Lift the pieces of meat out of the cooking liquid with any vegetables clinging to them and set aside, covered tightly. Skim off the fat from the liquid remaining in the pot.

Place a strainer over a bowl and pour the liquid through it. Discard the cayenne chile and bay leaves. Lift out the pieces of ñora. Use a spoon to scrape the pulp from the inside of the ñoras or chile pod. Put the pulp in a blender or food processor (discard the skins). Scrape the pulp from the piece of bell pepper and discard the skin. Add the pulp to the blender with any pieces of onion, tomato, and garlic remaining in the strainer.

> . . . *se fue tras el olor que despedían de sí ciertos*
> *tasajos de cabra que hirviendo al fuego,*
> *en un caldero estaban.* . . .
>
> . . . he set off on the trail of the smell wafting from some
> hunks of goat meat bubbling in a stew pot over the fire . . .
>
> SANCHO PANZA AT THE GOATHERDS' CAMP

Add the almonds to the blender with the pimentón and 1 cup of the strained liquid. Blend or process until the almonds are ground to a smooth paste.

Return the liquid to the stew pot and add the almond mixture. Bring to a boil, stirring. Return the lamb to the pot and cook gently for 20 minutes longer.

TO CHAR-ROAST A HEAD OF GARLIC

Spear the head of garlic on a fork or grasp it with tongs (protect your hands with an oven mitt) and hold over a gas flame or put under the broiler. Turn the garlic until it is charred on all sides. Peel the garlic cloves and rinse in water.

LAMB SHANKS BRAISED *with* BEANS

Cordero Estofado con Alubias

This is a satisfying dish that can be made with any bony cut of lamb—shanks, necks, riblets. If you use shanks, you may wish to strip the meat from the bones after cooking to facilitate serving.

SERVES 4

½ pound dried cannellini beans (1¼ cups), soaked overnight

2 bay leaves

1½ teaspoons salt

2 tablespoons olive oil

4 lamb shanks (about 3 pounds)

1½ cups chopped onion

3 garlic cloves, chopped

½ cup drained canned diced tomato

1 teaspoon black peppercorns, coarsely crushed

Pinch of ground cloves

½ teaspoon dried thyme

1 fresh rosemary sprig (optional)

Chopped fresh cilantro, parsley, or mint for garnish

Drain the beans and put them in a pot with 1 quart water. Bring to a rolling boil. Drain the beans, rinse them in cold water, and return them to the pot. Add 1 quart water, the bay leaves, and 1 teaspoon of the salt. Bring to a boil and simmer for 15 minutes.

Heat the oil in a heavy skillet over medium-high heat. Brown the lamb shanks on all sides, about 5 minutes. Remove them and reserve. Add the onion and garlic to the skillet and sauté until the onion begins to brown, 4 minutes. Add the tomato and sauté for 2 minutes. Add the pepper, cloves, thyme, rosemary if you're using it, remaining ½ teaspoon salt, and 2 cups water and stir.

Add the tomato mixture to the beans with the browned shanks. Bring to a boil, then reduce the heat so the beans bubble very gently. Cover and cook until the beans and lamb are very tender, about 1 hour.

If desired, strip the meat from the bones to serve. Serve the lamb and beans in bowls, garnished with chopped cilantro.

LAMB CHOPS SIZZLED with GARLIC

Chuletas de Cordero al Ajillo

Calling this by the diminuitive *ajillo,* meaning a wee bit of garlic, is rather tongue in cheek. In reality it's a whopping quantity of garlic. I had these delectable lamb chops in Las Pedroñeras, a La Mancha town that bills itself as the garlic capital. I learned that garlic gradually loses its punch. So when made with July's newly picked garlic, the ration of cloves is minimal (one per lamb chop). But later in the year, when the flavor is milder, the number is increased (two to three cloves per chop). I prefer chops cut from the leg for this dish. If you're using rib lamb chops, have them "frenched," or trimmed of all fat.

꒰ **SERVES 4**

8 to 12 lamb chops, cut ½ inch thick (2 pounds)

Salt and freshly ground black pepper

Pinch of dried thyme

10 garlic cloves

3 tablespoons olive oil

1 tablespoon chopped fresh parsley

2 tablespoons fresh lemon juice

Sprinkle the chops with salt, pepper, and thyme. Cut the unpeeled garlic cloves in half crosswise.

Heat the oil in a large skillet over medium heat. Add the lamb chops and garlic. Brown the chops on one side, about 3 minutes. Stir and turn the pieces of garlic. Turn the chops and brown on the other side, 3 to 4 minutes.

Transfer the chops to a serving platter. Add 2 tablespoons water, the parsley, and the lemon juice to the remaining oil and garlic. Heat until sizzling. Pour over the chops and serve immediately.

LAMB ROLL WRAPPED *in* CHARD LEAVES

Rollo de Cordero con Acelga

This is a delicious "meat loaf" cooked on top of the stove. Spiced ground lamb braises in a wrap of chard leaves with a surprise in the middle—nuggets of hard-cooked egg. This can also be prepared as individual packets instead of a large roll, in which case you will need three rather than two hard-cooked eggs, allowing ½ egg per packet. If the lamb is very lean, it will benefit from the addition of pancetta or bacon. Omit it if you like. The recipe also works quite well with ground turkey. Potatoes Mashed with Green Garlic (page 270) or plain steamed rice would be a good side dish with the lamb roll and its sauce.

SERVES 6

1 bunch of chard (18 to 24 leaves)	Salt and freshly ground black pepper
1 cup fresh bread crumbs (white or whole wheat)	2 eggs, 1 separated
1½ pounds ground lamb	2 hard-cooked eggs, halved lengthwise
2 garlic cloves, crushed	3 tablespoons olive oil
¼ cup chopped fresh parsley	1 cup coarsely chopped onion
⅓ cup diced pancetta or bacon (optional)	½ cup diced carrot
¼ cup minced onion	1 cup drained canned diced tomato
¼ cup seedless raisins	1 tablespoon all-purpose flour
Pinch of ground cloves	1 teaspoon sugar
⅛ teaspoon ground cinnamon	¾ cup dry white wine
Grating of fresh nutmeg	1 bay leaf
⅛ teaspoon ground coriander	

Cut off the chard stems and discard (or save for another use). Bring a large pot of water to a boil and blanch the leaves just until wilted, about 30 seconds. Drain the leaves.

Soak the bread crumbs in water to cover until softened. Squeeze out the water and put the softened bread in a mixing bowl. Add the ground lamb, garlic, parsley, bacon, minced onion, raisins, cloves, cinnamon, nutmeg, coriander, ½ teaspoon salt, pepper to taste, the whole egg, and 1 egg yolk.

With a large wooden spoon (or your hands), mix the meat thoroughly with the other ingredients.

Spread half of the chard leaves, shiny side down, in an overlapping layer on a work surface or on a platter. Divide the meat in half. Pat half of the meat into an oblong (about 9 inches). Place the cooked eggs, cut side down, in a row down the middle. Pat the remaining meat on top of the eggs. With your hands, shape the meat into a loaf, sealing in the eggs.

Fold the chard leaves up over the meat roll. Cover with the remaining chard leaves and tuck them under the roll, completely enclosing the meat roll. Pat the roll to firm it. It is not necessary to tie it.

Beat the egg white lightly with 1 teaspoon water. Place in a shallow pan. Turn the meat roll in the egg white to coat all sides.

Heat the oil in a deep skillet or casserole big enough to hold the roll. Brown the roll on all sides over medium heat, about 6 minutes. Remove and reserve.

Add the coarsely chopped onion and carrot to the oil and sauté until the onion begins to brown, 5 minutes. Add the tomato and cook over high heat for 3 minutes. Stir in the flour, sugar, and ½ teaspoon salt. Add the wine, bay leaf, and ½ cup water. Return the meat roll to the skillet. Bring to a simmer, cover, and cook slowly for 35 minutes.

Turn the roll and cook for 35 minutes more. Remove from the heat and let stand for 15 minutes. Use a sharp serrated knife to cut the roll into ¾-inch slices. The sauce can be strained or left chunky. Serve it with the meat roll.

Vegetables *and* Other
Side Dishes

Vegetables get star billing at a typical Spanish family meal, making their appearance either as a first course or incorporated into the main dish. A good example is the signature dish of La Mancha, *pisto manchego*, a medley of tomatoes, peppers, and zucchini. In La Mancha it's served in small, individual *cazuelitas* as a starter, with crusty bread for dipping. But, if you prefer to serve it as a side, go right ahead. It makes a delightful accompaniment to roast chicken, grilled lamb chops, broiled fish, or pan-fried pork.

Other substantial vegetable dishes, such as Cazuela of Potatoes and Chard, are actually entrees, whether for vegetarian meals or embellished with small quantities of meat, fish, or eggs. You'll find they make tasty lunch dishes, as hearty as a bowl of soup.

However you choose to serve these vegetable dishes—as starter, entree, or side dish—you will find some enticing recipes and new ways of putting flavors together. A pinch of caraway with eggplant is a revelation!

I've included in this chapter the peasant dishes of *migas,* fried bread crumbs, and *gachas,* garlicky "porridge," because, although in La Mancha they are breakfast dishes, they can be served as sides.

Also here are recipes for some zingy pickles that seem to embellish every salad, pâté, and relish platter in La Mancha.

MEDLEY OF SUMMER VEGETABLES

Pisto Manchego

You might recognize this dish—a medley of tomatoes, peppers, zucchini, and sometimes eggplant—as Provençal *ratatouille*, but *pisto* is authentically La Mancha, very possibly where ratatouille began. Its origins are Moorish—*alboronia*—although in those times it was a slow-cooked stew with onions, eggplant, and meat juices.

Pisto is a fine side dish with grilled fish, roast meat, and chicken. It makes a quick meal when paired with fried eggs (call it breakfast or supper). In La Mancha it is often served as a first course with toast or chunks of bread for dipping in the savory juices. Pisto also makes the sauce for chicken or lamb (see Chicken with Peppers and Tomatoes, Toledo Style, page 153).

If you prefer a "refined" version of pisto, roast and skin the green bell peppers before chopping them. While not absolutely essential, peeling the peppers prevents curls of pepper skin from coming loose in the vegetable medley. Feel free to embellish with favorite herbs and spices. Personally, I like ground cumin and hot pimentón.

SERVES 8

¼ cup olive oil	1 teaspoon salt
2 cups chopped green bell pepper	Freshly ground black pepper
1 cup chopped onion	½ teaspoon dried oregano
1 garlic clove, chopped	6 cups diced zucchini (4 medium zucchini)
3 cups peeled, seeded, and chopped tomato	

Heat the oil in a large skillet over medium heat and sauté the green pepper, onion, and garlic until softened, 15 minutes. Raise the heat and add the tomato, salt, pepper, and oregano. Cook until the tomato releases juice, 8 minutes.

Add the zucchini and cook, uncovered, until the zucchini is tender and most of the liquid has cooked off, about 30 minutes. Serve hot or at room temperature.

VARIATION: *Use 3 cups diced eggplant and 3 cups diced zucchini in place of the 6 cups zucchini. Sauté the eggplant first with the green pepper, onion, and garlic.*

FLAME-ROASTED GARDEN VEGETABLES

Asadillo de la Huerta

This is a wonderful dish to make with end-of-summer tomatoes and peppers from the garden or farmers' markets, but a quick version could be put together with fire-roasted vegetables from the grocery store. In La Mancha *asadillo,* which just means "roasted," is generally served as a starter, but I like it as a side dish with grilled or roasted meats.

SERVES 6

5 red bell peppers	1 teaspoon salt
5 large tomatoes (about 2 pounds)	½ teaspoon ground cumin
2 garlic cloves	¼ cup olive oil

Roast the peppers in a single layer over charcoal or a gas flame or under the broiler, turning to char them on all sides. Roast the tomatoes, turning once, until they are charred in places and the skins are split.

Place the roasted vegetables in a bowl and cover until they are cool enough to handle. Scrape off the charred pepper skins; remove and discard the stems and seeds. Tear the peppers into strips. Slip the skins off the tomatoes, cut out the stem and core, and chop the tomatoes. Combine with the peppers.

Crush the garlic with the salt in a mortar. Add the cumin. Gradually stir in the oil. Pour over the peppers and tomatoes and combine well. Serve at room temperature.

VARIATION: *To serve hot, heat 1 tablespoon olive oil in a skillet. Add the roasted and peeled tomatoes and peppers and fry over high heat only until heated through.*

ARTICHOKE SAUTÉ

Salteado de Alcachofas

These artichokes don't get dunked in lemon-water, so prepare them immediately before cooking so they don't darken. They are delicious as a side dish with roast lamb or chicken but also may be served as a warm salad atop greens, drizzled with a little Sherry vinegar. The artichokes most commonly found in Spain reach only fist size, even when mature. If you are using very large artichokes, cut them in half and nip out the choke with the tip of a very sharp knife.

SERVES 6

2 pounds artichokes (6 small)	Coarse salt
½ cup olive oil	

Pull off and discard the outer layer of artichoke leaves. Cut off the stems. Use a serrated knife to cut the top two-thirds off the artichokes. Discard leaves.

Begin to heat the oil in a heavy skillet over medium-high heat. Place the artichoke bottoms on a cutting board, cut edges down. With a sharp knife, cut the bottoms into ⅛-inch slices.

Add them to the hot oil as they are cut. Continue slicing until all the artichokes are in the sauté pan.

Fry the artichokes over medium-high heat until they are crunchy-tender, about 3 minutes. Remove them from the oil with a slotted spoon. Drain briefly and sprinkle with salt. Serve hot or at room temperature.

CHEESY ARTICHOKE GRATIN

Gratinado de Alcachofas con Queso

Artichokes with cheese make a substantial vegetable dish that you could serve as a luncheon entree. This dish can also be prepared with cardoons, a vegetable thistle related to artichoke. While artichokes consist of the thistle's flower bud, cardoons are thick stems, looking like oversized stalks of celery. They need to be peeled, then cooked slowly until very tender.

If you cook the artichokes in a clay cazuela or ovenproof skillet, they can go from the top of the stove to the oven. Otherwise, transfer the cooked artichokes to a baking dish.

SERVES 4 AS A LUNCHEON ENTREE OR 6 TO 8 AS A SIDE DISH

1 tablespoon fresh lemon juice

8 medium-large artichokes (3 pounds)

3½ tablespoons olive oil

½ cup chopped onion

1 garlic clove, chopped

⅓ cup diced bacon (2 ounces)

¼ cup dry white wine

½ teaspoon salt

1 cup coarsely grated Manchego (about 3 ounces)

½ cup fresh bread crumbs

Fill a bowl with cold water and add the lemon juice.

To trim the artichokes: cut off the stem close to the artichoke bottom. Snap off the first 3 layers of leaves (about 12 leaves). Use a sharp knife to slice the artichokes about 1¼ inches from the bottoms, discarding all the upper leaves. Cut the bottoms in half. Use the tip of a knife or a melon baller to scoop out the fuzzy choke. Drop the artichoke bottoms into the lemon water. Artichoke stems can be peeled down to the pale centers and cooked with the bottoms.

Heat 3 tablespoons of the oil in a medium skillet or cazuela over medium-heat. Sauté the onion, garlic, and bacon for 5 minutes.

Drain the artichoke bottoms. Add them to the skillet and sauté over medium-high heat for 5 minutes. Add the wine, salt, and ¼ cup water. Cover the pan and simmer until the artichokes are tender, 15 minutes.

Preheat the oven to 375°F.

Place the artichokes and all of their remaining liquid in an oven dish. Spread the grated cheese on top. Sprinkle with the bread crumbs. Drizzle the remaining 1½ teaspoons oil over the crumbs.

Bake until the mixture is bubbling and the crumbs are light golden, 15 minutes. Serve hot.

CASTILIAN GREEN BEANS with RED PEPPERS

Judías Verdes a la Castellana

These green beans are so delicious you may want to serve them as a main course. If possible, use flat romano beans. Should you choose to use frozen beans, skip the first step, in which the beans are blanched. Canned or jarred roasted red peppers can be used in this recipe.

SERVES 6

1½ pounds green beans, topped and tailed and cut into 2-inch lengths

2 tablespoons olive oil

½ cup diced pancetta, bacon, or serrano ham (3 ounces)

2 garlic cloves, sliced

Pinch of cumin seeds

Pinch of hot red pepper flakes

½ teaspoon salt

Freshly ground black pepper

3 roasted and peeled red bell peppers, cut into thin strips

Cook the beans in boiling salted water until crisp-tender, 5 minutes. Drain, saving ½ cup of the liquid. Refresh the beans in cold water and drain again.

Heat the oil in a large skillet or cazuela over medium heat. Sauté the pancetta for 2 minutes, until it begins to crisp. Add the garlic and fry until light golden, 1 minute. Stir in the cumin and red pepper flakes. Add the beans and sauté over medium heat for 3 minutes. Sprinkle with the salt and pepper to taste.

Stir in the strips of bell pepper and ¼ cup of the reserved bean liquor. Cook, uncovered, over medium heat, stirring occasionally, until the beans are very tender and most of the liquid is cooked off, about 12 minutes. (Add more bean liquid if needed.)

CHARD SAUTÉ

Mojete de Acelgas

Chard is such a satisfying vegetable because, with the leafy greens and substantial stems, it adds up to much more than spinach. In Spain, chard is usually grown huge, with leaves like palm fronds and stems as broad as pork chops.

This typical Manchegan chard dish would typically be served as a starter or a simple supper dish—with eggs folded into the vegetables. I prefer it without the eggs, as a side dish.

SERVES 6

2 pounds fresh chard	½ cup diced tomato, well drained if canned
2 tablespoons olive oil	1 teaspoon salt
2 garlic cloves, sliced crosswise	Freshly ground black pepper
1 teaspoon pimentón	1 tablespoon wine vinegar

Wash the chard, remove strings, if necessary, and chop the leaves and stems. Bring a large pot of salted water to a boil and cook the chard until tender, about 10 minutes. Drain, rinse in cold water, and drain well.

Heat the oil in a skillet over medium heat and fry the sliced garlic until golden, about 1 minute. Remove the pan from the heat and add the pimentón and tomato. Return to medium heat and cook for 3 minutes.

Stir in the chard, salt, pepper to taste, and 2 tablespoons water. Cook until the chard begins to simmer. Stir in the vinegar. Serve hot.

SPINACH with GARLIC, INIESTA STYLE

Espinacas a la Iniestense

Iniesta is a village in the Manchuela region of the province of Cuenca, where the spinach is said to be especially tasty due to being irrigated with saline water. This recipe comes from a study of the culinary heritage of the region by Javier Cuéllar Tórtola and Pedro Pardo Domingo.

SERVES 4 TO 6

1½ pounds fresh spinach

3 tablespoons olive oil

1 egg, separated

2 garlic cloves, peeled

½ teaspoon coarse salt

Pinch of ground cloves

Pinch of ground ginger

Freshly ground black pepper

½ cup milk

Wash and trim the spinach. Place in a large pot over high heat. Cover and steam until wilted, about 5 minutes. Drain in a colander, pressing out as much liquid as possible. Use kitchen scissors to cut up the spinach.

Heat the oil in a large skillet over medium heat and add the spinach. Toss it in the oil for 1 minute, then stir in the egg white and stir it around.

Crush the garlic with the salt in a mortar. Add the cloves, ginger, pepper, and 2 tablespoons water. Stir into the spinach.

Beat the egg yolk with the milk and add to the spinach. Cook, uncovered, until most of the liquid cooks away, 10 minutes. Serve hot.

PAN-SAUTÉED CABBAGE *with* CUMIN

Coles Salteadas

Spiked with garlic and cumin, simple cabbage becomes a delicious side dish. Serve it with pork chops, roast chicken, or salmon.

SERVES 6

2 pounds green cabbage	Pinch of cumin seeds
Salt	Freshly ground black pepper
2 tablespoons olive oil	1 tablespoon white wine vinegar
2 garlic cloves, slivered lengthwise	Pomegranate seeds (optional)

Slice the cabbage crosswise. Bring a pot of salted water to a boil and cook the cabbage until tender, about 10 minutes. Drain and refresh in cold water. Drain well.

Heat the oil in a large skillet over medium heat and sauté the garlic until light golden, 1 minute. Add the cumin seeds and sauté for 30 seconds. Stir in the cabbage. Season with pepper and ½ teaspoon salt. Sauté the cabbage until thoroughly heated, 5 minutes. Stir in the vinegar immediately before serving. If desired, scatter a few pomegranate seeds on top of the cabbage.

BATTER-FRIED CAULIFLOWER

Coliflor Rebosado

Served with a piquant tomato sauce for dipping, these tidbits of cauliflower make a nice appetizer. Or serve them as a side dish with simple grilled meat or poultry.

🦌 SERVES 4 TO 6

Salt

4 cups cauliflower florets (about 1¼ pounds)

1 tablespoon finely chopped fresh parsley

1 tablespoon fresh lemon juice

Olive oil for frying (about 1½ cups)

About ½ cup flour for dredging

¼ teaspoon caraway seeds

⅛ teaspoon cayenne

1 egg

Bring 2 quarts water to a boil with 2 teaspoons salt. Add the cauliflower, bring again to a boil, and cook until crisp-tender, about 5 minutes. Drain, cover with cold water, and drain again. Place the cauliflower in a bowl and sprinkle with the parsley and lemon juice. Toss the cauliflower and allow to stand for 15 minutes.

Heat oil to a depth of ¼ inch in a heavy skillet over medium-high heat until very hot but not smoking. Combine the flour with caraway and cayenne in a shallow dish. Beat the egg with 1 tablespoon water in a small bowl.

Dredge the florets in seasoned flour, coat them in beaten egg, and lift them into the hot oil. Fry them, in 2 or 3 batches, until golden on all sides, about 3 minutes. Remove with a slotted spoon or skimmer and drain on paper towels. Sprinkle with salt if desired. Serve hot.

NOTE: *The cauliflower may be prepared 1 hour in advance and reheated in a 400°F oven for about 8 minutes.*

CAULIFLOWER or BROCCOLI with GOLDEN GARLIC and ALMONDS

Coliflor o Brócoli con Ajo Dorado y Almendras

You can prepare this vegetable dish with both cauliflower and broccoli. Cook them separately and place them together in a heated serving bowl before spooning the garlic dressing over both.

❧ SERVES 6 TO 8

1¾ pounds cauliflower and/or broccoli

Salt

3 tablespoons olive oil

4 garlic cloves, sliced crosswise

1 tablespoon slivered almonds

1 teaspoon sweet pimentón

1 tablespoon wine vinegar

1 tablespoon chopped fresh parsley

Cut the cauliflower into 2-inch florets. Cut the broccoli into 2-inch pieces. Peel the stem, cut in half lengthwise, and cut crosswise into 2-inch pieces.

Cook the cauliflower and broccoli separately in boiling salted water until tender, 10 minutes. Drain, saving 3 tablespoons of the cooking water. Keep warm in a serving bowl.

While the cauliflower and broccoli are cooking, heat the oil in a small skillet over medium-high heat. Add the sliced garlic and almonds and fry them until they begin to turn golden, about 30 seconds. Remove the skillet from the heat.

Stir in the pimentón, then immediately add the vinegar and reserved cooking liquid. Add the parsley.

Spoon the garlic and almond dressing over the cauliflower and broccoli and serve immediately.

MINTED CARROTS

Zanahorias con Hierbabuena

Fresh mint adds a sprightly touch to carrots. They are also good as a salad—add a bit of Sherry vinegar to the cold carrots and serve atop greens with a sprinkling of chopped scallion.

SERVES 4 TO 6

1 pound carrots, peeled and thinly sliced

1 tablespoon olive oil

1 tablespoon chopped onion

1 tablespoon pine nuts

1 small garlic clove, minced

1 tablespoon raisins (optional)

1 tablespoon fresh lemon juice

Salt and freshly ground black pepper

1 tablespoon chopped fresh mint leaves

Cook the carrots in boiling salted water until just tender, about 5 minutes. Drain and refresh in cold water. Drain.

Heat the oil in a small saucepan over medium heat and sauté the onion for 2 minutes. Add the pine nuts and garlic and sauté for 2 minutes more. Add the carrots and raisins, if you're using them, and sauté until the carrots are heated through, about 2 minutes. Stir in the lemon juice and season with salt and pepper. Remove from the heat and add the mint leaves.

FAVA BEANS *with* ESCAROLE *and* MINT

Cazuela de Habas

Springtime is so fleeting! Tender fava beans, spring onions, and mint come and go. Salad greens such as escarole bolt to seed with the first hot days. Here is a dish to celebrate the season. It makes a fine side dish to serve with lamb.

If small fava beans are freshly picked and shelled, their outer skins are perfectly edible. Only dry favas or old beans need to be blanched and then skinned.

SERVES 6

2 tablespoons olive oil

2½ cups shelled fava beans (from about 3¼ pounds in their shells)

½ cup chopped spring onion or scallion

1 fresh mint sprig

4 cups shredded escarole (6 to 8 large leaves)

1 teaspoon salt

1 tablespoon wine vinegar

Chopped fresh mint for garnish

Heat the oil in a cazuela or heavy skillet over low heat. Add the fava beans, onion, and mint. Cook, uncovered, stirring occasionally, for 20 minutes.

Remove the mint. Add the escarole, salt, vinegar, and ¼ cup water. Cover and simmer for 15 minutes. Serve garnished with chopped mint.

SAUTÉ OF FRESH PEAS *and* CARROTS

Salteado de Guisantes con Zanahorias

Made with sweet, freshly shelled garden peas, this dish is exceptional. In Spain it might be served as a first course, with a garnish of chopped egg. But it makes a fine side dish, with fish, chicken, or meat.

You will need about 3 pounds of peas in their shells to make 2 cups shelled peas. Frozen peas can be substituted. Other vegetables—fava beans, chopped asparagus, green beans—can be used in place of peas, although cooking time may need to be adjusted.

SERVES 4

2 tablespoons olive oil	1 tablespoon chopped fresh parsley
½ cup diced carrot	Pinch of dried thyme
½ cup diced serrano ham or bacon (3 ounces)	½ teaspoon salt
½ cup chopped onion	Freshly ground black pepper
1 garlic clove, chopped	2 tablespoons chopped scallion
¼ cup diced red bell pepper	1 hard-cooked egg, chopped (optional)
2 cups fresh or frozen peas	

Heat the oil in a cazuela or medium skillet over medium heat. Add the carrot, ham, and onion and sauté for 5 minutes. Add the garlic and red pepper and sauté for 2 minutes longer.

Add the peas to the pan and sauté them for 3 minutes. Season with parsley, thyme, salt, and pepper to taste. Add ½ cup water. Bring to a boil, cover, and simmer until the peas are tender, about 5 minutes. (Some peas may require longer cooking. If so, add more water and simmer them until tender.)

Remove the cover and cook for 1 minute, until most of the liquid is cooked away.

Serve immediately, garnished with scallion and, if desired, chopped egg.

MARKET DAY IN ALCÁZAR DE SAN JUAN

Monday is *mercadillo,* street market day, in Alcázar de San Juan, a town in the very heart of La Mancha. From Roman times this was a crossroads for legionnaires and for trade. The Arabs followed the Romans, bequeathing the town the first part of its name, Alcázar, meaning "fortress," although nothing remains of the Arab fortifications. After the reconquest by Christian kings the town was repopulated by the military order of San Juan, the Knights of St. John. Thus the second part of the name. In the thirteenth century, King Sancho IV declared Alcázar de San Juan a market town. In more recent history, Alcázar emerged as an important railway hub. Today it is a thriving center of agribusiness—wine (the offices of the regulating board for DO La Mancha wine are located in Alcázar), cheese (one of the country's biggest cheese producers is here), and fresh produce from market gardens.

Every Monday vendors spread out their wares across dozens of open-air stalls on the edge of town. Most of them are selling shoes and underwear, baby clothes and dish towels, pots, pans, and screwdrivers. But just past a trailer with cages of live baby chicks, ducks, and turkeys dyed in Day-Glo pink, yellow, and purple begin the food stands.

A prickly smell that tickles the taste buds announces the pickle vendors. Their stalls have vats of brine-cured olives, pickled eggplant, pickled onions in several colors and sizes, pickled peppers, both hot and sweet.

The vendor of *chucherías,* kiddie candy in a riot of different colors and shapes—pink and green sugar chews, gumdrops, foil-wrapped caramels, lemon balls, strawberry twists, licorice sticks—scoops the sweets into bags and weighs them on an old-fashioned balance scale. Next to his stand is one selling *frutos secos,* all manner of dried fruits and nuts. There are five kinds of almonds (whole, shelled, skinned, toasted, and fried and salted); hazelnuts, walnuts, peanuts, pine nuts, toasted chickpeas; *pipas,* sunflower seeds; dried chestnuts, edible acorns, figs, dried apricots called *orejones,* little ears; prunes, raisins, honey. A nearby spice vendor has wooden boxes heaped with pungent spices and aromatic herbs, both culinary and medicinal. Bunches of thyme hang above the table. Thyme flavors the olives gathered in the autumn to be home-cured in brine.

On the back loop of stalls is the farmers' market. (No fresh meat or cheese is sold at the

Monday market.) Mercedes Martín sells farm produce at the market with her two brothers, Julián and Jesús. They also have a stall in the Alcázar municipal market, bringing produce from the family farm in nearby Herencia. On one September morning Mercedes had two kinds of eggplant, green beans, spinach, tomatoes, peppers, zucchini, pumpkin, cauliflower, spinach, chard, peppers, garlic, leeks, cabbages, carrots, potatoes, melons, watermelons, and plums. Only apples, pears, and some other fruits came from outside the region.

She proffered slivers of melon for tasting. Juicy and sweet, it was a delight. The melon grown here is a variety known as *piel de sapo,* "toad skin." It has dark green, hard, ridged skin and pale yellow flesh. It's commercialized under the protected label of Indicación Geográfica Protegida Melón de la Mancha.

Mercedes had sun-dried tomatoes—*tomatillas*—from the farm.

"Split them in half, put them in the sun for one week," she said. The sun of La Mancha is powerful. Add a couple of sun-dried tomatoes to a slow-cooked stew, she suggested.

She also had strings of skinny dried sweet peppers plus hot chiles.

The dried peppers, she said, go into *tiznao,* a favorite La Mancha dish of roasted peppers, onions, and cod. A customer filling her market basket at Mercedes' stall offered her recipe for white beans cooked with the dried peppers, sun-dried tomatoes, onion, pig's foot, and jowls. Julián, Mercedes' brother, said the *guindillas,* dried chiles, were an essential ingredient in the sauce for cooking snails.

And those tiny eggplants? "In Almagro they pickle them," offered another shopper, "but I cook them whole with tomatoes and cumin."

An elderly man was picking out some freshly dug potatoes. "These will be good in a *mojete* with asparagus and mushrooms," he said. *Mojete* is a vegetable stew served soupy, for dunking bread into. He also bought some spinach, to be sautéed in olive oil with garlic, then scrambled with eggs.

A pretty young woman carrying a huge bouquet of yellow and white flowers selected gem-like plums in green, pink, and violet. The local greengage plums were in their moment of glory, juicy, tart, and sweet.

By 1:30 P.M. the constant stream of shoppers had lessened. It was time to pack up the merchandise and the portable tables and head back to the farm.

EGGPLANT *with* TOMATO *and* CARAWAY

Berenjena Guisada con Alcaravea

In Alcázar de San Juan this is prepared with a variety of tiny green eggplant, cooked whole. Caraway seed, a spice used in several La Mancha dishes, adds an interesting flavor. You could substitute cumin seed. Serve the eggplant with lamb chops or roast chicken.

SERVES 6

2 medium eggplants (about 1½ pounds)

2 teaspoons salt

1 bay leaf

2 tablespoons olive oil

2 garlic cloves, chopped

1½ cups peeled, seeded, and diced tomato

⅛ teaspoon caraway seeds

Freshly ground black pepper

2 teaspoons fresh lemon juice or wine vinegar

Chopped fresh mint or parsley for garnish

Peel the eggplants and cut into ¾-inch cubes. Bring 1 quart water to a boil with 1½ teaspoons of the salt and the bay leaf. Add the eggplant and cook until barely tender, 3 to 4 minutes. Drain. Discard the bay leaf.

Heat the oil in a skillet over medium heat. Add the garlic and sauté until golden, 1 minute. Raise the heat to high, add the eggplant and tomato, and sauté for 1 minute. Season with caraway, pepper, and the remaining ½ teaspoon salt. Reduce the heat and cook until most of the liquid has cooked away, 10 minutes.

Remove from the heat and stir in the lemon juice. Sprinkle with chopped mint to serve.

BAKED EGGPLANT *with* CHEESE

Berenjenas con Queso al Horno

This easy dish can bake alongside a roast. The spices and wine make candy of the slow-roasted eggplant. The eggplant skins are like a terrine, not meant to be eaten. While authentic Manchego is best, you could substitute Parmesan, Gruyère, or pecorino.

SERVES 8

4 medium eggplants (about 3 pounds)

Salt

¼ cup olive oil

¼ teaspoon ground cinnamon

Pinch of ground cloves

Pinch of ground ginger

Grating of fresh nutmeg

Pinch of dried oregano

Freshly ground black pepper

1 cup dry white wine

6 ounces Manchego, grated (about 2 cups)

Cut off and discard the stems and leaves from the eggplants. Cut each eggplant in half lengthwise. With a sharp knife, make deep cuts in the flesh lengthwise and crosswise. Salt the eggplants and leave them, cut side down, to drain for 1 hour.

Preheat the oven to 350°F.

Rinse the eggplants in water, drain well, then pat dry with paper towels. Place the eggplant halves, cut side up, in a single layer in a baking pan. Drizzle with the olive oil. Combine the cinnamon, cloves, ginger, nutmeg, oregano, and pepper to taste. Sprinkle the spices over the eggplant. Bake for 15 minutes.

Pour the wine over the eggplants. Return to the oven for 15 minutes. Turn the eggplants cut side down and bake for 30 minutes longer, or until they are fork-tender.

Turn cut side up again and spoon the pan juices over the eggplants. (If the pan is dry, add about ¼ cup water.) Spread the grated cheese on top of the eggplant halves. Return to the oven and bake until the cheese is melted and lightly browned, 12 to 15 minutes. Serve hot.

FRIED EGGPLANT *with* A DRIZZLE OF HONEY

Berenjena con Miel

Salty fried eggplant paired with sweet, sticky honey makes a tantalizing combo of flavor and texture. In Spain, the eggplant slices, heaped on a platter, are served as a tapa or starter.

⁂ SERVES 4 TO 6

2 medium eggplants (1½ pounds)

Salt

About 1 cup all-purpose flour for dredging

About 3 cups olive oil for frying

2 teaspoons honey

Peel the eggplants and cut them crosswise into ³⁄₁₆-inch-thick slices. Layer them in a bowl, sprinkling liberally with salt. Allow to stand for 1 hour.

Rinse the eggplant slices in water and drain. Dredge them in flour and shake off the excess.

Heat ½ inch oil in a large skillet until almost smoking. Working in 2 or 3 batches, add slices of eggplant to the oil. Fry them, turning once, until golden, about 1 minute per side. Remove and allow to drain on paper towels.

Heap the eggplant on a platter and drizzle with the honey. Serve hot.

CHAR-GRILLED EGGPLANT *with* LEMON DRESSING

Berenjena a la Parilla con Aliño

These grilled eggplants are the perfect accompaniment to a barbecue meal. They can be served hot off the coals but are even better if the dressing is allowed to soak in for 30 minutes. The tangy lemon dressing is also good tossed with cooked green beans.

SERVES 6

3 medium eggplants (2 to 2½ pounds)

Salt

⅓ cup olive oil, plus oil for the grill

2 tablespoons fine dry bread crumbs

2 garlic cloves, chopped

Pinch of hot red pepper flakes

⅓ cup fresh lemon juice

¼ cup chopped fresh parsley

½ teaspoon dried oregano

Cut off the stems and leaves from the eggplants. Cut each eggplant in half lengthwise. Make 2 to 3 slashes in the flesh side. In a large bowl, combine 6 cups water with 1½ tablespoons salt. Place the cut eggplant in the brine and place a saucer on top to keep them submerged. Allow to stand for at least 1 hour and up to 3 hours.

While the eggplants are soaking, prepare the dressing. Heat ⅓ cup olive oil in a small skillet over medium heat. Add the bread crumbs, garlic, ½ teaspoon salt, and the red pepper flakes and stir until they begin to turn golden, about 2 minutes. Immediately add the lemon juice and ¼ cup water. Stir until the sauce thickens and emulsifies. Remove from the heat and allow to cool for 5 minutes. Stir in the parsley and oregano.

Drain the eggplants and discard the water. Light a charcoal grill. When the coals are medium-hot and uniformly covered with gray ash, brush both sides of the eggplant halves with oil. Set them skin side down on the grill and grill for 5 minutes. Turn the eggplant cut side down and grill until the eggplants are tender when tested with a skewer and the surface is golden brown, about 5 minutes.

Transfer the eggplants to a platter and spoon the dressing over them. Serve hot or at room temperature.

PAN-GRILLED VEGETABLES

Verduras a la Parrilla

This assortment of pan-grilled vegetables makes a good starter, in place of a salad. Use either a ridged grill pan or a flat griddle. Cooking time will vary for each vegetable, depending on thickness, but all should cook in 8 minutes or less. Grill the eggplant until very tender, but allow asparagus and onion to stay somewhat crisp. The vegetables are so delicious with nothing more elaborate than extra virgin olive oil. However, if you like, serve *aji-aceite,* garlic sauce (page 115), as an accompaniment.

SERVES 4

1 medium eggplant (about ¾ pound)

1 medium zucchini (about ¾ pound)

Coarse salt

¼ cup olive oil

1 red bell pepper

8 asparagus spears

1 onion

4 mushrooms, such as portobello, oyster, or porcini (cèpes)

1 firm plum tomato, quartered

4 garlic cloves

1 tablespoon plus 1 teaspoon extra virgin olive oil

Fresh parsley or basil sprigs for garnish

Peel the eggplant and cut off the stem end. Cut lengthwise into ¾-inch-thick slices. Place in a shallow pan. Trim the ends of the zucchini and slice it lengthwise into ½-inch-thick slices. Place in a single layer in the pan. Sprinkle the eggplant and zucchini on both sides with salt. Let it stand for 1 hour. Drain the eggplant and zucchini in a colander for 15 minutes. Pat dry.

Wipe out the shallow pan. Spread the eggplant and zucchini slices in it. Brush them on both sides with oil.

Cut the pepper into quarters, discarding the stem and seeds. Use a vegetable peeler to shave the outer skins from the asparagus. Slice the onion ½ inch thick. Spread the pepper, asparagus, onion, mushrooms, tomato, and unpeeled garlic in another shallow pan and brush them with oil.

Brush a ridged grill pan or flat griddle with oil and heat until very hot. Cook each of the vegetables until tender, turning slices with tongs to grill both sides. Eggplant will need about 8 minutes; zucchini, 6; asparagus, 8; onion, 5; mushrooms, 8; tomato, 3.

Arrange slices of each vegetable on 4 plates. Sprinkle with coarse salt and drizzle 1 teaspoon extra virgin olive oil over each serving. Garnish with parsley or basil. Serve warm or at room temperature.

Mirad, señor doctor; de aquí adelante,
no os curéis de darme a comer cosas regaladas,
ni manjares exquisitos, porque será sacar a mi estómago
de sus quicios, el cual está acostumbrado a cabra,
a vaca, a tocino, a cecina, a nabos y a cebollas. . . .

Look, Doc, from now on, don't even think about feeding me dainties, nor fancy foods, because you'll just upset my stomach, which is used to goat meat, beef, salt pork, jerky, turnips and onions. . . .

SANCHO PANZA, COMPLAINING ABOUT THE FOOD
HE IS SERVED AS GOVERNOR OF AN ISLAND

BRAISED TURNIPS *with* PIMENTÓN

Nabos Guisados al Pimentón

These turnips go nicely with roast turkey or roast pork. Smoky pimentón de la Vera gives them a special nuance.

SERVES 6

1¼ pounds turnips

½ red bell pepper

2 tablespoons olive oil

1 garlic clove, sliced crosswise

1 teaspoon sweet pimentón, preferably smoked

Hot red pepper flakes

Pinch of dried oregano

½ teaspoon salt

1 tablespoon Sherry vinegar

Peel the turnips and cut them into 2-inch pieces. Cut the pepper into 2-inch strips. Heat the oil in a skillet or cazuela over medium heat and sauté the turnips until lightly browned, 5 minutes. Add the pepper and garlic and sauté for 2 minutes longer.

Remove the pan from the heat and stir in the pimentón, red pepper flakes, oregano, salt, and vinegar. Add 1¼ cups water. Return the pan to the heat. Bring to a boil, cover, and simmer, turning the turnips occasionally, until they are very tender and most of the liquid has cooked away, about 35 minutes.

MUSHROOM and POTATO STEW

Guisado de Setas y Patatas

La Mancha is Spain's biggest producer of cultivated mushrooms.

A real forager might return to the kitchen with two or even three varieties of wild mushrooms. (*Níscalos, Lactarius sanguifluus,* and *setas de cardo, Pleurotus eryngii,* are the most common.) But, if your foraging takes place at the supermarket, that's fine too. You can select several varieties if you like, or make this stew with just one—woodsy portobellos and shiitakes, delicate chanterelles, or oyster mushrooms. A satisfying vegetarian main dish.

SERVES 6

⅓ cup olive oil

½ cup chopped onion

2 garlic cloves, 1 chopped, 1 crushed

2 bay leaves

1½ pounds sliced mushrooms (can be a mixture)

1 teaspoon sweet pimentón

¼ teaspoon saffron threads, crushed (optional)

½ cup chopped red bell pepper

½ cup peeled and chopped tomato

3 pounds baking potatoes, peeled and cut into 1½-inch chunks

½ cup dry white wine

2 teaspoons salt

2 tablespoons chopped fresh parsley

Pinch of hot pimentón for garnish

In a cazuela or deep sauté pan over high heat, heat the oil and sauté the chopped onion, chopped garlic, bay leaves, and mushrooms for 5 minutes, or until the mushrooms begin to sizzle. (Some varieties of mushrooms will release more liquid and take longer to cook.)

Stir in the pimentón, saffron if you're using it, red pepper, tomato, potatoes, and wine. Continue to cook over high heat for 10 minutes.

Add 1 cup water and the salt. Bring to a boil, cover the cazuela, and simmer for 20 minutes. Add the crushed garlic to the stew. Uncover and cook until the potatoes are tender, about 10 minutes more. Let stand for 5 minutes before serving. Sprinkle with the parsley and pimentón.

CAZUELA OF POTATOES *and* CHARD

Patatas con Acelgas en Cazuela

The distinctive flavors of chard, leeks, and fennel meld nicely with potatoes in this dish, which goes especially well with fish. Bake it in a flameproof cazuela or gratin dish. A topping of grated Manchego is optional.

Leftovers make an admirable cold dish. Spike the potatoes and chard with fresh lemon juice and serve with a sprinkling of chopped scallion and parsley.

SERVES 6 TO 8

3 tablespoons olive oil

2 pounds baking potatoes

4 cups chopped chard stems and leaves (about ½ pound)

½ cup chopped leek

Freshly ground black pepper

¼ teaspoon fennel seeds

1 teaspoon salt

2 tablespoons wine vinegar

1 garlic clove, crushed

½ cup grated cheese (optional)

Preheat the oven to 350°F. Oil the cazuela.

Peel the potatoes and slice them ¼ inch thick. Mix together the sliced potatoes, chopped chard, and leek and spread in the cazuela. Sprinkle with pepper, fennel seeds, and salt.

In a small bowl, combine the remaining oil, the vinegar, crushed garlic, and ½ cup water. Pour this mixture over the vegetables.

Cover the cazuela with foil. Set the cazuela over medium heat on top of the stove until the liquid begins to bubble. Then place it in the oven and bake for 30 minutes.

Remove the foil, add the grated cheese if desired, and return to the oven for 15 minutes.

Allow the vegetables to sit for 10 minutes before serving.

POTATOES MASHED with GREEN GARLIC

Palotes con Patatas

Palotes are garlic scapes—stems with flower buds—that are removed from the garlic plants so the bulbs develop fuller. Green garlic shoots or scallions can be used in this recipe in place of scapes. Serve this dish with poached eggs if desired. This recipe comes from Las Pedroñeras, a village in Cuenca famed for its garlic.

SERVES 6

2 pounds baking potatoes

3 tablespoons olive oil

½ cup chopped scapes, green garlic shoots, or scallions

1 garlic clove, chopped

1 teaspoon sweet pimentón

Hot red pepper flakes

½ teaspoon salt

Freshly ground black pepper

Peel the potatoes, cut them into pieces, and cook them in boiling salted water until very tender. Drain the potatoes, saving 1 cup of the liquid.

Heat the oil in a heavy skillet over medium heat and gently sauté the chopped garlic shoots and garlic for 5 minutes. Remove the pan from the heat and stir in the pimentón and red pepper flakes.

Return the skillet to the heat and add the drained potatoes. Chop and mash them in the oil until almost pureed. Stir in ½ cup of the reserved potato water, the salt, and pepper to taste. Keep stirring and mashing the potatoes, adding as much of the remaining liquid as needed to make a mixture the consistency of mashed potatoes. A few lumps in the potatoes are fine.

HOT POTATOES

Patatas Bravas

These potatoes are hot as in spicy. Accompanied by a chile-spiked tomato sauce, they are the *patatas bravas* that originated in the Madrid tapa bar Café Brava. This version, without the sauce, is good served alongside steak, roast lamb, grilled chicken, or fried fish.

The potatoes can be peeled and cut several hours in advance. Leave them covered with water. Then drain and pat them dry on kitchen towels. Fry the potatoes in olive oil for best flavor. If using extra virgin oil, select one of the Picual variety blends, for they are especially stable at high temperatures. After the oil has cooled, strain it and reserve in a dark place for a second use.

SERVES 4 TO 6

2 pounds baking potatoes, peeled and cut into 1-inch cubes

About 1 quart olive oil for frying

½ teaspoon ground cumin

1 teaspoon salt

Cayenne to taste

Pat the potatoes dry. Heat the oil in a large, deep straight-sided skillet to a depth of ½ to ¾ inch. When the oil is shimmering and almost smoking (360°F), add the potatoes. Fry them, turning occasionally, until they are golden brown and tender when pierced with a skewer, about 12 minutes.

Remove the potatoes to a bowl lined with paper toweling. Sprinkle them with cumin, salt, and cayenne. Serve immediately.

HASH BROWN POTATO CAKE

Hartatunos

The Spanish name of this dish, *hartatunos,* means "fill the rascals up." It makes a good side with roast meat or game stews.

🦌 SERVES 6

¼ cup olive oil

4 cups peeled potatoes in ¼-inch-thick slices (about 1½ pounds)

⅓ cup diced bacon

1 garlic clove

1½ teaspoons sweet pimentón

⅛ teaspoon cayenne

½ teaspoon salt

Freshly ground black pepper

Pinch of cumin seeds

Six ½-inch-thick baguette slices

1 fresh mint sprig for garnish

Heat the oil in a large heavy skillet over medium heat. Add the potatoes and bacon. Cut a slit in the unpeeled garlic and add it whole to the skillet. Cook the potatoes, turning them frequently, for 10 minutes. Don't let them brown. As the potatoes begin to soften, use the edge of a spatula to begin breaking them into smaller pieces. Continue cooking and breaking up the potatoes until they are completely tender and lightly browned, about 15 minutes more.

Remove the skillet from the heat. Tip the skillet so the remaining oil drains to one side. Lift out the potatoes, bacon, and garlic with a spatula and reserve them.

Stir the pimentón, cayenne, salt, pepper to taste, and cumin seeds into the oil remaining in the skillet. Add ¼ cup water and stir to blend the spices well. Add ¼ cup more water. Place the baguette slices in the skillet and return the skillet to medium heat. Break up the pieces of bread with the edge of a spatula. Cook until the bread begins to dry and toast.

Return the potatoes, bacon, and garlic to the skillet. Cook, tossing the mixture together for 3 minutes. Discard the garlic. Press the potato-bread mixture into a round, flat cake, 8 to 9 inches in diameter. Firm the edges with a spatula. Cook until browned. Loosen the potato cake with a spatula. Invert it onto a serving plate, cut it into wedges, and garnish it with the mint.

THAT SPECIAL TOUCH—
EXTRA VIRGIN OLIVE OIL

In my kitchen cupboard are four or five bottles of different extra virgin olive oils from several regions of Spain. That's in addition to the "house" olive oil, my everyday cooking oil.

It's such a pleasure to have a palette of flavors to choose from. When I want nuances of flavor, I dab and dribble from my collection of fine oils. Sometimes I know exactly what flavor I'm looking for to complement a dish. Other times I relish experimenting, sampling the range of possibilities.

I love the Spanish way of drizzling a little extra virgin olive oil over a finished dish—cooked vegetables, grilled fish, sliced cold meat. It lends style and, by varying the chosen oil, changes the focus of a dish. Simple grilled salmon takes on different hues as you splash through the spectrum from sweet and fruity Hojiblanca to almondy Arbequina to peppery Picual.

Olive oils from Spain usually are not single varietals. In most regions the oil is blended to combine the best characteristics of several varieties. For example, Arbequina is prized for its delicate, almondy flavor, but it is somewhat unstable (prone to oxidation). Picual, fruity and somewhat bitter, is remarkably stable, even at high temperatures. When blended with Picual, Hojiblanca lends a sweetness that balances the bitterness.

Olive oil is the singular cooking fat in my kitchen—no butter or margarine, no lard, no vegetable shortening, no other vegetable oil. So, I use it in quantity. Yes, on breakfast toast, on popcorn, in cakes and pies, as well as in every single Spanish dish I cook. Happily, I live at the source, so this is not an extravagant gesture. While olive oil is more expensive than most vegetable fats, I feel it's worth the price. I know it has healthful benefits, but it's mainly about taste. I'm willing to pay the price.

My "house" oil is local, pressed at a town several miles away. Over the Christmas holidays and during the first couple weeks of January, I pick my own olives and haul them to a trucking point. A middleman weighs my sacks and gives me a chit. At the end of the season of *recolección*, I return and find out how many liters of oil I've earned.

Because it is the fruit of my own labor, I am careful to store it properly and use it within a year. No tag-ends of bottles in my cupboard! (Keep extra virgin olive oil moderately cool and—most important—protected from the light.)

I also collect olive oil on my travels in Spain, so I can sample many terroirs. In the United States you might not have available the huge selection that I do in Spain, but you will find in stores there some of the absolute best in quality from various regions.

I find more and more organic olive oils available, and I use them as much as possible. But I haven't switched completely. For one thing, the bulk of the virgin oil I use is my local one, which comes from growers of all sorts. And, of course, organics off the shelf are more expensive.

SHEPHERDS' GARLIC-FRIED BREAD CRUMBS

Migas del Pastor

Shepherds in the field prepare this simple dish with stale bread and bits of salt pork, cooked in a large skillet over a wood fire. They eat it straight from the pan. During the *vendimia*, grape harvest, sweet grapes accompany the migas. In this rendition raisins replace the grapes. Their sweetness makes a nice counterpoint to the garlic and salty sausage. Pomegranate seeds could be used instead.

The technique of making migas is simple—soak the diced bread (start preparations at least eight hours before serving), then fry it slowly in oil until crumbly and crunchy, chopping it as it fries into very small crumbs.

Migas make a delicious breakfast served with fried eggs or a side dish with roast meat or grilled pork chop.

SERVES 4

---

8 cups day-old bread in ½-inch dice (about 1 pound)

1 teaspoon salt

⅓ cup olive oil

½ cup diced pancetta or bacon (3 ounces)

1 Spanish hard chorizo (2 ounces), casing removed and sausage chopped

8 garlic cloves

⅛ teaspoon cumin or caraway seeds

Hot red pepper flakes

½ teaspoon sweet pimentón

¼ cup raisins or pomegranate seeds

Place the diced bread in a bowl. Stir the salt into ¾ cup warm water. Sprinkle the bread with the water, tossing to dampen the bread evenly. Place the bread in a kitchen towel that has been dampened. Tie the bread tightly and allow to stand for 8 hours or overnight.

Heat the oil in a deep skillet over medium heat and fry the pancetta and chorizo for 2 minutes. Skim out and reserve.

Lightly crush the garlic cloves to split the skins, but do not peel them. Add to the oil in which the pancetta fried. Add the cumin, red pepper flakes to taste, and bread.

Fry the bread over medium heat, turning it frequently. Keep cutting the bread with the edge of a wooden paddle or heatproof spatula, gradually reducing the dice to loose crumbs. Cook until the crumbs are lightly crunchy, 20 minutes.

Add the pimentón, raisins, and reserved pancetta and chorizo. Cook for another 2 minutes and serve.

VARIATION: *Fry the bread crumbs as directed, omitting the pancetta, chorizo, garlic, and spices. Serve them in bowls with thick drinking chocolate (page 365) poured over.*

CHICKPEA PORRIDGE

Gachas

This is a stick-to-the-ribs breakfast for a winter's day. Served to the helpers at a hog slaughtering, it would probably incorporate chunks of fried liver, and the liquid used might be the "broth" in which the blood sausages were cooked.

Gachas makes a good side dish with fried meat, sausages, or roast chicken, or it could be served as a dip, a sort of Spanish hummus. In La Mancha it is made with *harina de almorta*, vetch flour. This adaptation switches legume flours, using chickpea flour instead.

SERVES 4

3 tablespoons olive oil

½ cup diced unsmoked bacon or pancetta (3 ounces)

4 garlic cloves

2 cups chickpea flour

1 tablespoon sweet pimentón

2 teaspoons salt

1 clove

⅛ teaspoon ground cumin

Freshly ground black pepper

1 teaspoon dried oregano

1 quart water or broth

Chopped fresh parsley or cilantro for garnish

Heat the oil in a cazuela or pan over medium-high heat and fry the diced bacon until crisped, about 1½ minutes. Skim it out and set aside. Peel 2 of the garlic cloves, add to the oil, and fry until golden, about 30 seconds. Remove and reserve. Give the other 2 cloves a light blow with a mallet to split the skins and put them in the oil.

Stir in the chickpea flour. Stir it for a minute to toast it slightly, but do not let it scorch. Remove from the heat and stir in the pimentón.

In a blender, combine the fried garlic, salt, clove, cumin, pepper to taste, and oregano with ½ cup of the water. Blend until smooth. Stir it into the chickpea flour. Add ½ cup more of the liquid and stir to dissolve the lumps.

Put the cazuela back on the heat and continue stirring. As the porridge thickens, continue to add liquid, ½ cup at a time, stirring continuously, until all the liquid is incorporated, about 15 minutes. The mixture should have the consistency of whipped potatoes.

Serve the porridge hot, sprinkled with the reserved bacon bits and parsley.

NOTE: *The gachas can be reheated in a microwave. Beat in additional water to thin it before heating.*

POLENTA *and* CRUNCHY CROUTONS

Gachasmigas Manchegas

Serve this with fried eggs for a sturdy farmer's breakfast, as a base for grilled portobello mushrooms, or as a side with grilled or roasted meat. As in the previous recipe, Manchegan *gachas* are made with a fine flour from the legume vetch. In this version, cornmeal stands in for vetch.

❧ SERVES 4 TO 6

2 cups diced bread (4 slices)

6 ounces fatty pork, such as pork belly or jowls

¼ cup plus 2 tablespoons olive oil

1 tablespoon sweet pimentón

Pinch of cayenne

1 cup coarse cornmeal or polenta (not instant)

1 quart boiling water

Pinch of ground cloves

¼ teaspoon caraway seeds

1 teaspoon salt

Cut the bread and pork into ½-inch dice. Heat ¼ cup oil in a heavy skillet over medium-high heat. Fry the bread and pork until browned and crisped, about 2½ minutes. Remove and reserve.

Add 2 tablespoons oil to the skillet. When the oil is hot, remove the skillet from the heat and stir in the pimentón and cayenne. Add the cornmeal. Return the skillet to the heat and add the boiling water, cloves, caraway, and salt.

Cook the cornmeal over low heat, stirring frequently with a wooden spoon. It is cooked when it begins to pull away in a mass from the bottom of the skillet, about 20 minutes.

Serve the polenta topped with the croutons and pork bits.

PICKLED EGGPLANT, ALMAGRO STYLE

Berenjenas de Almagro

Almagro is a gem of a town, with a Plaza Mayor enclosed by graceful old buildings, one of which houses the Corral de Comedias, a sixteenth-century theater. The famous pickled egg-plant are made with tiny (two-inch) round green eggplants. Speared on short lengths of wild fennel, they are prepared whole, with stem and some of the calyx attached. The egg-plants are served as a tapa. You pick them up by the stem and eat the eggplant nubbin.

This is an adaptation of the classic Almagro recipe. It is not meant to be a conserve, so keep it, refrigerated, for up to three weeks. It's a good relish with roast lamb. If you serve the eggplants as an aperitif, spear the pieces with toothpicks.

MAKES 4 CUPS

2 medium eggplants (1½ pounds)	1 tablespoon ground cumin
Salt	½ teaspoon fennel seeds
2 tablespoons sweet pimentón	¼ teaspoon ground cinnamon
½ teaspoon cayenne	⅓ cup white wine vinegar

Peel the eggplants. Cut them lengthwise into quarters, then slice crosswise into 1½-inch wedges. In a large pot, bring 2 quarts water with 3 tablespoons salt to a rolling boil. Have ready a pan of ice water. Add the eggplants to the boiling water. When the water returns to a boil, cook the eggplant for 2 minutes. Drain and plunge into ice water. When it is cooled, drain well.

In a bowl, combine the pimentón, cayenne, cumin, fennel, cinnamon, and ½ teaspoon salt. Stir the vinegar into the spices until smooth. Add this mixture to 1½ cups water in a saucepan. Bring to a boil and cook for 1 minute. Add the eggplant and bring again to a boil. Remove the pan from the heat.

Place the eggplant and liquid in a heatproof bowl or jar. Cover tightly. When cool, refrigerate. The eggplant will be ready to eat in 24 hours.

PICKLED MUSHROOMS

Setas en Escabeche

Where country folk pick wild mushrooms, they have ways of preserving them, by drying, by pickling. This recipe, while not a real preserve, makes a tasty mushroom pickle that goes well with grilled meat or fish or as an addition to salads or soup. Oyster mushrooms work especially well, but you can use any variety of wild or cultivated mushroom. Slice thick ones crosswise to an even thickness.

MAKES 2½ CUPS

1 pound oyster mushrooms	⅛ teaspoon dried thyme
¼ onion, sliced from stem to root	Pinch of celery seeds
2 garlic cloves, slivered	1 bay leaf
¼ cup slivered red bell pepper	¼ cup extra virgin olive oil
One 1-inch piece dried red chile	¼ cup Sherry vinegar
1 strip lemon zest	2 teaspoons salt
⅛ teaspoon black peppercorns	

Rinse the mushrooms and drain. Trim away hard stems. Cut large mushrooms into 2 or 3 pieces.

Place the onion, garlic, bell pepper, chile, lemon zest, peppercorns, thyme, celery seeds, bay leaf, oil, vinegar, salt, and 2 cups water in a pan. Bring to a boil and cook for 5 minutes.

Add the mushrooms to the pan. Bring again to a boil, then simmer, uncovered, until the mushrooms are very tender, about 30 minutes.

Let the mushrooms cool in the liquid for 30 minutes. Ladle the mushrooms into a glass jar or other nonreactive container. Add enough of the pickling liquid to cover them completely. Cover the container and allow to marinate, refrigerated, for at least 24 hours. Keeps up to 2 weeks.

To serve, drain the mushrooms from the liquid and serve at room temperature.

SCARLET-PICKLED ONIONS

Cebolletas Escarlatas

In La Mancha, any presentation of pâté comes garnished with scarlet pickled onions. Colored with red beets, the onions make a nice contrast to smooth and unctuous foods such as pâté, but they also add pizzazz to salads. Pickled garlic is another zingy relish. Cloves of white garlic are pickled in the same manner as onions, but without the beet to color them.

Soaking the whole onions in brine makes it easier to slip off the skins—and fewer tears, too.

ﾀ MAKES ABOUT 2 PINTS

1½ pounds small (1½-inch) yellow or white onions (about 32)

1½ tablespoons coarse salt

1 medium beet (5 ounces), peeled and quartered

4 cloves

1½ cups wine vinegar

Sprinkle the onions with 1½ teaspoons of the salt and cover with water. Let soak for 3 hours. Drain the onions. Peel them, trimming the root ends and cutting a thin slice off tops.

Place the onions in a nonreactive bowl and add water to cover. Sprinkle with 1½ teaspoons of the remaining salt. Allow the onions to soak for 24 hours. Drain and rinse them.

In a saucepan, combine the remaining 1½ teaspoons salt, quartered beet, cloves, vinegar, and 2¼ cups water. Bring to a boil and cook for 5 minutes. Add the onions and cook gently for 10 minutes.

Skim out the beets and discard (or reserve for another use).

Ladle the onions into sterile jars and pour the pickling liquid over them. Seal tightly. Clean the jars and allow to cool.

Refrigerate the jars of pickled onions. The onions will be ready to eat in 5 days. They keep, refrigerated, for up to 3 months.

Cookies, Cakes, Pastries, *and* Puddings

In every village where I stop, I make a point to visit the local pastry shop to sample the specialties. Every town seems to have its beloved holiday cookies or favorite pudding or confection rooted in tradition. In Valdepeñas I discovered *mostillo,* a candy made during the grape harvest from boiled-down grape must. In Almagro, on the holiday of All Saints and All Souls, I tasted "saints' bones," edible reliquary of marzipan with cream filling. In Toledo convents I bought sweets from the *torno,* turnstile, where cloistered nuns sell their confections. In La Roda I sampled the town's famed *miguelitos,* flaky pastries with a cream filling. My collection of recipes (and my waistline) kept expanding at an alarming rate.

I have included recipes for the most authentic cakes, puddings, and other sweets of La Mancha, many of which come from the region's rich heritage of Arab and Sephardic cooking. Here are also some new takes using La Mancha ingredients. Saffron ice cream is a winner.

CINNAMON-WINE RINGS

Roscos de Vino

The olive oil makes a crispy cookie, not too sweet. The soft dough is easy to knead. You will hardly need any flour on the board, as the oil content keeps the dough from sticking. Serve the rings with coffee, tea, or sweet wine.

✺ MAKES 24

3¼ cups all-purpose flour plus more for board

3 teaspoons baking powder

½ teaspoon ground cinnamon

1 cup mild-flavored olive oil

½ cup dry white wine

¼ cup granulated sugar

1 teaspoon grated lemon zest

1 teaspoon sesame seeds, toasted

Pinch of salt

About ⅓ cup confectioners' sugar for dusting

Preheat the oven to 350°F.

Sift together the flour, baking powder, and cinnamon.

Combine the oil, wine, and granulated sugar in a mixing bowl and whisk to blend. Add the zest, sesame seeds, and salt. Stir in the dry ingredients to make a soft dough.

Turn the dough out on a lightly floured board and knead until the dough is shiny, about 4 minutes.

Divide the dough into 24 walnut-sized balls. Roll each ball into a cord, about 6 inches long and ½ inch thick. Pinch the ends together, forming a ring. Place the rings on baking sheets lined with parchment or Silpats.

Bake in the middle of the oven, switching the position of the sheets once, until the rings are lightly golden, 40 to 45 minutes.

Cool the rings on a rack. Sift confectioners' sugar over them.

ALMOND RINGS

Melindres

Here is a variation on Toledo marzipan. Formed into tiny rings, this sweet is especially appreciated for holiday giving.

Almond meal or flour is available from many Internet sources.

One egg white makes enough glaze for a double batch of melindres. If preferred, use ½ egg white, ½ cup confectioners' sugar, and 1½ teaspoons lemon juice for the glaze.

MAKES THIRTY 2-INCH RINGS

2½ cups almond meal (unsweetened)

1 cup plus 2 tablespoons granulated sugar

1 egg white

1 cup confectioners' sugar, sifted

1 tablespoon fresh lemon juice

Combine the almond meal and granulated sugar in a blender or processor and grind until very smooth. Add 7 to 8 teaspoons of water, 1 teaspoon at a time, processing until the almond mixture forms a smooth mass that sticks together. Turn it out onto a marble slab and knead briefly.

Preheat the oven to 300°F.

Divide the almond mixture into balls about the size of a pecan. Roll each one into a cord, 4½ inches long and about ⅜ inch in diameter. Bend the cord to make a circle, pinching the ends together. (If the cord breaks, just pinch together the broken bits.) Place the rings on a baking sheet lined with parchment or a Silpat.

Bake the rings for 12 minutes. Cool them on a rack.

Combine the egg white and sifted confectioners' sugar. Beat at high speed for 3 minutes. Add the lemon juice and beat for 2 minutes longer.

Dip the rings into the egg white glaze. Use a skewer to drag the rings through the egg white. Lift the rings out and let excess drip off. Place them on a baking sheet and return to the oven for 10 minutes. Remove and cool the rings on a rack.

MARZIPAN—A SWEET TRADITION IN TOLEDO

Sor Sagrario and Sor Isabel, two nuns of the Cistercian Order, sit behind a table just inside the massive doors to the sixteenth-century convent of Santo Domingo el Antiguo in Toledo's historic old town. They sell admission tickets to the convent's church, which contains an altarpiece and paintings by Toledo artist El Greco, whose tomb is in the church. The nuns also sell marzipan and other sweets, all prettily packaged, that they make in the convent kitchen.

"We put on aprons over our habits," said Sor Sagrario. *Orar y trabajar,* pray and work. "We tell the rosary while we work in the kitchen."

At the San Antonio convent, on the edge of the Jewish quarter, Franciscan sisters also confect a variety of sweets. Two nuns tending the shop explain that the *corazones*—hearts of marzipan with an egg yolk cream filling—are made from a very old convent recipe. At another convent cloistered nuns sell the sweet marzipan from a *torno,* a turnstile. Customers approach the grilled window and place their order with a nun inside a cage like a bank teller.

Etymologists have never traced how the word *marzipan—mazapán* in Spanish—came into current language. If they could, they might be able to explain the origins of this delectable sweet. One theory is that the word derives from the Arabic *mauthabán,* meaning "seated king," because, supposedly, the bars of marzipan were stamped with a logo of a king on a throne. As Islamic peoples generally did not use the human image in pictures, this seems to stretch the point. But, undoubtedly, marzipan devolved from an Arabic sweetmeat, for the Arabs introduced the cultivation of both almonds and sugar to Spain after their domination of Iberian lands in 711.

But marzipan making may also come from Sephardic Jewish confectionary traditions. Toledo had an important Sephardic community during the Moorish reign and after. When in 1492 the Catholic kings, Ferdinand and Isabella (the same monarchs who conquered the last Moorish kingdom of Granada and funded Columbus's scheme to sail west to find the Spice Islands), proclaimed the expulsion of the Jews from Spain, many converted rather than flee. The *conversos* took many of their customs, traditions, and foods with them into Christianity, even into the convents. Those who fled Spain took their Spanish customs with them to other parts of the world. Sephardic Jewish families in many parts of the world today still serve marzipan for holidays and on festive occasions such as weddings and bar mitzvahs.

In Toledo the art of confecting marzipan was kept alive in convents. Cloistered nuns prepared the sweet almond candy as gifts to their benefactors, usually members of the nobility. In another legend, marzipan was invented by nuns as a substitute for bread in a time when invading troops had destroyed wheat fields. Mazapán looks a lot like bread dough: *masa*—dough—and *pan*—bread.

In the shadow of Toledo's grand cathedral is the *obrador* or workshop of restaurateur Adolfo Muñoz. His master *pastelero,* confectioner, Julián de Haza, rolls out a slab of marzipan—50 percent almonds, 50 percent sugar—breaks off little pieces and with sleight of hand, a sculptor's nimble fingers, shapes them into tiny mice, snails, and swans. With a tiny hooked knife, he incises eyes, noses, scales, tails. Once dried, they will be glazed with colors.

Julián moves on to larger works—the *anguila* or eel, the most typical marzipan confection of Toledo. He starts with a simple spiral pattern. The marzipan paste is shaped and cut to fit the pattern. He dimples it with his fingers. The filling is spread on top—half "angels' hair," a sweet pumpkin jam, and half *yema,* candied egg cream mixed with marzipan. Julián rolls out a top slab of marzipan paste, using his hands to form it over the base. He cuts away the excess with a sharp knife. With his fingers he makes indentations to form the scales. With edible silver balls and candied fruits tucked into the coils, this is one of the most emblematic sweets of a Spanish Christmas.

At the family table, Adolfo explains, the eel is cut into small portions, starting from both the tail and the head, so that everyone gets a piece with both fillings.

Why eels? Adolfo says it's because the confectioners wanted to imitate nature—the eels in the River Tajo, snails, birds.

Next Julián prepares trays of *delicias.* These are little rounds of marzipan paste folded over an egg yolk filling. After drying, they are brushed with egg, placed on wooden trays, and baked in a very hot oven (570°F) for two minutes. They emerge glazed a rich brown.

Adolfo's workshop produces marzipan almost daily. Some goes to the restaurant, some for banquets catered by the restaurant (for a wedding, Julián shapes a massive marzipan book, inscribed with the names of the bride and groom). Artisanal marzipan is made from two varieties of sweet almonds, the oval Largueta, which contributes intense aroma, and the round Marcona, exceptionally rich in oil. Spanish marzipan does not contain bitter almonds.

Marzipan is traditional for Christmas celebrations everywhere in Spain. The sumptuous supper on *Nochebuena,* Christmas Eve, usually begins with shrimp and other shellfish, proceeds through a whole baked fish, and continues to roast baby lamb. With a dozen or more family members in attendance, dinner reaches the high point of the evening with the appearance of a silver tray with delicacies of marzipan and other sweets. Some of the family will go off to church for midnight mass celebrating the birth of the Christ child; others to the *discoteca* to dance until dawn, while the youngest may, finally, head to bed. But all ardently adhere to traditional observances: Nochebuena is family and sweet marzipan.

LEMON COOKIES

Pelusas

These light-as-fluff cookies are typical of El Toboso, the village that was the home of the fictional Dulcinea—"Sweetie"—Don Quixote's ladylove. The recipe was given to me by the Clarisa nuns at the San Benito monastery in El Toboso. The sisters make this and other sweets to sell to visitors. Their recipe calls for thirteen dozen eggs, nine kilos of flour, five kilos of sugar, and five liters of oil! I have downsized just a bit. The cookies are pressed together, two by two. They keep well stored in an airtight container. Place parchment paper between the layers so the cookies don't stick to each other.

⁓ MAKES **30** COOKIES

4 eggs

2 egg yolks

1 cup granulated sugar

¾ cup mild-flavored olive oil

1 teaspoon grated lemon zest

1 teaspoon anisette (optional)

3½ cups sifted all-purpose flour

1 cup sifted confectioners' sugar

Preheat the oven to 400°F.

Separate one of the eggs and combine the 3 remaining whole eggs and 3 yolks in a mixing bowl with the granulated sugar. Beat on high speed until thickened and very pale, about 5 minutes. Beat in the oil, lemon zest, and anisette if you're using it. Fold in the flour, mixing thoroughly.

Transfer the cookie batter to a pastry bag fitted with a ½-inch tip. Pipe the batter in 3-inch circles onto baking sheets lined with parchment paper or Silpats. (Or simply spoon the batter onto lined baking sheets.)

Bake for 5 minutes and rotate the baking sheets. Bake until the edges of the cookies are golden and a cookie springs back if pressed in the center, 4 to 5 minutes longer. Remove the baking sheets from the oven and let the cookies cool.

Beat the remaining egg white until stiff. Beat in the confectioners' sugar. Dribble squiggles of icing over the cookies. Allow to dry.

CHEWY WALNUT COOKIES

Mostachos de Nuez

This macaroon-type cookie from La Mancha is remarkably similar to *mustachudos,* a walnut sweet found in Sephardic cooking. Probably they share common roots in the Arabic-influenced pastries of medieval Spain.

MAKES FORTY-EIGHT 2-INCH COOKIES

¾ pound walnut meats (about 3 cups)

3 eggs, separated

¼ teaspoon fresh lemon juice

½ teaspoon grated lemon zest

½ teaspoon ground cinnamon

¾ cup sugar

2 tablespoons all-purpose flour

Grind the walnuts medium-fine in a food processor.

Preheat the oven to 350°F.

Beat the egg whites until stiff and beat in the lemon juice. Reserve. Combine the lemon zest and cinnamon in a small bowl.

Beat the yolks and sugar until light, 1 minute. Stir in the flour and the ground walnuts.

Fold half of the egg whites thoroughly into the walnut mixture. Fold in the remaining whites.

Lightly oil baking sheets. Using 2 teaspoons, drop mounds of the walnut mixture 2 inches apart on baking sheets. The mixture will spread out as it bakes.

Bake until the rims of the cookies are brown, 20 minutes. Place the sheets on racks to cool. Use the edge of a spatula to loosen the cookies once they are cooled.

BIGGER-THAN-LADYFINGERS

Tortas de Alcázar de San Juan

Maybe these should be called "macho-fingers." They are ladyfingers with muscle! In Alcázar de San Juan, the town where they originate, the cookies are baked in ovals, 5 inches × 3½ inches. A light, fat-free sponge cookie, they are delightful with coffee, tea, or hot chocolate. They also are combined with custard sauce for a typical dessert, *natillas* (page 320).

✕ MAKES 16 COOKIES

4 eggs at room temperature

½ cup sugar

½ teaspoon vanilla extract

1 cup cake flour, sifted

Pinch of salt

Preheat the oven to 400°F. Line baking sheets with parchment or Silpats.

Beat the eggs and sugar at high speed until very pale, thick, and doubled in volume, about 6 minutes. Beat in the vanilla. Sift a third of the flour and the salt over the eggs and fold it in with a spatula. Repeat with the remaining flour.

Spoon or pipe the batter onto baking sheets to make 5-inch ovals. Bake until lightly golden on the edges. The cookies are done when, if pressed in the center, the sponge springs back, 10 to 12 minutes.

Allow to cool. Loosen the cookies from the parchment and press the cookies together, two by two.

COCONUT COOKIES

Cocos

This recipe comes from the Clarisa nuns in El Toboso. On the days they bake Lemon Cookies, which require numerous egg yolks (page 290), they follow with these coconut cookies to use up the whites. The potato in the mixture helps keep the cookies moist and chewy.

MAKES **60 COOKIES**

1 small baking potato (¼ pound)

¼ cup milk

3 egg whites at room temperature

1 large egg at room temperature

1½ cups sugar

4 cups grated unsweetened coconut (10 ounces)

3 tablespoons all-purpose flour

⅛ teaspoon baking soda

Pinch of salt

Peel and quarter the potato and cook it in boiling water until tender, about 6 minutes. Drain. Mash the potato until smooth and beat in the milk.

Preheat the oven to 425°F.

In a large mixing bowl, beat the egg whites, egg, and sugar until almost doubled in volume, 5 minutes. Beat in the mashed potato and beat for 2 minutes more.

Place the coconut in a bowl, sift the flour, baking soda, and salt over it, and toss to combine.

Fold the coconut lightly into the egg mixture. Place in 1½-inch mounds on baking sheets lined with baking parchment or Silpats. Bake in the top of the oven until lightly golden on top, about 10 minutes. Turn off the oven and leave the cookies 10 minutes longer. Allow to cool before removing from the baking sheets.

ORANGE-SCENTED LARD COOKIES

Mantecados

These are typical Christmas cookies in Spain. The holiday coincides with cool weather and the season for hog slaughtering. After the hams are salted and the sausages hung to cure, pork fat is rendered to make pure white lard. Lard makes a tender cookie, but you could use part butter if preferred. These cookies keep for up to 3 weeks in an airtight container.

꩜ **MAKES ABOUT SIXTY 2-INCH COOKIES**

2 cups lard or a mixture of lard and butter

1 cup plus 2 tablespoons granulated sugar

3 egg yolks

2 eggs

1 teaspoon grated orange zest

½ cup fresh orange juice

7 cups all-purpose flour, plus flour for rolling out the dough

½ cup chopped almonds (optional)

2 tablespoons confectioners' sugar

Cream the lard in a large mixing bowl until fluffy. Beat in 1 cup of the granulated sugar, the egg yolks, and one of the whole eggs. Add the orange zest and juice. Using a large wooden spoon, gradually stir in the flour. Turn the dough out on a lightly floured board and knead it only until the flour is thoroughly combined with the lard. Cover with plastic wrap and refrigerate the dough for at least 4 and up to 24 hours.

Preheat the oven to 375°F. Line 2 baking sheets with parchment or Silpats.

Divide the dough into quarters. With a floured rolling pin, roll out one piece of dough ½ inch thick. Cut into 2-inch circles or squares and place them on the baking sheets. Gather scraps of dough together and roll out again. Roll and cut the remaining dough.

Beat the remaining whole egg with the remaining 2 tablespoons sugar. Brush the tops of the cookies with the egg mixture. If using, sprinkle almonds on the surface and lightly press them into the dough.

Bake until the tops of the cookies are golden, about 25 minutes. Cool the cookies before sifting confectioners' sugar over them.

WALNUT CAKE

Torta de Nueces

This recipe is of Sephardic origin. Not overly sweet, it makes a lovely teacake.

⁂ SERVES 12

---

2 cups walnuts

8 tablespoons (1 stick) butter

1 cup milk

1½ cups granulated sugar

3 cups all-purpose flour

3 teaspoons baking powder

Pinch of salt

2 eggs

1 tablespoon grated orange zest

Confectioners' sugar for sprinkling

Finely chop the walnuts in a food processor. Butter and flour a 9-inch springform pan.

Combine the butter, milk, and granulated sugar in a saucepan and heat until the butter is melted and the sugar dissolved. Cool slightly.

Sift together the flour, baking powder, and salt.

Preheat the oven to 350°F.

Beat the eggs in a mixing bowl. Beat in the butter mixture. Beat in the orange zest. Beat in the flour mixture. Fold in the chopped walnuts.

Pour the cake batter into the prepared pan. Bake until a skewer comes out clean, about 50 minutes.

Cool the cake on a rack for 10 minutes. Release the sides of the pan and cool the cake completely. Sift confectioners' sugar over the top.

LAYER CAKE with APRICOTS and MARZIPAN, TOLEDO STYLE

Bizcocho de Toledo

Here's a cake that starts out absolutely simple—a *bizcocho*, or sponge cake—which is so typical in Spanish homes. It goes way back in history—it is called *pan de españa,* "Spanish bread," by Sephardic Jews. The basic sponge cake is delightful with nothing more than fresh fruit—a perfect base for strawberries, for example. Soaked in wine-laced syrup, it becomes *bizcochos borrachos,* "drunken cakes."

This very fancy cake puts together layers of simple sponge with apricots, cream filling, and a topping of almond marzipan. In the original Toledo cake, the filling is made with *yema,* an egg-rich cream consisting of a dozen egg yolks! In my modification, the cream filling requires only a modicum of eggs.

Almond marzipan, so typical of Toledo, is simple to make at home. Ideally, you start with freshly shelled almonds, blanched (and skinned), then ground. You won't need all of the almond paste for the cake, so call in the kids, who will enjoy shaping this sweet almond playdough.

The cake is finished with a crisscross decoration made by caramelizing sugar with red-hot rods. Use metal skewers heated over a gas flame. Carefully lay them across the surface until the sugar bubbles. If this seems like too much trouble (or danger), simply serve the cake without this flourish.

You will have not only more marzipan than you need for one cake but also more syrup and cream filling.

SERVES 12

FOR THE SPONGE CAKE

1 cup cake flour

4 large eggs at room temperature

½ cup sugar

1 teaspoon grated lemon zest (optional)

Preheat the oven to 350°F. Butter an 8-inch springform pan, dust it with flour, and tap out the excess.

Sift the cake flour into a bowl.

Place the eggs in a large mixing bowl with the sugar and beat at high speed until the mixture thickens, becomes very pale in color, and more than doubles in volume, about 6 minutes. Beat in the lemon zest if you're using it.

Sprinkle ¼ cup of the sifted cake flour over the egg-sugar mixture and fold it in with a rubber spatula. Continue adding flour ¼ cup at a time until all is incorporated.

Pour the batter into the springform pan and bake until a skewer inserted in the center comes out clean, about 30 minutes. Cool the cake on a rack.

FOR THE APRICOT-BRANDY SYRUP (MAKES 1 CUP)

1½ cups dried apricots (¾ pound)

1 cup sugar

1 strip lemon zest

3 tablespoons brandy

Chop the apricots coarsely. Rinse them and reserve.

Combine the sugar and lemon zest with 1 cup water in a saucepan. Bring to a boil and simmer for 2 minutes. Add the apricots and simmer for 10 minutes.

Pour the apricot syrup through a strainer into a heatproof bowl. Discard the lemon zest and reserve the apricots. Add the brandy to the syrup and set aside. You will need only half of the syrup for the cake; save the remaining ½ cup for another use.

FOR THE MARZIPAN TOPPING

2 cups blanched almonds (about 10 ounces)

1¼ cups sugar

1 egg white, lightly beaten

1 egg yolk, mixed with ½ teaspoon water

Grind the almonds with the sugar in a food processor, blender, coffee grinder, spice grinder, or grain mill to make a paste that—with the addition of egg white or a little water—can be kneaded and molded until the consistency of very fine meal. Place in a mixing bowl and combine with the egg white. Turn out onto a pastry board and knead the mixture until smooth, 2 minutes.

Preheat the oven to 500°F.

Roll out the marzipan on a sheet of plastic wrap to a thickness of ½ inch. Cut an 8-inch round to fit the top of the cake. Place it on baking parchment on a baking sheet. Use the remaining marzipan to mold flowers, rabbits, mice, etc., to decorate the cake. Or save it for another use.

Brush the marzipan round and any molded pieces with the egg yolk. Place in the oven for 3 minutes. Remove and let the marzipan cool.

FOR THE CREAM FILLING (MAKES 2 CUPS)

2 cups milk

1 strip lemon zest

⅓ cup cornstarch

2 egg yolks

1 egg

½ cup sugar

Place 1½ cups of the milk in a saucepan with the lemon zest and bring to a boil. Remove from the heat and discard lemon zest.

Combine the cornstarch with the remaining ½ cup milk, stirring until smooth.

Beat the yolks and egg in a heatproof mixing bowl with the sugar. Add the cornstarch and milk mixture.

Whisk the hot milk into the egg mixture. Strain into a clean pan. Place over a pan of boiling water and cook the egg mixture, whisking constantly. It will thicken in about 2 minutes. Continue cooking and whisking for 3 minutes more.

Remove the pan from the heat and whisk occasionally as it cools, for 10 minutes. Spread the filling while warm.

You need only 1 cup of the cream filling for this cake. Freeze the rest, thawing and then blending it smooth in a blender before using it.

TO ASSEMBLE THE TOLEDO CAKE

2 teaspoons confectioners' sugar

Remove the sponge cake from the springform cake pan. Use a serrated knife to split the sponge cake in half horizontally. It helps to mark the halfway point by sticking toothpicks into it as a guide for the slicing knife.

Place the bottom half of the cake on a serving plate. Spoon ½ cup of the apricot-brandy syrup over it.

Spread the bottom layer with 1 cup of the cream filling. Spread the reserved apricots on the cream filling, reserving a few for garnish.

Place the top of the sponge cake over the cream filling.

Top the cake with the round of marzipan. Spoon confectioners' sugar in a grid across the top of the marzipan.

Heat steel pokers or metal skewers until red-hot. Lay them across the surface of the marzipan to caramelize the sugar and create a crisscross pattern. Let the cake cool. Use a brush to remove any excess sugar.

Decorate the cake with the marzipan flowers, mice, rabbits, and reserved pieces of apricot.

"LITTLE MICKEYS"
(PASTRY SQUARES *with* PUMPKIN CREAM FILLING)

Miguelitos con Crema de Calabaza

The little town of La Roda (Albacete province) is renowned for these delectable flaky pastry squares with a cream filling. They were invented by a local baker who named them after his appreciative friend, Miguelito ("little Mickey"). The original puff pastry was made not with butter but with lard, which produces a wonderfully flaky pastry. Frozen puff pastry is easier. I've changed the cream filling for one with cinnamon-spiced pumpkin.

🦌 **MAKES 18 PASTRY SQUARES**

½ cup milk

¼ cup cornstarch

2 egg yolks

2 cups pumpkin puree (from a 29-ounce can)

½ cup granulated sugar

½ teaspoon ground cinnamon

Pinch of ground cloves

1 teaspoon grated lemon zest

One 17-ounce package frozen puff pastry, thawed (2 sheets)

2 tablespoons confectioners' sugar

For the pumpkin cream filling, combine ¼ cup of the milk with the cornstarch in a small bowl and stir until smooth. Stir the egg yolks in a bowl. Add the milk and cornstarch mixture.

Combine the remaining ¼ cup milk with the pumpkin puree and granulated sugar in a saucepan over medium heat. Heat, stirring, until the mixture begins to bubble, about 3 minutes.

Stir some of the hot pumpkin mixture into the egg and cornstarch mixture, then whisk the egg into the pan with the pumpkin.

Place the pan over boiling water and cook, stirring, until the custard thickens and is smooth, 5 minutes. Add the cinnamon, cloves, and lemon zest.

Cool to room temperature. (The cream can be prepared up to a day in advance and kept covered and refrigerated. Bring to room temperature before spreading.)

Preheat the oven to 425°F.

For the pastry squares, use a sharp knife or pastry cutter to cut each sheet of puff pastry into nine 3-inch squares. Place them 1 inch apart on a baking sheet and bake for 5 minutes. Lower the oven temperature to 375°F and bake until the pastry is golden, 20 to 25 minutes.

Transfer the pastries to a rack to cool.

When cool, split the pastries in half horizontally, using the tip of a knife to separate the layers. Spread the bottoms thickly with pumpkin cream and press the tops on lightly to sandwich the cream.

Sift confectioners' sugar over the tops of the pastries.

WALNUT TURNOVERS *with* HONEY GLAZE

Empanadillas de Nueces

These delicious pastries appear on both La Mancha and Sephardic holiday menus. The honey glaze stays somewhat sticky. Separate the turnovers with wax paper so they don't stick together.

✳ MAKES **36** TURNOVERS

FOR THE PASTRY DOUGH

2 cups all-purpose flour, plus flour for rolling out the dough

⅛ teaspoon salt

2 tablespoons sugar

2 eggs, beaten

⅓ cup olive oil

FOR THE FILLING

2 cups walnuts

¼ cup sugar

2 teaspoons ground cinnamon

Pinch of ground cloves

⅓ cup raisins

1 egg

FOR THE GLAZE

¼ cup honey

¾ cup sugar

1 teaspoon fresh lemon juice

To make the turnover dough, combine the flour, salt, and sugar in a mixing bowl. Make a well in the center and pour in the eggs and oil. Stir the flour into the egg mixture little by little, making a soft dough.

Gather the dough together and turn out onto a lightly floured board. Knead very briefly to combine. Place in a bowl, cover with plastic wrap, and refrigerate for 2 hours.

While the dough is resting, prepare the filling. Grind the walnuts, sugar, cinnamon, and cloves in a food processor. Add the raisins and egg and process until uniformly chopped (not pureed).

Preheat the oven to 350°F.

Divide the dough in half. Roll out one piece of dough on a floured board to ⅛-inch thickness.

Use a cookie cutter to cut into 3-inch rounds. Place a teaspoonful of the walnut mixture on each round. Fold over and crimp the edges together with a fork. Place the turnovers on a lightly oiled baking sheet. Gather scraps of dough to roll out again.

Roll out the remaining dough, fill, and fold the turnovers in the same manner.

Bake the turnovers until golden brown, about 25 minutes. Transfer them to a rack to cool.

For the glaze, combine the honey, sugar, lemon juice, and ½ cup water in a small skillet. Bring to a boil and cook for 5 minutes.

Working with 5 to 6 turnovers at a time, dip them into the honey syrup in the skillet, turning them to coat both sides. Skim them out and place on a rack. Continue dipping turnovers in the syrup, keeping the syrup over low heat.

When all of the turnovers have been dipped, raise the heat and boil the remaining syrup for 2 to 3 minutes. Spoon it over the tops of the turnovers. Allow them to cool.

SWEET BREAD ROLL

Pan Dulce

I enjoyed this lovely sweet bread in the village of Quintanar de la Orden, where it is called *borrachos*. But never did I find out why it had that name, which means "drunken." Various sweets in the Spanish repertoire are called *borrachos*, because they have wine or liquor in their dough or else are soaked in wine syrup. But this bread has not a trace of alcohol. Could it be that only a drunk might have folded the dough over on itself into a twisted shape? Or is *borrachos*, perhaps, a corruption of *brioche*?

The same dough, studded with candied fruits and with a trinket baked in it, can be used for *roscón de reyes*, Three Kings' Day cake, served on January 6. The roscón is usually split and filled with whipped cream.

Sugar makes the dough very sticky. Using a large wooden paddle, stir as much flour as possible into the dough. Then use one hand to knead in the remaining flour, keeping one hand clean. Before turning the dough out, lightly oil the board and your hands. Knead the dough, brushing the board with additional oil to prevent the dough from sticking.

MAKES 2 LOAVES, SERVING 16 TO 20

1 cup sugar

½ cup warm water (110°F)

One ¼-ounce envelope active dry yeast

1½ teaspoons salt

8 cups sifted all-purpose flour

2 eggs

¾ cup olive oil

1 teaspoon grated lemon zest

1½ cups very hot water

¼ teaspoon saffron threads, crushed (optional)

1 egg yolk

Reserve 2 tablespoons of the sugar for the bread topping. Place 1 teaspoon of the remaining sugar in a small bowl. Add the warm water to the sugar and sprinkle the yeast over it. Allow to stand for 10 minutes, until bubbly.

Place the remaining sugar in a large mixing bowl. Add the salt and 3 cups of the flour and mix. Make a well in the center of the flour.

Beat the whole eggs in a bowl. Beat ½ cup of the oil into the eggs with the lemon zest. Pour the very hot water over the saffron, if you're using it, and allow to infuse for 3 minutes.

Add the egg mixture, saffron water, and yeast to the flour in the mixing bowl. Beat the batter with an electric mixer or wooden paddle for 5 minutes. Cover the bowl with a dampened cloth and place in a warm, draft-free place to ferment for 1 hour, to make a sponge batter.

Place the remaining ¼ cup oil in a shallow bowl.

Stir the sponge batter. Begin stirring in the remaining 5 cups flour. When the dough is too stiff to stir, dip a hand into the oil and knead the dough with one hand. Lightly oil the board and turn the dough out. With oiled hands, knead the dough for 10 minutes, until it is smooth and very elastic. Shape into a ball. Oil a clean bowl. Place the dough in the bowl and turn it to coat all sides lightly with oil.

Cover with a damp cloth and allow to rise until almost doubled in volume, 2 hours.

Preheat the oven to 375°F.

Punch down the dough and divide it into 2 equal balls. Roll out one ball into a large oval, about 12 × 24 inches and ¼ inch thick. Brush the surface with oil. Prick all over with a fork. Fold the short ends to the middle, overlapping them so the dough resembles an envelope. Roll the envelope out with a rolling pin to seal, making a flattened loaf. Transfer the dough to a baking sheet sprinkled with ½ teaspoon flour.

Roll out the second ball of dough. Brush the surface with oil and repeat the process, pricking all over with a fork again, and folding the ends to the middle, overlapping them. Roll out again to seal the folds. Transfer to a baking sheet sprinkled with ½ teaspoon flour.

Beat the egg yolk with 1 teaspoon water. Brush the tops of the two loaves with the yolk. Sprinkle them with the reserved 2 tablespoons sugar.

Bake the bread in the middle of the oven, changing the position of the baking sheets after 15 minutes. The bread is done when it is golden on top and it sounds hollow if tapped on the bottom, 35 to 40 minutes.

VARIATION: *Roscón de Reyes. The one who finds the tiny trinket baked in this cake, served for Three Kings' Day, January 6, is assured a year's good fortune.*

Prepare the dough as directed. Instead of rolling out the dough, insert a metal or other nontoxic, heat-proof trinket or coin in each ball. Shape each ball into a ring by flattening the ball, then inserting a finger in the center and gently easing the dough outward to create a hole in the center. Stuff the hole with crumpled foil and place on a baking sheet.

Brush with beaten egg yolk, sprinkle the top with slivered almonds, and decorate with candied fruits. Sprinkle with sugar and bake until browned.

SWEET POTATO BUNS

Tortas de Boniato

Sweet potatoes give a lovely color and moistness to these buns. Serve them with cream cheese and marmalade for breakfast or split crosswise and filled with sliced turkey for a very special lunch.

You will need about 1 cup mashed sweet potato. You can use leftover cooked sweet potato. If your leftovers have been spiced, that's fine; but if the potatoes have been sweetened, eliminate the sugar from the bread recipe.

MAKES **12 LARGE BUNS**

1 medium sweet potato (14 ounces), peeled and cut into pieces (to make 1 cup mashed sweet potato)

One ¼-ounce envelope active dry yeast

½ cup olive oil plus oil for the bowl and baking sheets

2 eggs

5 tablespoons sugar

1 teaspoon salt

⅛ teaspoon aniseeds (optional)

1½ cups warm milk (110°F)

8 cups all-purpose flour, plus flour for kneading

1 egg yolk

1 tablespoon plus 1 teaspoon milk

Cook the sweet potato in boiling water to cover until fork-tender. Drain, reserving ½ cup of the water.

Cool the cooking water to 110°F. Place in a small bowl and sprinkle the yeast over it. Allow to stand until bubbly, 10 minutes.

Mash the sweet potato or put through a ricer. Stir the ½ cup oil into it.

Beat the eggs in a large mixing bowl with 2 tablespoons of the sugar, the salt, and the aniseeds if you're using them. Add the sweet potato, yeast, and warm milk. Use a large wooden spoon to stir in about 6 cups of flour. Knead in the remaining 2 cups flour.

Turn the dough out onto a floured board and knead until smooth and shiny, 5 minutes. Sprinkle the board with additional flour as needed to keep the dough from sticking. Gather the dough into a ball.

Oil a large clean bowl. Place the dough in the bowl, turning it to coat all sides lightly with oil. Cover the bowl with a damp cloth and place in a warm place until the dough has doubled in volume, about 2 hours.

Lightly oil 2 baking sheets and dust them with flour.

With a floured hand, punch down the dough. Knead briefly on a floured board. Divide the dough into 12 balls (about 5½ ounces each). Roll or pat them into disks about 5 inches in diameter and ½ inch thick. Place on the baking sheets. Cover the buns with plastic wrap and set in a warm place to rise for 1 hour.

Preheat the oven to 400°F.

Combine the egg yolk with the milk and brush the tops of the buns with it. Sprinkle them with the remaining 3 tablespoons sugar.

Bake the buns in the middle of the oven, rotating the sheets after 10 minutes, until they are golden on top and sound hollow when tapped on the bottom, 18 to 20 minutes.

Cool the buns on wire racks.

CRISPY LEAVES

Hojuelas

The fried dough that Cervantes refers to, called *frutas de la sartén,* or "fruits of the frying pan," are typical sweets in areas of Spain such as La Mancha and Andalucía, where olive oil reigns supreme. The simple dough, flavored with aniseeds and sesame, is rolled out and shaped into rings, twists, ears, leaves, rosettes, and turnovers, fried until golden in olive oil, then dipped in boiled honey or sugar syrup.

Some popular fried pastries, such as *flores,* flowers, require special iron molds for shaping the dough. But these "leaves"—really just strips of dough—are simple to prepare.

Francisca Mompó in Quintanar de la Orden served me these crisp fried pastries when I visited her to chat about recipes. She says she makes a double batch of the dough and keeps it in the refrigerator, frying up each day only enough to serve to her painting class, grandchildren, or visitors.

❧ MAKES ABOUT **36 LEAVES**

⅓ cup mild-flavored olive oil

1 slice lemon

1 teaspoon sesame seeds

2 cups plus 2 tablespoons all-purpose flour

1 egg

1 egg yolk

¼ teaspoon salt

2 tablespoons rum, brandy, or anisette

¼ cup fresh orange juice

½ to ¾ cup olive oil for frying

⅓ cup granulated sugar

1 tablespoon confectioners' sugar

Heat the mild-flavored olive oil in a small pan over medium heat with the lemon slice until the lemon begins to sizzle. Remove from the heat and strain the oil. Add the sesame seeds to the hot oil. Allow to cool.

Place the flour in a mixing bowl and make a well in the center.

Beat together the egg, yolk, salt, rum, and orange juice. Pour into the well in the flour. Mix the flour gradually into the liquid ingredients to make a soft dough. Turn out on a pastry board and knead for 5 minutes. Pat into a ball, cover with plastic wrap, and allow the dough to rest at room temperature for 2 hours. (The dough may be wrapped and refrigerated for up to 3 days. Bring it to room temperature before rolling it out.)

Divide the dough into 2 pieces. Leave one covered. Break off pieces of dough and roll into 1-inch balls. Roll them out very thinly, almost transparent, into rectangles or ovals. Alternatively, roll out the dough into a large rectangle, approximately 10 × 18 inches, and cut strips on the diagonal, 2½ × 3½ inches.

Place a medium skillet over medium-high heat. Add enough oil to cover the bottom to a depth of ⅛ inch. When the oil is hot but not smoking, fry the leaves, 2 or 3 at a time, until golden on both sides, about 40 seconds per side.

Drain each batch on paper towels briefly. Then transfer them to a tray and sprinkle with granulated sugar. Continue frying the remaining strips of dough, replenishing the oil as needed.

Once cooled, serve the leaves dusted lightly with confectioners' sugar.

. . . dos calderas de aceite, mayores que las de un tinte servian de freir cosas de masa, que con dos valientes palas las sacaban fritas y las zambullian en otra caldera de preparada miel.

. . . two cauldrons of oil bigger than a dyer's vat served to fry doughnuts that were scooped out golden from the oil with two awesome paddles and plunged into another kettle of honey syrup.

DON QUIXOTE AND SANCHO PANZA
WATCHING COOKS PREPARING SWEETS FOR
THE WEDDING FEAST FOR RICH MAN CAMACHO

ANISE-FLAVORED DOUGHNUTS

Rosquillas

These doughnuts are especially loved at Christmastime. Neighbors get together to pool resources to make hundreds of them, sufficient to last the twelve days of Christmas. Working in tandem, one shapes the doughnuts, and the other drops them into the hot oil and skims them out. If you're on your own in the kitchen, cut all the doughnuts and place them on a baking sheet. Then proceed with the frying. If you don't have a doughnut cutter, cut rounds with a cookie cutter and improvise another tool (such as a thimble, bottle cap, or round tip of pastry gun) to cut out the center hole.

You will be surprised by how little oil is absorbed in frying the dough—that is, if you use olive oil.

MAKES **18**

½ cup olive oil plus oil for deep-frying	Pinch of salt
½ teaspoon aniseeds	2 eggs
1 teaspoon grated orange zest	1 cup sugar
5½ cups all-purpose flour	½ cup fresh orange juice
1 tablespoon plus 1 teaspoon baking powder	

Heat ½ cup oil in a small skillet until hot but not smoking. Remove from the heat and add the aniseeds. Allow to cool. Stir in the orange zest.

Combine the flour, baking powder, and salt.

With an electric mixer, beat the eggs and ½ cup of the sugar until thick and pale, 2 minutes. Beat in the oil with aniseeds, then the orange juice. With the mixer, beat in 2 cups of the flour mixture.

Using a wooden spoon, stir in the remaining flour to make a soft dough. Turn out on a board and knead briefly to thoroughly mix the flour into the dough. Cover with plastic wrap and allow to stand at room temperature for at least 1 hour and up to 3 hours.

Roll the dough out to a thickness of ⅜ inch. Cut rings using a 2½-inch doughnut cutter. Gather holes and scraps and roll out and cut the remaining dough.

Place enough oil in a deep, heavy frying pan to measure 1 inch deep (about 5 cups). Heat the oil until shimmering hot but not smoking (360°F). Carefully slide the doughnuts, 5 or 6 at a time, into the oil. Don't crowd them. Turn them to brown both sides. Remove when golden brown after about 3 minutes. Continue frying the remaining doughnuts, modulating the heat so the oil doesn't smoke.

Drain the doughnuts on absorbent paper and dredge in the remaining ½ cup sugar. Allow to cool before serving.

ALMOND FRITTERS

Tortillitas de Almendras

If you love almonds, these fritters are for you. Serve them like cookies, to be eaten out of hand. They keep very well in an airtight container.

If possible, grind blanched almonds immediately before preparing these fritters. If you purchase ground almonds, store in the refrigerator to prevent rancidity of the oil-rich nuts.

MAKES ABOUT TWENTY-FOUR 1½-INCH FRITTERS

1½ cups finely ground almonds

2 teaspoons all-purpose flour

¼ teaspoon ground cinnamon

Pinch of salt

2 eggs, separated

1 tablespoon granulated sugar

1 teaspoon fresh lemon juice

About ½ cup olive oil for frying

1 tablespoon confectioners' sugar

Combine the almonds, flour, cinnamon, and salt in a mixing bowl. Add the egg yolks and mix thoroughly.

Place the egg whites in another mixing bowl and beat at high speed until stiff. Beat in the granulated sugar, then the lemon juice.

Mix half of the egg whites with the almond mixture. Fold the remaining whites into the almonds.

Heat the oil in a medium skillet over medium-high heat until hot but not smoking (360°F). Drop teaspoonfuls of the almond mixture into the oil, flattening them slightly with the back of a spoon or wooden spatula. Fry until golden brown, then turn to brown the reverse side, about 1½ minutes total.

Drain on paper towels and allow to cool. When cool, sift confectioners' sugar over the fritters.

PUFFS OF WIND (FRITTERS)

Buñuelos de Viento

Food as entertainment—that's what these fritters are. A bunch of friends and neighbors get together to make *buñuelos*. They are typically seen at fiestas and are delicious accompanied by thick hot chocolate (page 365). They are best enjoyed the same day they are made.

To double the recipe, use twice the amount of milk, butter, salt, sugar, and flour, but only 3 eggs.

MAKES TWENTY-FOUR 1½-INCH PUFFS

½ cup milk or water

1 teaspoon aguardiente de anís or anisette (optional)

2 tablespoons butter

Pinch of salt

1 tablespoon sugar

½ cup plus 2 tablespoons all-purpose flour

2 eggs

About 4 cups olive oil for frying

Confectioners' sugar for dusting

Combine the milk, anisette if you're using it, butter, salt, and sugar in a saucepan. Bring to a boil and swirl the liquid to melt the butter.

Add all of the flour and stir hard with a wooden spoon until the paste thickens and comes away from the sides of the pan.

Remove from the heat and beat in 1 egg until it is completely absorbed. Add the second egg and beat until the batter is smooth.

Place oil in a heavy skillet to a depth of 1 inch and heat to 360°F (shimmering but not smoking). Drop teaspoonfuls of the batter into the hot oil, using a second spoon to push the batter off. The balls of batter will bob to the surface of the oil and turn themselves over. Remove the puffs when golden brown, 2 to 3 minutes.

Drain on paper towels. When cool, sift confectioners' sugar over the puffs.

FIGGY FRITTERS

Buñuelitos de Higos

These sweet fritters would make a delightful breakfast treat. They should be enjoyed the same day they are made.

SERVES 6 TO 10

½ pound small dried figs, such as Calimyrna

½ cup all-purpose flour

⅛ teaspoon salt

½ teaspoon baking soda

¼ teaspoon grated lemon zest

½ cup milk

1½ to 2 cups olive oil for frying

2 teaspoons confectioners' sugar

Wash the figs and drain on paper towels. Use kitchen scissors to snip out the stems. Cut the figs in half if they are small or quarters if they are larger.

Combine the flour, salt, and baking soda in a mixing bowl. Add the lemon zest and milk and stir to make a light batter. Add the figs to the batter and mix well.

Place oil in a heavy skillet to a depth of ½ inch. Heat until the oil is hot but not smoking (360°F). Scoop spoonfuls of batter into the hot oil. Turn the fritters as they brown, frying them for about 1 minute.

Drain on paper towels. Sift confectioners' sugar over the fritters. Serve warm or at room temperature.

SWEET TOASTS

Torrijas

These toasts are much like "French toast," but in Spain they are served as dessert, not breakfast. Everywhere in La Mancha, *torrijas* are absolutely essential during Holy Week and Easter holidays. I wonder if this derives from the Jewish tradition of using up all of the *hametz*, or leavened bread, before Passover—the springtime festival that usually coincides with Holy Week. Possibly *conversos*, converts to Christianity, brought with them to a new religion some of the customs of the former.

SERVES 6

12 slices stale bread (¾ pound)

2 cups milk

½ cup sugar

1 strip lemon zest

¼ cup dry red or white wine

2 eggs, well beaten

¼ cup olive oil

1 teaspoon ground cinnamon

1 tablespoon sugar or 2 tablespoons honey mixed with 1 tablespoon water

Place the slices of bread in one layer in a pan.

In a saucepan over medium heat, heat the milk with the ½ cup sugar and the lemon zest until the sugar is dissolved. Remove from the heat and add the wine to the milk. Pour this liquid over the bread and allow to stand until the liquid is absorbed, about 10 minutes. Discard the zest.

Place the beaten eggs in a dish. Heat some of the oil in a large, heavy skillet over medium-high heat. Dip the slices of bread into the egg on both sides. Fry them until browned on both sides, about 2½ minutes total. Transfer to a platter.

When all the bread slices are fried, sprinkle them with cinnamon and sugar or honey that has been boiled with water for 1 minute. Serve the toasts hot or cold.

SWEET CINNAMON DUMPLINGS *in* CARAMEL SAUCE

Rellenos Dulces con Canela

This is the sort of homespun dessert that children love. And it's a great way to use up stale bread. Typical of Cuenca, these bread-based dumplings are first fried, then simmered in caramel sauce. In another version the sauce is made with honey and wine boiled down to a syrup.

❧ MAKES ABOUT **24** DUMPLINGS, SERVING **6**

---

8 to 10 slices stale bread (about ½ pound)

1 cup milk

2 eggs

2 tablespoons sugar

¼ teaspoon baking soda

½ teaspoon ground cinnamon

⅛ teaspoon aniseeds

½ cup olive oil for frying

Caramel sauce (recipe follows)

Whipped cream for serving (optional)

Place the bread in a shallow pan. Drizzle with half the milk. Turn the slices and pour on the remaining milk. Allow to stand for 30 minutes, until the bread is softened.

Chop the bread in a food processor with the eggs, sugar, baking soda, cinnamon, and aniseeds. It does not need to be completely pureed.

Heat the oil in a large skillet over medium-high heat. Drop the batter by tablespoons into the pan and brown well, about 1½ minutes. Use a spatula to turn the dumplings and brown on the other side, another 1½ minutes. Remove to drain on a paper towel.

Heat the caramel sauce in a saucepan and add the fried dumplings. Cook them in the sauce for 5 minutes. Remove the dumplings with a slotted spoon and allow to cool.

Serve the dumplings drizzled with some of the sauce and accompanied by whipped cream if desired.

❦ CARAMEL SAUCE   *Salsa de Caramelo*

❦ Makes 2 cups sauce

1 cup sugar

1 tablespoon fresh lemon juice

2 teaspoons ground cinnamon (optional)

Place the sugar, lemon juice, and ¼ cup water in a heavy saucepan over medium heat. Melt the sugar, stirring. Raise the heat to medium-high and cook the melted sugar without stirring, tilting the pan occasionally, until the sugar turns a medium-dark caramel color, 8 to 10 minutes.

Remove the pan from the heat and very carefully pour in 2 cups water. The caramelized sugar will bubble and splatter. Add the cinnamon if you're using it. Return the pan to the heat and cook over low heat, stirring to dissolve any lumps of caramel. Sauce will keep, covered and refrigerated, for 6 weeks.

CHRISTMAS ALMOND SOUP

Sopa de Almendras para Navidad

In Toledo, this divine dessert is traditional for the Christmas Eve family dinner. The soup is a thick cream while hot. Cooled, it reaches custard consistency. This recipe makes four generous servings, but, if part of a copious holiday meal, it could be divided among eight small pudding bowls instead of soup bowls. Almond paste can be purchased ready to use. But you can also make your own; see the note following the recipe.

SERVES 4

4 thick slices brioche	1 strip orange or lemon zest
½ pound sweetened almond paste	¼ teaspoon ground cinnamon
1 quart whole milk	Whipped cream for serving (optional)

Preheat the oven to 350°F.

Place the brioche slices on a baking sheet. Bake them for 8 minutes. Turn the slices and bake for 6 to 8 minutes longer, until golden brown on both sides. Remove from the oven and place a slice in each of 4 shallow soup bowls.

Cut the almond paste into chunks. Dissolve it in 2 cups of the milk. (This is quickly accomplished in a blender.) Place the dissolved almond paste in a saucepan and stir in the remaining milk. Add the orange zest. Place over high heat and stir frequently until the soup begins to foam up. Turn the heat to low and simmer, stirring occasionally, for 15 minutes. The soup will thicken to the consistency of heavy cream. Discard the orange zest.

Ladle the soup over the toasted brioche. Sprinkle the cinnamon on top of the soup. Serve hot or at room temperature, accompanied by whipped cream if desired.

NOTE: *To make almond paste, combine ¼ pound (½ cup) sugar with ¼ pound ground almonds (1⅓ cups) in a blender or food processor. Grind them. Add 1 tablespoon water to make a paste. The paste can be stored in the refrigerator for up to 2 weeks or in the freezer for up to 3 months.*

CUSTARD PUDDING *with* MERINGUE TOPPING

Natillas

In Alcázar de San Juan, a town in central La Mancha, this pudding is so absolutely simple—warmed sheep's milk is thickened with egg and poured over *tortas,* sponge cookies, then sprinkled with sugar and cinnamon. This custard, which doesn't require sheep's milk, thickens to the consistency of heavy cream. It's luscious poured over ladyfingers or a layer of sponge cake. Traditionally it is flavored with lemon and cinnamon. However, the milk can be infused with alternative flavors—vanilla bean; orange zest and rosemary; mint. Vanilla custard is particularly good finished with a dribble of chocolate sauce instead of the sprinkled cinnamon. The meringue topping is optional. If you have another use for the egg whites, simply omit it.

SERVES 6

3 cups milk

One 2-inch cinnamon stick

2 strips lemon zest

½ cup granulated sugar

1 tablespoon cornstarch

4 eggs, separated

12 Bigger-Than-Ladyfingers (page 292) or 24 store-bought ladyfingers

1½ tablespoons ground cinnamon

2 teaspoons fresh lemon juice

½ cup confectioners' sugar, sifted

Combine 2 cups of the milk, the cinnamon stick, zest, and granulated sugar in a saucepan and bring to a boil. Remove from the heat and strain into a heatproof bowl.

Stir the remaining 1 cup milk with the cornstarch until smooth. Beat in the 4 egg yolks. Whisk in the hot milk. Place the mixture in the top of a double boiler and cook over boiling water, stirring, until it is as thick as cream, 10 minutes.

Place 2 tortas de Alcázar (or 4 ladyfingers) in each of 6 shallow bowls. Spoon the custard over the tortas. Sprinkle with cinnamon. Chill the puddings.

Preheat the oven to 300°F. Line a baking sheet with parchment.

Place the egg whites in a mixing bowl and beat at high speed until stiff. Beat in the lemon juice. Fold in the confectioners' sugar and beat at high speed until combined.

Heap mounds of the meringue on the baking sheet (divide into 6 or 12) and bake until the peaks are golden, 12 minutes. Turn off the oven and allow the meringues to dry for 30 minutes.

Place a meringue on top of each pudding. (Depending on the size of the meringues, there may be more than required for the 6 puddings.)

MOLDED MANCHEGO CHEESE FLAN
with CARAMEL SAUCE

Bizcochá con Flan de Queso Manchego

This luscious dessert can be made a day or two in advance of a dinner party. A mold is coated in caramel and lined with a layer of sponge cake, brioche, or ladyfingers. When the cheese custard is poured in, the cake pieces float to the top. When unmolded, the cake forms the base of the dessert. Garnish the flan with a few currants or raspberries. Or pair it with quince sorbet (page 343) for a classic combo. Use a large loaf pan, 9 × 5 × 3 inches, for this recipe.

SERVES 8

1 cup sugar	1 strip lemon zest
5 ounces sponge cake or brioche, sliced ¾ inch thick	3½ ounces Manchego, grated (about 1½ cups)
1 cup milk	4 large eggs
1 cup cream	1 egg yolk
1 bay leaf	

Place ½ cup sugar and 3 tablespoons water in a heavy saucepan. Bring to a boil and stir to dissolve sugar. Cook without stirring over medium heat, swirling pan occasionally, until sugar melts and turns a deep gold color, 4 to 6 minutes. Pour the caramel into a 9 × 5-inch loaf pan, tilting to coat the bottom with the caramel. Cool until caramel hardens.

Place a layer of the sponge or brioche on top of the caramel in the loaf pan.

Preheat the oven to 350°F.

Combine the milk, cream, bay leaf, lemon zest, and remaining sugar in a saucepan. Bring to a boil, stirring to dissolve the sugar. Remove from the heat. Skim out and discard the bay leaf and zest. Stir in the grated cheese.

Beat the eggs in a heatproof bowl. Beat the hot milk and cheese mixture into the eggs, little by little. Carefully pour the mixture over the cake and caramel in the loaf pan. (The pieces of cake will bob to the top.) Cover the loaf pan with foil.

Set the loaf pan in a larger baking pan. Add boiling water to reach halfway up the sides of the loaf pan. Carefully transfer the pans to the oven. Bake until a skewer inserted in the custard comes out clean, about 1 hour.

Remove from the oven and transfer the loaf pan to a rack to cool. When cool, loosen the sides with a knife and turn the flan out onto a serving dish. Slice crosswise to serve, spooning on some of the caramel sauce.

"FRIED MILK"

Leche Frita

How do you fry milk? First turn it into a thick custard. Served warm, the custard squares are crisp on the outside, creamy on the inside. They may also be served cold, in which case the custard sets up fairly solid.

Traditionally, fried milk is sprinkled with sugar and cinnamon, but at the Restaurante Sucot in Valdepeñas I enjoyed it with a sublime orange syrup (page 325).

A slotted fish spatula with a thin, curved edge works well for lifting the custard squares out of the beaten egg and into the crumbs and for scooping them out of the frying oil.

MAKES SIXTEEN 2-INCH SQUARES, SERVING 4 TO 8

FOR THE CUSTARD	2 eggs
2¼ cups milk	⅓ cup all-purpose flour
One 6-inch strip lemon or orange zest	¼ cup cornstarch
One 2-inch cinnamon stick	⅓ cup sugar

Generously oil an 8-inch square cake pan or plastic container.

Place 1¾ cups of the milk in a heavy saucepan with the lemon zest and cinnamon stick. Bring to a boil. Remove from the heat and let infuse for 5 minutes. Strain the milk into a heatproof pitcher.

Combine the remaining ½ cup milk, the eggs, flour, cornstarch, and sugar in a blender and blend until completely smooth. With the blender running, pour in the hot milk.

Return the custard mixture to the saucepan and place over boiling water. Cook, stirring constantly, until the custard barely begins to thicken. (This happens very rapidly.) Remove it from the heat and beat it hard to prevent lumps from forming. Place the pan over boiling water again and cook, stirring constantly, for 5 minutes. Remove from the heat and beat the custard until very smooth.

Immediately spread the custard to an even thickness in the cake pan. Cover with plastic wrap and refrigerate for at least 4 and up to 24 hours.

TO FRY THE CUSTARD

1 egg

1 cup fine dry bread crumbs

About ½ cup olive oil for frying

1½ tablespoons sugar (optional)

1 teaspoon ground cinnamon (optional)

Intensely Orange Syrup (optional; recipe follows)

Cut the custard into sixteen 2-inch squares. Beat the egg with 2 teaspoons water in a shallow bowl. Spread half the bread crumbs in a shallow tray.

Dip each custard square into beaten egg, then lift it out and place it in the bread crumbs. Sprinkle the remaining bread crumbs over the custard squares. Shake the tray gently to coat the edges of the custard. Place the breaded custard squares on a cookie sheet and refrigerate for at least 30 minutes and up to 4 hours.

Heat the oil in a large, heavy skillet over medium heat until hot but not smoking. Fry the custard squares, in 2 batches, until browned on both sides, 1 to 2 minutes per side. Transfer them to a tray lined with paper towels to drain.

If you're using the sugar and cinnamon, sprinkle them over the fried custard squares while still warm. If you're using the orange syrup, spoon it over the squares immediately before serving. Serve warm or cold.

INTENSELY ORANGE SYRUP *Jarabe de Naranjas*

Slow reduction of pure orange juice makes an intensely flavored syrup. Spoon it over puddings, sponge cake, ice cream, or breakfast toast or use it in mixing cocktails. Combined with bubbly cava, it is sensational.

Makes 1½ cups

Zest from 1 orange

3 cups fresh orange juice (from 8 to 10 oranges)

3 tablespoons fresh lemon juice

1 cup sugar

Cut the orange zest into fine julienne slivers. Blanch the zest in boiling water for 2 minutes. Drain. Blanch again for 2 minutes and drain. Reserve the zest.

Combine the orange juice, lemon juice, and sugar in a saucepan. Bring to a boil and skim off the froth from the top.

Finely chop the orange zest. Add it to the pan. Lower the heat so the orange juice bubbles gently. Cook until thickened and reduced by half, about 40 minutes.

Cool the syrup. Store, tightly covered, in the refrigerator. The syrup keeps for several months.

FIGS POACHED *in* VANILLA SYRUP

Higos con Jarabe de Vanilla

These vanilla-scented figs are especially good served with ice cream or whipped cream. They keep well, refrigerated, for up to three weeks. Should any syrup remain, combine it with chilled white wine and pour over ice for delicious wine coolers.

SERVES 8

---

2 pounds firm, ripe fresh figs (about 5 dozen)

½ vanilla bean

2 cups sugar

4 cloves

3 tablespoons fresh lemon juice

Wash the figs and nip off the stems.

Split the half vanilla bean lengthwise. Place in a large pan with the sugar, cloves, lemon juice, and 1 quart water. Bring to a boil and boil for 2 minutes. Add the figs, bring again to a boil, and cook for 3 minutes.

Remove the figs with a slotted spoon and place in a heatproof bowl. Bring the syrup to a boil and cook until reduced by half, about 15 minutes. Pour the hot syrup through a strainer over the figs. Allow to cool, then refrigerate, covered.

Allow the figs to macerate in the syrup for 24 hours before serving.

CINNAMON PUMPKIN SLICES

Hojarascas de Calabaza

Thinly sliced pumpkin fried in oil and sprinkled with sugar makes a surprisingly easy dessert or breakfast treat—sort of like French toast without the toast. (Incidentally, I also love it sprinkled with salt and oregano as a savory side dish.) Don't expect the pumpkin to be crisp. It should be tender but not overly soft. Use small pie pumpkins in this recipe. If they are not available, substitute acorn or other winter squash.

⅗ SERVES 6

¼ small pumpkin (1 pound 6 ounces)	¼ to ⅓ cup olive oil
1 egg, beaten	1 tablespoon sugar
⅓ cup all-purpose flour	1 teaspoon ground cinnamon

Scoop out and discard the pumpkin seeds and membrane. Cut the pumpkin crosswise into ⅜-inch-thick slices (approximately 24 slices, 4 × 1½ inches). Pare the slices, discarding the skin.

Place the egg in a shallow dish. Place the flour in a shallow pan. Dip the pumpkin slices in beaten egg, then dredge them in flour, patting off the excess.

Heat the oil in a heavy skillet over medium heat. Fry a third of the pumpkin slices until speckled brown on both sides, 4 to 5 minutes. The pumpkin should be fork-tender but not overly soft. Remove the pumpkin and drain it on paper towels. Continue frying the remaining pumpkin slices in the same manner, adding oil as needed.

Fan the pumpkin slices on a serving dish and sprinkle them with sugar and cinnamon. Serve warm or at room temperature.

QUINCE JELLY

Dulce de Membrillo

Thick enough to cut with a knife, quince jelly (also called *quince paste*) can be served with breakfast breads, makes a delightful addition to a cheese platter, and works as appetizer or dessert. The sweetness of the fruit contrasts beautifully with creamy or salty cheeses. Quince jelly is available at specialty foods stores. But should you have a windfall of this lovely fruit, here is how to prepare the jelly.

MAKES 3¾ POUNDS QUINCE PASTE, PROVIDING TWENTY-TWO 1 × 3¼ × 1½-INCH SLICES.

4½ pounds quinces (5 or 6)

1 tablespoon fresh lemon juice

About 6 cups sugar

Wash the quinces. Place them in a large pan with the lemon juice and water to cover. Bring to a boil and cook over medium heat, covered, until the quinces are easily pierced with a knife, about 30 minutes. Drain, saving ½ cup of the cooking liquid.

When cool enough to handle, peel the quinces and remove the seeds and cores. Puree the fruit in a food mill or food processor, adding the reserved liquid as needed. You should have about 6 cups of puree.

Measure the pureed fruit. For every cup of puree add 1 cup sugar. Place in a heavy saucepan over high heat until it begins to bubble. Continue to cook over medium-high heat, stirring frequently, for 15 minutes. As the mixture begins to thicken, stir constantly so it doesn't scorch on the bottom. Cook until, when stirred, the puree pulls away in a solid mass from the bottom of the pan, 20 to 30 minutes longer. A spoonful dropped on a cold plate solidifies immediately.

Spread the quince jelly to a depth of 1½ inches in one or more molds (a 7 × 11-inch rectangular cake pan is perfect). The quince paste solidifies as it cools.

Once cool, the quince can be cut into smaller portions, each wrapped in plastic wrap and foil, and stored refrigerated for up to several months.

Slice 1 inch thick to serve.

MOORISH DELIGHT

Mostillo

This sweet is remarkably similar to the one more commonly known as *Turkish delight,* which in turn is a variation on *halvah,* which, long ago, was also made with thickened grape juice. The Spanish sweet, *mostillo,* derives from the Moorish heritage.

At the *vendimia,* grape harvest, La Mancha is awash in grape juice—*mosto.* Boiled down to a sweet syrup, the juice is thickened with flour and cooked again until it sets up almost solid. Spiced with cinnamon, aniseeds, and lemon zest, it makes a confection that lasts for many months if stored in a cool place. Another version of the same confection contains no mosto but caramelized sugar syrup.

This small-scale version with nuts isn't made for keeping. Serve it on a dessert tray with cream cheese.

MAKES ABOUT FIFTEEN 1½-INCH PIECES

1 quart unsweetened red grape juice (not Concord)

3 strips orange zest

1 strip lemon zest

¼ teaspoon aniseeds

½ cup sugar

1 cup all-purpose flour

½ teaspoon ground cinnamon

Blanched almonds, pine nuts, or walnut halves

Combine the juice, orange and lemon zest, aniseeds, and sugar in a saucepan. Bring to a boil, then cook, uncovered, until reduced to 2 cups (about 30 minutes). Strain the juice and discard the zest. Let the juice cool.

Place the flour in a bowl. Stir in the cooled juice 2 tablespoons at a time, mixing very well. Continue stirring to form a smooth paste. Strain the paste to eliminate any lumps.

Place the paste in a saucepan over medium heat. Stirring constantly, cook until the paste comes away from the sides of the pan and is so stiff that it is difficult to stir, about 15 minutes. (Test by putting a spoonful on a plate; turn the plate upside down. If the mixture doesn't fall off, it is done.)

Remove from the heat and stir in the cinnamon. Spread the paste in a 7-inch square or round pan or 2 smaller molds. Use an offset spatula dipped in hot water to smooth the top.

Stud the top with almonds or pine nuts or walnut halves, pressed into the surface. Allow to cool completely. Store tightly covered in the refrigerator. The sweet will keep for up to 1 month.

Serve cut into squares or thin wedges.

SWEET POTATOES CANDIED in GRAPE SYRUP

Arrope con Boniatos

Arrope is a syrup produced from boiled-down grape must, which is newly pressed, unfermented grape juice, a commodity much available in La Mancha during the September wine harvest. Various fruits and even vegetables are cooked in the syrup to preserve them.

One La Mancha recipe book (*Recetario Gastronómico de Castilla–La Mancha,* by Enrique García Moreno) gives instructions for making arrope from the very beginning:

> *Tread the grapes and strain out the skins and seeds. Put in some firebrands and leave until the following day. Remove the brands and let the must rest awhile. Change it several times from one recipient to another, discarding the sediment. Put the juice to cook, skimming off the scum that rises. Add egg white to the simmering must. When it turns black, strain the juice and return it to cook.*
>
> *Cut a pumpkin into small pieces and put it into* cal viva *[calcium hydroxide, the same substance used to whitewash houses; culinarily known as pickling lime, which hardens the pumpkin so it won't fall apart in the arrope]. Then wash the pumpkin well.*
>
> *When the arrope has cooked down to the consistency of honey, add the pumpkin.*

Other fruits and vegetables cooked in arrope are melon, eggplant, pears, figs, carrots, and sweet potatoes. Sweet potatoes don't need hardening in pickling lime.

As a child I never cared for the candied sweet potatoes that accompanied holiday turkey dinners. But, moved over to dessert, I think they are lovely. For a real treat, serve these sweet potatoes and their syrup with whipped cream and a scattering of walnuts or with almond ice cream.

MAKES 2 PINTS

10 cups unsweetened white grape juice
¾ cup sugar
5 cloves
1 small orange
4 cups sweet potato in ¾-inch cubes (1½ pounds)

Combine the grape juice, sugar, and cloves in a large, heavy saucepan. Bring to a boil. Reduce the heat to medium so the juice keeps bubbling. Cook until reduced by half, about 1 hour. Skim out the cloves and discard.

Slice the ends off the orange and discard. Cut the orange in half and slice it crosswise. Discard any seeds. Add the orange slices to the reduced grape juice with the sweet potato.

Bring to a boil. Cook over medium heat until juice is as thick as syrup and the sweet potatoes are tender, about 40 minutes. Place the hot mixture into 2 sterile 1-pint glass jars. Seal and cool. Store, refrigerated, for up to 1 month.

CUENCA-STYLE HONEY-ALMOND NOUGAT

Alajú

This almond candy, famous in Cuenca, is of Arabic origin and quite similar to *turrón*, another nougat of honey and almonds. Turrón, a specialty of Toledo and of Jijona (Alicante), is usually purchased, but *alajú* is simple to confect at home. So sweet that it is served in slivers, it makes a lovely addition to a candy tray and a fine holiday gift.

The cooked honey and almond mixture is spread between edible paper-thin wafers so that it's not too sticky to pick up. (The wafers can be ordered from baking-craft Web sites.) Otherwise, spread it on nonstick baking parchment. Peel off the parchment to cut the nougat. When cool, the candy is slightly flexible, not hard as brittle.

Honey is easier to measure and pour if warmed very slightly in a microwave and poured into a measuring cup that has been oiled lightly with almond or olive oil. Walnut halves can be used in place of almonds.

MAKES THREE 5-INCH PATTIES, 8 TO 10 SLICES EACH

1 cup blanched whole almonds

1 cup fine dry bread crumbs

Six 5-inch-diameter wafers (or squares of nonstick baking parchment)

1 cup multifloral honey

1 teaspoon grated orange zest

Preheat the oven to 375°F.

Place the almonds in a baking pan and the crumbs in another baking pan. Toast them, stirring frequently, until light golden (do not allow to brown), about 14 minutes. Cool the almonds and crumbs.

Arrange 3 wafers on a marble slab or individual china dishes. Have the remaining 3 wafers ready.

Place the honey in a saucepan and position a candy thermometer in the honey. Heat over medium-high heat until the honey bubbles and begins to foam up. Let it cook to the soft-ball stage (238°F), 2 to 3 minutes.

Stir in the almonds. Stir in the bread crumbs. Cook over low heat, stirring constantly, for 1 minute. Stir in the orange zest.

Spread a third of the honey-almond mixture on each of 3 wafers. Place another wafer on top of each and gently press the patties to spread the filling to an approximate thickness of ½ inch. Allow them to cool. The nougat is ready to eat immediately, but it can be kept, wrapped tightly in plastic wrap and foil and stored in an airtight container, for up to 3 months.

Use a cleaver to cut the disks of nougat crosswise into ½-inch slivers. Serve on a candy tray.

CHOCOLATE-FIG BONBONS

Bombones de Higos con Chocolate

Figs plus chocolate equal divine. This artisanal gourmet product—figs with a chocolate cream filling, bathed in bittersweet chocolate—can be made at home without too much trouble. Don't worry if your bonbons don't have a slick professional finish—they will still taste wonderful. Chocolate-covered figs make great holiday gifts. Place them in fluted bonbon papers or simply wrap them individually in tissue paper.

MAKES 75 BONBONS

---

1 pound small dried figs, such as Calimyrna

1 cup plus 2 tablespoons sugar

¼ cup brandy

1 pound bittersweet chocolate, chopped or grated

2 tablespoons extra virgin olive oil

⅓ cup boiling water

With a sharp knife, cut a slit in the bottoms of the figs, leaving the stems intact.

Combine 1 cup of the sugar and 3 cups water in a saucepan. Bring to a boil, stirring to dissolve the sugar. Cook for 3 minutes. Add the brandy, bring again to a boil, and stir in the figs. Remove the pan from the heat and let the figs macerate for 15 minutes.

Drain the figs in a colander, saving the brandy sugar syrup for another use. Spread the figs on a rack and allow to dry in a well-ventilated place for 2 hours.

Prepare the chocolate cream filling. In the top of a double boiler over boiling water, melt ¼ pound of the chocolate. Stir in the olive oil, the remaining 2 tablespoons sugar, and the boiling water. Place the pan over medium, direct heat and cook, stirring, for 3 minutes. Scrape into a heatproof bowl. Cool the chocolate, then refrigerate.

To stuff the figs with the chocolate cream filling, poke a finger or wooden dowel into the slit to make a hollow and use the tip of a small knife to push about ⅛ teaspoon of the chocolate cream into the center. Place each fig on a tray as it is filled. (You may not need all of the chocolate cream. Reserve unused chocolate for another use.) Set aside in a cool place (not the refrigerator) for at least 30 minutes and up to 6 hours.

Place the remaining ¾ pound chocolate in the top of a double boiler. Stir frequently with a wooden spoon until melted. The chocolate is ready when it's warm to the touch but not hot. Dip one fig at a time into the chocolate, rolling it around with a toothpick until it is completely coated. Spear the fig with the toothpick or use 2 forks to lift it out, letting excess chocolate drip off. Place on a baking sheet lined with wax paper and let sit at room temperature. The candies are ready when the chocolate hardens completely.

Place the figs in individual bonbon papers or in a box lined with wax paper. They are ready to eat immediately but may be kept, refrigerated, for up to 1 month.

LAVENDER HONEY ICE MILK

Helado de Miel de Espliegas

The provinces of Guadalajara and Cuenca are famed for their delectable honeys. This ice milk is very subtly flavored with lavender flowers and lavender honey. (The ice milk will be a golden honey color—not lavender.) You might try variations—sprigs of rosemary with rosemary honey, thyme and thyme honey, orange blossoms with orange blossom honey.

SERVES 6

2⅓ cups whole or 2% milk	1 clove
½ cup lavender honey	4 egg yolks
12 lavender flowers or 1 tablespoon dried culinary lavender	Pinch of salt

Combine 2 cups of the milk and the honey in a saucepan over medium heat. Heat, stirring, until the honey is dissolved. Remove from the heat and add the lavender flowers and clove. Cover the pan and let the lavender steep for 30 minutes.

Blend the yolks and salt with ⅓ cup of the remaining milk and pour into a clean saucepan. Strain the lavender-infused milk into the eggs. Cook over medium heat, whisking, until the custard reaches 180°F, about 5 minutes. Remove from the heat and whisk in the remaining ⅓ cup cold milk.

Chill the mixture. Freeze in an ice cream maker according to the manufacturer's instructions.

SAFFRON ICE CREAM with PINE NUT PRALINE and CHOCOLATE SYRUP

Helado de Azafrán con Guirlache de Piñones y Sirope de Chocolate

La Mancha saffron lends a golden color and an aromatic, subtly bitter flavor to the rich ice cream. Saffron has a real affinity for chocolate, while the pine nuts provide a crunchy contrast to the smooth cream. Altogether a delightful combination. Ice cream, praline, and syrup can all be made several days in advance of serving.

SERVES **8**

FOR THE ICE CREAM

2 cups milk

1 strip orange zest

1 teaspoon saffron threads, crushed

6 egg yolks

Pinch of salt

⅔ cup sugar

1¾ cups whipping cream

FOR THE PINE NUT PRALINE

⅓ cup sugar

½ cup pine nuts

FOR THE CHOCOLATE SYRUP (MAKES ¾ CUP)

¼ pound bittersweet chocolate, broken into pieces

2 tablespoons extra virgin olive oil

½ cup boiling water

1 tablespoon sugar

Bring the milk and orange zest to a boil. Pour the milk through a strainer into a heatproof bowl and discard the orange zest. Add the crushed saffron to the milk and allow to infuse for 20 minutes.

Beat the egg yolks, salt, and sugar in a bowl. Lift off the skin from the top of the milk and beat the warm milk into the yolks. Transfer to the top of a double boiler and cook the custard mixture over hot water until foamy and thick enough to coat a spoon. Remove from the heat and allow to cool.

Whip the cream until it holds soft peaks. Fold it thoroughly into the custard mixture and chill.

Freeze the mixture in an ice cream maker according to the manufacturer's instructions.

To prepare the praline, place 3 tablespoons of the sugar and 2 tablespoons water in a heavy skillet or round-bottomed wok over high heat. Dissolve the sugar, stirring.

When the sugar is bubbling, stir in the pine nuts. Cook, stirring, until the sugar begins to caramelize and adhere to the kernels. Add 2 tablespoons more sugar and stir until it melts and turns golden. Add the remaining sugar and continue stirring and cooking until the pine nuts are coated in caramel.

Spread the mixture out onto an oiled plate or a sheet of parchment. Allow to cool. When completely cool, break the praline up into small bits. Store in a covered container for up to 1 week.

To prepare the chocolate syrup, melt the chocolate in the top of a double boiler over hot water. Stir until smooth. Stir in the oil, then the boiling water, then the sugar.

Place the saucepan over direct heat and cook, stirring, until it begins to bubble. Cook without stirring for 3 minutes. Remove and cool.

The syrup keeps refrigerated for up to 1 week. It can be reheated in a microwave to bring to pouring consistency.

To serve, allow the ice cream to soften for 20 to 30 minutes. Scoop the ice cream into small bowls. Drizzle with chocolate syrup and scatter the praline on top.

FROZEN FIG MOUSSE

Tarta Helada de Higos

Fig trees grow widely in La Mancha. The dried fruit provides a ready source of sweetness in winter meals. This luscious dessert, combined with honey and cream, makes a grand finale for Christmas dinner. Dessert chefs like to create composite sweets that play off flavors and textures. If you'd like to custom-design your dessert, try the frozen fig mousse with a drizzle or swirl of chocolate syrup (page 339), orange syrup (page 325), caramel sauce (page 318), or Sweet Potatoes Candied in Grape Syrup (page 332). Then add a crisp fried cookie, such as Crispy Leaves (page 309) or Almond Fritters (page 313). Scatter with Pine Nut Praline (page 339). Very festive.

SERVES 8

½ pound dried figs (about 1¼ cups)	½ cup sugar
1½ cups boiling water	2 tablespoons honey
⅛ teaspoon aniseeds	Pinch of ground cloves
3 egg yolks	1½ cups whipping cream
½ cup milk	

Rinse the figs, place them in a heatproof bowl, and pour the boiling water over them. Allow the figs to soak for 3 hours. Drain, saving some of the liquid.

Nip out the fig stems with a knife and cut the figs in half. Put the figs in a blender with ½ cup of the reserved soaking liquid and the aniseeds. Puree the figs in a blender until smooth. Place the puree in a mixing bowl.

Beat the egg yolks in another bowl. Combine the milk, sugar, honey, and cloves in a saucepan. Bring to a boil, stirring to dissolve the honey. Remove from the heat. Whisk the hot milk into the yolks.

Return the milk-yolk mixture to the pan and place over boiling water. Cook over boiling water, whisking constantly, until the mixture thickens, about 4 minutes. The custard will be thick enough to coat a spoon.

Remove the pan from the heat and whisk for 1 minute as the custard cools.

Fold the custard into the fig puree. Chill the mixture.

Chill beaters and bowl before beating the cream until it holds soft peaks. Stir some of the cream into the fig mixture. Then fold the remaining whipped cream thoroughly into the fig puree.

Place the fig-cream mixture in an 8-inch springform pan. Cover with plastic wrap and freeze for 8 hours, or until the mousse is solid.

The frozen mousse can be removed from the springform, wrapped in plastic wrap and foil, and returned to the freezer for up to 2 weeks.

To serve, remove from the freezer at least 10 minutes before serving. Dip a serrated knife into hot water to slice.

Variation: Instead of freezing the mousse, serve it chilled, dolloped into dessert coupes.

QUINCE SORBET

Sorbete de Membrillo

Quince is a full-flavored, old-fashioned fruit that looks like an oversized, knobbly apple. Somewhere between apple and pear in flavor and texture, the quince has a leathery skin rich in pectin. Cooked with sugar, the fruit sets up as a stiff jelly (also called *quince paste*) that can be cut into slices. (Should you have a windfall of quince, the recipe for quince jelly is on page 329.) Imported quince jelly (see Sources) is an easy starting point for this sorbet. Although the fruit has a pleasing graininess, the pectin makes a creamy ice without any fat.

A classic pairing is quince jelly with either aged Manchego or *queso fresco*, fresh white goat cheese. So this sorbet goes especially well with Molded Manchego Cheese Flan (page 322).

SERVES 8

1½ cups quince jelly (14 ounces)

¼ cup sugar

1 teaspoon grated orange zest

2 tablespoons fresh lemon juice

Pinch of ground cloves

Allow the quince jelly to come to room temperature.

In a saucepan, combine 2½ cups water with the sugar. Bring to a boil and simmer for 2 minutes. Add the quince jelly and stir over low heat until it is dissolved. Stir in the orange zest, lemon juice, and cloves.

Cool the quince mixture, stirring occasionally, and then chill it. Place in an ice cream maker and process according to the manufacturer's directions. Place the frozen quince sorbet in a container with a tight seal and freeze at least 2 hours.

Soften the sorbet before serving.

RED WINE GRANITA

Granizado de Vino Tinto

Use an unaged Tempranillo wine for this frosty dessert. A bottle of wine, three-quarters of a liter, contains about 3¼ cups of liquid. One cup of uncooked wine added to the cooked syrup contains just enough alcohol to keep the mix from freezing solid.

SERVES 6

1 bottle red wine

1¼ cups sugar

1 vanilla bean

One 5-inch strip orange zest

One 5-inch strip lemon zest

1 clove

Fresh mint sprigs

Pour all but 1 cup of the wine into a heavy saucepan with the sugar, vanilla, orange zest, lemon zest, and clove. Bring to a boil and simmer gently for 10 minutes.

Pour the reserved cup of wine into the cooked wine. Pour through a strainer and discard the solids. Cool the wine.

Place in an 8-inch cake pan and freeze for 2 hours. Stir the mixture and return to the freezer. Freeze, stirring every 2 hours. Serve the granita while still slushy. If the mixture freezes solid, break it up and puree in a food processor.

Serve in dessert cups garnished with mint sprigs.

ORANGE ICE

Granizado de Naranja

A *granizado* is an iced drink, served slushy with a straw. But it can also be served frozen, much like Italian granita.

SERVES 6

---

4 to 5 oranges (to make 1½ cups juice) Fresh mint sprigs for garnish

1 cup sugar

Remove strips of zest from 1 orange. Grate enough zest from another orange to make 1 teaspoon. Juice the oranges and pass the juice through a fine-meshed strainer.

Place the sugar, strips of zest, and 1½ cups water in a saucepan. Bring to a boil and simmer for 5 minutes. Cool. Strain the sugar syrup, discarding the strips of zest. Combine the syrup, orange juice, and grated zest.

Pour into a glass or metal pan and freeze for 1 hour. Stir the frozen bits into the liquid and return to the freezer. Repeat the stirring several more times. Transfer to a covered container and freeze.

To serve as an ice, scrape or scoop the ice into dessert cups. To serve as a tall drink, place the ice in a blender with 2 cups cold water and blend until slushy. Serve in tall glasses. Garnish the ice or drink with mint sprigs.

Wine and Other Drinks

Nueve meses de invierno y tres meses de infierno. "Nine months of winter and three months of hell" is how they characterize the climate of Castilla–La Mancha, Spain's central plateau. Blazing-hot summers and frigid winters are hard on people, but good for vines. In this sunny, dry climate, they've never heard of grapes not ripening, as sometimes happens in more northern lands following a cold summer.

This is big wine country. In fact, it is the biggest area of vineyards on earth—about 8 percent of all lands worldwide planted in vines and almost half of all the vineyards in Spain are within La Mancha. Miles and miles of vineyards keep the landscape verdant through hellishly hot summers.

Wine has been made in the La Mancha region continuously since pre-Roman times. By the nineteenth century, La Mancha wines, in particular those of Valdepeñas, had become the wine of choice for the taverns of Madrid, supplied by muleteers who hauled it to the capital in wineskins. With the coming of the railroad in 1861, a daily "wine train" delivered carloads of wine to the capital.

The wine of the old days, called *clarete,* was made by mixing quantities of white wine—produced in prodigious quantity—with enough red to give it color. Having cornered the market in "ordinary" wine, for most of the twentieth century winemakers in La Mancha didn't pay much attention to world market trends toward quality wines at higher prices—specifically, aged reds. And growers balked at ripping out white-grape vines and replanting with red-wine grapes.

The 1980s and '90s brought massive restructuring of vineyards and wineries, with government subsidies to ease the pain of radical change. Acres of Airén white wine grapes were replaced with red varieties. Relegated to museums are the *tinajas,* huge earthenware vats in which grape must used to be fermented. Wineries replaced them with stainless-steel tanks allowing temperature-controlled fermentation. Underground *cavas,* cellars for keeping wines, were expanded to include oak barrels for aging wine. Forward-thinking winemakers, with an eye to world markets, pioneered the planting of new grape varietals. Gradually, the tradition-bound regulating boards of the various *denominaciones de origen* have come to allow "foreign" grapes, such as Cabernet Sauvignon, in winemaking. The region, sometimes likened to a slumbering giant, is taking huge strides toward modern wines, with an emphasis on quality instead of quantity. Big money is being invested in La Mancha by some of the important wineries from other parts of Spain.

✑ Grape Varieties

The principal white wine grape varieties in La Mancha are Airén—the most abundant grape in Spain—and Macabeo. Grown in very small quantities are Verdejo, Merseguera, Albillo, Sauvignon Blanc, Viognier, and Chardonnay. Though less and less white wine is made, Airén grapes continue to be important for distillation. The resulting grape alcohol is used in *aguardiente,* an anise-flavored liqueur, and it goes to Sherry bodegas for use in making Brandy de Jerez.

Of red-wine grapes, Tempranillo—also called *Cencibel* in La Mancha—is far and away the most widely used, both in monovarietal and blended wines. Tempranillo is the same grape that has made the fame of La Rioja. It lends itself to fruity young reds and full-bodied oak-aged wines. Other red-wine grapes grown in the region are Garnacha (Grenache), Monastrell, Bobal, Graciano, Cabernet Sauvignon, Merlot, Syrah, and Petit Verdot. Blending of varietals opens up opportunities for originality in winemaking.

✑ Denominations of Origin

Castilla–La Mancha encompasses eight denominations of origin, a designation equivalent to French *appellation contrôlée,* plus the relatively new categories of Vinos de la Tierra de Castilla and Vinos de Pago, or single-estate wines.

DO ALMANSA.   Situated on the eastern edge of Albacete province, bordering Valencia, Alicante, and Murcia. Whites of Macabeo and Verdejo; reds of Monastrell with Tempranillo.

DO JUMILLA.   Centered in the province of Murcia with vineyards in Albacete. Red wines of Monastrell, Tempranillo, Syrah, and Cabernet Sauvignon.

DO LA MANCHA.   The biggest of the wine regions, it spreads across the provinces of Ciudad Real, Albacete, Cuenca, and Toledo. Wineries within this denomination range from gigantic cooperatives to single-estate operations. While Airén for whites and Tempranillo for reds make up most vineyard acreage, Chardonnay, Cabernet Sauvignon, and Syrah are allowed.

DO MANCHUELA. Occupies the eastern part of Cuenca and Albacete provinces. Constituted in 2000, the sector has attracted new investments and experimenters. Bobal is the primary grape, but other varieties are being increased.

DO MÉNTRIDA Situated in the north of Toledo province, bordering Madrid and Ávila. Garnacha has been the preferred varietal, but Tempranillo, Cabernet Sauvignon, Merlot, Syrah, and Petit Verdot are grown also. Macabeo and Sauvignon Blanc are the white varieties.

DO MONDÉJAR. Within the province of Guadalajara. White grapes are Malvar and Macabeo; red are Tempranillo and Cabernet Sauvignon.

DO RIBERA DEL JÚCAR. In the south of Cuenca province. The newest denomination concentrated on red wines of Tempranillo, Cabernet Sauvignon, Merlot, Syrah, and Bobal.

DO VALDEPEÑAS. A pocket within the huge DO La Mancha, encompassing the lands around the town of Valdepeñas in the south of Ciudad Real province. The wines of this region are, historically, second in popularity only to those of La Rioja. Valdepeñas has huge "factory" wineries turning out well-made, inexpensive wines, as well as small boutique bodegas making superb wines on a very small scale. White wines of Airén, Macabeo, and Chardonnay; rosé *(rosado)* of Tempranillo; and reds of Tempranillo, Garnacha, and Cabernet Sauvignon.

VINOS DE LA TIERRA DE CASTILLA. This category was created for wines made within Castilla–La Mancha that don't necessarily fit into one of the denominations. They may fall outside of the geographical limitations; be made of varietals not authorized by the regulating boards; produce yields not authorized; or use techniques in growing or vinification not allowed by the denominations. The intention was to allow winemakers to produce wines that could compete on the world market. Many of the new generation of La Mancha wines carry this label, including some of the most critically acclaimed. Some bodegas make both—wines with a denomination label and another with the Vinos de la Tierra (V.T.) label.

VINOS DE PAGO. *Pago* means an estate, domain, *chateau*. This denomination is given to single-estate wines that meet stringent quality requisites.

✍ Pairing Wine with Food

In most of Spain's wine regions, including Castilla–La Mancha, red-wine vintages are classified as *jóven,* young; *crianza,* slightly aged; *reserva,* aged; and *gran reserva,* long aged. Wines with denomination labels must adhere to minimum aging requirements. For example, DO Valdepeñas specifies that crianza wines must be aged in oak barrels for at least six months and in bottle for at least eighteen months, and reserva wines must have at least twelve months in barrel and two years in bottle. Traditionally, this has meant that when you buy a bottle of wine, it's ready to drink. You don't have to cellar it and wait for the tannins to smooth out.

Some winemakers, aiming for a world market where crianza and reserva are terms less well understood than in Spain, avoid these classifications. Some of them claim long aging on oak changes a wine's personality and distorts the fruit. They may label their wines "aged in oak barrels" and, modeled after the French, allow the consumer to keep the wine in bottle for longer periods.

Drink young wines within a year of the time they are made. Good ones are fruity and fresh, with bright cherry color. Choose youthful wines to drink with tapas, especially with potato tortilla, meatballs, and Spanish sausages such as chorizo; with family meals of lentils, beans, chickpeas, or pasta; with paella; with breaded veal or pork cutlet; with roast chicken or turkey. La Mancha's inexpensive young reds are a good choice for making sangría.

Crianza wines, with just a touch of oak, go especially well with cheese of all sorts, especially aged Manchego. This is also the perfect wine with most meat dishes such as grilled steak or roast pork or lamb. Serve it with a lamb burger or hamburger of choice beef.

A reserva wine, as the word indicates, means "reserved," a term used in Spanish wine-making to distinguish the finest wines of a vintner's cellar, which are reserved, in bottle, until they are at their optimum for drinking. A reserva wine is made when the grapes in a particular year are of sufficient quality to produce a wine that will improve with aging. These wines, usually of a deep brick color, offer complex bouquet and taste. Choose them to accompany dishes such as stewed partridge, venison, duck, and beef.

White wines of La Mancha are usually young and simple. Macabeo varietals are rather better than Airén, although either one, when cold-fermented, makes a light and fresh white that, served chilled, accompanies fish and shellfish very nicely. Some winemakers are experimenting with Chardonnay and Viognier, giving them a brief passage through oak to lend sophistication and complexity.

Serve red wines at a cool room temperature. In hot weather, without a controlled-temperature cellar or room air-conditioning, give wines a sixty-minute cooling period in the refrigerator before opening. Crianza and reserva reds need a bit of time in the glass to open up. Some winemakers choose not to clarify and filter their wines. These benefit from being decanted carefully, leaving any sediment behind. Serve most rosés (*rosados*) and white wines well chilled.

❧ CHOICES

As I traveled around La Mancha, I sampled local wines in restaurants and bars. I met wine-makers and bought their wines right at the *bodegas,* wineries. I discovered much to like. My personal picks, listed below, include some of the region's priciest bottles ($60 and up) and others that are amazing bargains ($3.00). There are many more excellent wines—but I haven't tasted them yet. Quite a few of these are exported to the United States. The bodega's name and location are given first, then the name of one of its wines where it is different from the bodega's name. Incidentally, I just love reading the names of these little towns in La Mancha—Corral de Almaguer, Retuerta del Bullaque, Quintanar de la Orden, Argamasilla de Alba, Mota del Cuervo—any one of which could be *un lugar de la Mancha,* that mysterious someplace in La Mancha where Don Quixote lived.

Barreda, Corral de Almaguer (Toledo). *Torre de Barreda*; Vino de la Tierra de Castilla.

Centro Españolas, Tomelloso (Ciudad Real). *Allozo*; DO La Mancha.

Cooperativa Nuestra Señora del Rosario, El Provencio (Cuenca). *Canforrales*; DO La Mancha.

Cooperativa Nuestro Padre Jesús del Perdón, Manzanares (Ciudad Real). *Yuntero*; DO La Mancha.

Cooperativa Tintoralba, Alpera (Albacete). DO Almansa.

Dehesa del Carrizal, Retuerta del Bullaque (Ciudad Real). Vino de la Tierra de Castilla.

Dionisos, Valdepeñas (Ciudad Real). *Vinum Vitae*; DO Valdepeñas. Wine made from organic grapes.

Dominio de Malpica, Malpica del Tajo (Toledo). *Solaz*; Vino de la Tierra de Castilla. Division of the Osborne Sherry company.

Dominio de Valdepusa, Malpica del Tajo (Toledo). *Emeritus*; Vino de Pago. First-ever denomination for a single-estate wine.

El Vínculo, Campo de Criptana (Ciudad Real). DO La Mancha. Belongs to Alejandro Fernández Tinto Pesquera of Ribera del Duero fame.

Entremontes, Quintanar de la Orden (Toledo). DO La Mancha.

Finca Antigua, Los Hinojosos (Cuenca). DO La Mancha. The bodega is a division of Rioja bodega Martínez Bujanda.

Finca Sandoval, Ledaña (Cuenca). *Salia*; DO Manchuela.

Fontana, Fuente de Pedro Naharro (Cuenca). *Quercus*; DO La Mancha.

J. Santos, La Villa de Don Fadrique (Toledo). DO La Mancha.

Leganza, Quintanar de la Orden (Toledo). DO La Mancha. A division of giant Faustino bodega in La Rioja.

Manuel Manzaneque–Finca Elez, El Bonillo (Albacete). Vino de Pago.

Miguel Calatayud, Valdepeñas (Ciudad Real). *Vegaval Plata*; DO Valdepeñas.

Montalvo Wilmot, Argamasilla de Alba (Ciudad Real). DO La Mancha.

Pago del Ama, Toledo. Vino de la Tierra de Castilla.

Piqueras, Almansa (Albacete). *Castillo de Almansa*; DO Almansa.

S.A.T. Santa Rita, Mota del Cuervo (Cuenca). *Veronés*; DO La Mancha.

Vidal del Saz, Campo de Criptana (Ciudad Real). DO La Mancha.

Viña Albali Reservas, Valdepeñas. DO Valdepeñas. Division of the huge Félix Solís bodega.

MANCHEGAN WHITE WINE COOLER

Zurra Manchega

The traditional white wine of La Mancha is made from Airén grapes, the most abundant grape in Spain. Robust, disease-resistant vines yield heavily and produce wines with a pleasant aroma, no complexity, not much keeping power. Low in price, La Mancha whites are perfect for making this refreshing wine cooler with an intriguing hint of spice. You could use any dry white wine. This drink, called *cuerva* in Albacete, is traditionally made, like a punch, in a large earthenware bowl and served in small earthenware cups.

SERVES 6

⅓ cup sugar

Fresh mint sprigs plus 6 mint sprigs for garnish

1 celery stalk

One 2-inch cinnamon stick

1 lemon, sliced

1 orange, sliced

1 bottle dry white wine, chilled

1 peach, sliced

Soda water to taste (1 to 2 cups)

Ice cubes (optional)

Combine the sugar and 1 cup water in a small saucepan. Bring to a boil and cook for 5 minutes. Remove from the heat and add the mint, celery, cinnamon, and half of the lemon and orange slices. Let steep for at least 30 minutes.

Strain into a pitcher and add the wine, remaining lemon and orange slices, and peach slices. Dilute to taste with soda water. Serve in tall glasses, with ice if desired. Garnish with mint sprigs.

—Pero, dígame, señor—dijo Sancho—por el siglo
de lo que más quiere, ¿este vino es de Ciudad Real?

—¡Brabo mojón!—respondió el del Bosque—; en verdad que no
es de otra parte, y que tiene algunos años de ancianidad.

—¿No será bueno, señor escudero, que tenga yo un instinto tan
grande y tan natural en esto de conocer vinos, que en dándome
a oler cualquiera, acierto la patria, el linaje, el sabor y la dura
y las vueltas que ha de dar, con todas las circunstancias al
vino atañaderas? Pero no hay de qué maravillarse, si tuve en
mi linaje, por parte de mi padre, los dos más excelentes
mojones que en luengos años conoció La Mancha. . . .

"But, tell me, sir," said Sancho, "by the world you so
love, isn't this wine from Ciudad Real?"

"Good call, man!" replied the Squire of the Forest. "To
tell the truth it's from nowhere else, and it's got a few
years of aging too."

"And why do you suppose, sir squire, that I shouldn't
have a great natural instinct for knowing wines?" said
Sancho. "Give me a sniff of any wine and I can tell you
the vineyard it came from, its vintage, grape, and age,
how many turns the barrel had, and just about any other
detail concerning wine. But you shouldn't be so
surprised, for on my father's side of the family were two
of the foremost wine tasters ever known in La Mancha."

SANCHO PANZA, DRINKING WITH THE
KNIGHT OF THE FOREST'S SQUIRE

VENDIMIA LUNCH
WITH THE MARQUÉS

On a bright September morning on the first day of the *vendimia*, grape harvest, Carlos Falcó, the Marqués of Griñón, arrives early at his vineyards of Dominio de Valpusa to keep an eye on everything. A grandee of Spain whose name crops up in society and gossip columns, Don Carlos looks right at home in country clothes as he walks through the vineyards, talking with the workers.

He picks a cluster of the deep purple, almost black grapes and tastes one.

"This is how we know when to pick the grapes," he says. "We taste them. We do the chemical analysis too, but I don't have to wait for the lab tests. You can taste the sugars. These are fully ripened grapes. We start tomorrow with the Syrah."

The grape vines are trained high on wires. Don Carlos explains that this kind of canopy management—once unknown in most Spanish vineyards—allows more sunlight to reach leaves and the ripening fruit.

"That allows greater yield and better wine," he says.

Most of the clusters are at waist level, meaning the pickers don't have to stoop and bend to cut them. They heap the fruit into crates, which are loaded on a flatbed truck and hauled to the *bodega*, winery, only two hundred yards from the vineyards. The vinification process begins before the dew is hardly dried on the grapes.

This is at the heart of the making of *vino de pago*, single-estate wine.

"*Pago* means 'domain,'" explains Don Carlos. "It is the same as terroir."

Dominio de Valdepusa, where Don Carlos planted his experimental vineyards back in 1974, became in 2004 the first ever single estate in Spain, like the French *grands crus*, to be granted its own Denomination of Origin. The lands are west of Toledo, at Malpica de Tajo, situated on a plateau overlooking the broad valley of the River Pusa, a tributary of the Tajo. The property, which has been in the family since 1292, lies just outside the old, established wine denomination of Méntrida, one of eight denominations in Castilla–La Mancha.

"They invited us to join the Méntrida denomination," says Don Carlos. "But we preferred to stay out. We wanted to do something revolutionary."

Back in 1974, planting Cabernet Sauvignon, a "foreign" grape, in native Tempranillo and

Garnacha country was revolutionary. It was actually prohibited by the denominations that established which grape varietals could be used in the region's wines. He also set up drip irrigation in the vineyards—also prohibited by the governing wine boards.

Carlos Falcó, who studied agriculture at a Belgian university, then studied at the University of California at Davis, where he met Dr. Maynard Amerine, the late professor and wine guru.

"He introduced me to Cabernet Sauvignon, and it changed my life," says Don Carlos. The going wisdom was that you couldn't make good Cab in a hot climate such as in central Spain. But Dr. Amerine encouraged him to give it a try. New winery technology allowing temperature controls during fermentation, use of antioxidants such as ascorbic acid to allow wines to age gently, and cooling of cellars would make it possible.

"Then they told me I couldn't do this in Spain. I lost ten years wrangling with the authorities. Finally I decided to go ahead anyway." He smuggled in the outlaw vine cuttings in a truckload of apple trees.

"I never looked back."

Don Carlos was the first in Spain to plant Syrah (1991), a variety he considers especially suitable for Spain's hot zones, and Petit Verdot (1992), producing the first single varietal Petit Verdot wine in the world. He pioneered in the use of Australian vineyard consultant Richard Smart's systems of vine pruning and canopy management as well as sophisticated computer-managed watering systems that measure stress levels in the vineyards.

Don Carlos makes three single-varietal wines with the Dominio de Valdepusa label—Cabernet Sauvignon, Syrah, and Petit Verdot—plus Emeritus and Svmma Varietalis, both blends of all three, aged in French oak barrels from eleven to twenty-two months. He does not make Tempranillo.

"We're very famous in the wine world," he chuckles, "because anyone who wants to taste Petit Verdot can find it only here. In Bordeaux, where it is used in top-growth wines like Château Margaux, you can't taste it unless you go into the cellar and taste from the barrel."

What happens to Cabernet Sauvignon or other French grapes when they are planted in La Mancha?

"It takes four elements to make wine," says Don Carlos, "soil, climate, grape, and the person who makes the wine. The soil is Spanish, the climate is Spanish, and I am Spanish. Only the grape is not. That's three out of four, so it is a very Spanish wine." He adds that Jancis Robinson, well-known wine critic, even claimed, perhaps tongue-in-cheek, that Syrah wines from Spain finish tasting like Tempranillo.

If once he appeared a raving renegade, in retrospect Don Carlos looks like the prophet who pointed the way to restructuring of vineyards and winemaking and, most important, marketing wines internationally. The principal wine regions of Castilla–La Mancha now allow plantations of Cabernet Sauvignon, Syrah, Merlot, and Petit Verdot.

On the Dominio de Valdepusa estate are two rambling eighteenth-century buildings. The old *casa de labor*, or farm building, houses the winery's receiving center, offices, tasting rooms, and barrel room. The ochre *casa de vacas*, cow keeper's house, is used for family gatherings and entertaining guests (Carlos Falcó and his family live near Madrid).

Lunch is laid on the terrace overlooking a walled garden. With a twinkle, Don Carlos uncorks a white wine to sip as aperitif.

"This wine is made by a friend of mine, in the Montes de Toledo," he says as he pours. "It is a Viognier, very fragrant." Viognier! Another surprise. Can this really be La Mancha? He passes a plate of *cecina de ciervo*, venison "ham," also from the Montes de Toledo. It is sliced paper-thin, drizzled with extra virgin olive oil (the marqués's title also appears on olive oil produced on a nearby estate), and sprinkled with thyme.

Lunch begins with *ajo blanco*, a cold garlic-almond soup with the surprise of sweet melon. The entree, *tórtola*, wild dove, braised in a wine sauce, is the perfect foil for savoring the clean, bright flavors of Emeritus, Don Carlos's unique blend of Cabernet Sauvignon, Syrah, and Petit Verdot. It is silky, herbaceous, with a hint of licorice and toffee.

It is a lovely finish to a day in the terroir of Dominio de Valdepusa.

RED WINE SANGRÍA

Sangría

This classic party drink has many variations. Tourist restaurants often serve sangría syrupy sweet, while Spaniards enjoy it fairly dry, with a double punch of brandy or liqueur. Use any young red wine with no oak, preferably a Tempranillo from La Mancha. In Spain, sangría is diluted with *gaseoso,* lightly sweetened, slightly lemony fizzy water.

Use any combination of fruit in the sangría. Strawberries, oranges, melon, apples, pears, bananas, grapes, and peaches, sliced or chopped, are some of the best. Apples float, oranges sink. Serve the sangría in a pitcher with a long-handled spoon for ladling out the fruit. Pour into wide-mouthed juice glasses or goblets. Ice is optional—it dilutes the sangría as it melts.

Sangría goes nicely with some tapas and canapés but is too sweet to serve with a meal. I like it for summer entertaining al fresco, on the patio or poolside.

❧ SERVES 8 TO 10

¼ cup sugar	¼ cup brandy or liqueur such as Cointreau
1 strip orange zest	1 bottle red wine, chilled
2 cups chopped or sliced fruit	2 to 3 cups chilled soda water

Combine the sugar with the zest and 1 cup water in a small saucepan. Bring to a boil and simmer for 2 minutes. Allow the sugar syrup to cool. Strain it into a 2-quart pitcher. Discard the orange zest.

Add the fruit and brandy to the pitcher. The fruit can macerate, refrigerated, for up to 2 hours. Add the chilled red wine. Immediately before serving, add chilled soda water to taste.

WATERMELON SANGRÍA

Sangría de Sandía

This makes a fun party drink. It can be prepared in advance and chilled. Or, if preferred, serve it over ice cubes.

SERVES **8**

3 tablespoons sugar

1 strip orange zest

2 pounds ripe watermelon

3 tablespoons Cointreau or Triple Sec

1 bottle dry white wine, well chilled

A few strawberries

Fresh mint sprigs for garnish

Combine the sugar and zest with ½ cup water in a small saucepan. Bring to a boil and stir to dissolve the sugar. Remove from the heat and cool. Discard the orange zest.

Remove the seeds and green rind from the watermelon. Save a few chunks of flesh for garnish. Puree the flesh in a blender or food processor. Strain the puree and place in a pitcher with the sugar syrup, Cointreau, and white wine. Chill the sangría for 1 hour.

Serve the sangría, over ice if desired, garnished with the reserved cubes of watermelon, whole strawberries, and mint sprigs.

SWEET SPICED WINE

Místela

In bygone times in the vineyards it was customary to make this sweet wine with unfermented grape must. The addition of distilled alcohol stopped the fermentation of the sugars in the juice. It was allowed to steep for forty days, then filtered.

This recipe is an adaptation, using grape juice in place of must. Use any clear spirit, such as *aguardiente de orujo*, grappa, vodka, or gin. Serve it well chilled, in tiny liqueur glasses with cakes and cookies. Or turn it into a tall drink by diluting it with soda water and pouring it over ice.

MAKES 3 PINTS

1 strip orange zest

1 strip lemon zest

1 teaspoon aniseeds

One 1-inch cinnamon stick

¼ cup sugar

1 quart white grape juice

2 cups vodka or other clear liquor

Combine the strips of zest, aniseeds, cinnamon, sugar, and 1 cup water in a small saucepan. Bring to a boil and simmer for 3 minutes. Remove from the heat and allow to cool. Strain the sugar syrup and discard the solids.

Combine the sugar syrup, grape juice, and vodka in a container with a tightly fitting cap (jar, bottle, flask). Refrigerate until chilled.

LATE-NIGHT LIQUEUR

Licor de Trasnochá

Use your best cut-glass decanter to serve this liqueur. It is sweet, but not insipid, and aromatic with orange and spices—a fine after-dinner drink sipped neat. Mix it with soda water and ice for a tall drink or concoct a Spanish cocktail with it.

Remove the orange zest with a vegetable peeler in as few strips as possible, being sure to leave behind all the white pith. Leave the strips of zest to dry for several days. Once the orange-spice mixture is combined with the alcohol (vodka or grappa), the liqueur infuses for 2 weeks before being strained. Take care to use very clean utensils, jars, and bottles.

MAKES 2½ PINTS

Zest of 2 oranges

2 cups sugar

1 tablespoon aniseeds, coarsely crushed

1½ teaspoons coriander seeds, coarsely crushed

2 cloves

1 tablespoon fresh lemon verbena (optional)

3 fresh mint sprigs

1 quart vodka or grappa

Allow the orange zest to dry for about 4 days.

Combine the sugar with 1½ cups water in a saucepan. Bring to a boil and stir to dissolve the sugar. Add the orange zest, aniseeds, coriander seeds, and cloves. Cook gently for 5 minutes. Remove from the heat and add the lemon verbena, if you're using it, and mint. Allow to cool for 20 minutes.

Place the sugar syrup with the orange zest and spices in a clean glass jar (divide between 2 jars if necessary). Add the vodka. Cover tightly and leave in a cool, dark place for 2 weeks.

Strain the liqueur into a pitcher and discard the solids. Fit a filter paper into a coffee filter. Pour 1 cup boiling water through it. Discard the water. Place the filter over a bottle or decanter and pour in the liqueur. It will filter through very slowly. Continue adding liqueur until it has all been filtered. Again, use 2 bottles if necessary. Cap or stopper the bottles tightly. The liqueur is ready to drink but can be kept in a cool, dark place for up to 1 year.

COFFEE *and* SPICE LIQUEUR

Resolí

This delightful liqueur is traditional in the enchanting town of Cuenca, where "hanging houses" cling to sheer canyon walls high above the river valley. An Italian monk supposedly introduced the liqueur at the end of the fifteenth century. Although the name, *resolí*, is quite similar to Sicilian *rosolio*, a liqueur made with rose petals, the Spanish version contains coffee and spices, no roses.

In Cuenca the liqueur is made with distilled grape alcohol, *aguardiente de orujo*. Any clear alcohol—orujo, grappa, marc, or vodka—can be used.

MAKES ABOUT 4 PINTS

¼ cup finely ground dark-roast coffee	5 cloves
½ cup dried figs, washed	1 teaspoon aniseeds
Zest of 1 orange	2 cups sugar
One 3-inch cinnamon stick	5 cups vodka

Brew the coffee with 1 cup water.

Combine the figs, orange zest, cinnamon, cloves, aniseeds, and 1½ cups water in a saucepan. Bring to a boil and simmer for 2 minutes.

Place the sugar in a heavy saucepan over medium heat. Melt the sugar until it is golden and most of the lumps are dissolved, 6 minutes. Remove from the heat and stir until all the sugar is melted.

Very carefully pour the coffee into the melted sugar. The sugar will bubble up. Stir it with a wooden spoon until the coffee is absorbed. Add the liquid in which the figs cooked. Place the pan over low heat and stir until the sugar is completely dissolved in the liquid. Remove from heat and add the figs, zest, and spices to the sugar syrup. Cool.

Place the sugar syrup with spices in a clean 2-quart jar (or divide between two 1-quart jars). Add the vodka. Cover the jar tightly and allow to steep for 2 weeks.

Strain the liqueur into a pitcher, discarding all the solids. Line a coffee filter with filter paper. Pour 1 cup boiling water through the filter, discarding the water. Place the filter over a clean pitcher and gradually pour the liqueur through it. It will filter very slowly and may take up to 20 minutes.

After filtering, pour the liqueur into clean bottles or decanters. Stopper tightly and store in a dark place. The liqueur is ready to drink after 2 weeks. It keeps well for up to 1 year.

COFFEE WITH MILK
CAFÉ CON LECHE

In Spain, the café, where business is transacted and social engagements take place, is as basic to everyday life as the tapa bar. In fact, sometimes it is the same establishment—serving coffee with snacks in the morning and late afternoon, wine and tapas in the evening, and coffee and brandy in the late, after-dinner hour.

The most typical bar coffee is *torrefacto,* beans dark-roasted with sugar, giving a bittersweet caramel taste, and very finely ground (see Sources). Made in an espresso machine and served with frothy steam-heated milk, it is sort of like a latte, but better. Coffee begins the day at breakfast, served half and half with hot milk. It ends the day as strong espresso served black, *solo,* in tiny cups. In between are many degrees of tonality: a *sombra,* "shade," is more milk than coffee, but a *nube,* "cloud," is mostly hot milk with a touch of coffee; a *cortado,* "cut," is coffee with just a tinge of milk.

Coffee brewed at home may be made in an electric coffee maker, an espresso pot, or with a simple paper filter.

HOT CHOCOLATE

Chocolate a la Taza

Hot chocolate so thick it's almost a pudding is a favorite treat for the finale of late-night fiestas, served up at street stalls and accompanied by *churros*, fritters, for dunking. At home, hot chocolate is special for winter mornings during the Christmas season and for family Sunday breakfasts.

In Spain you buy a bar of *chocolate a la taza*, drinking chocolate, which already contains sugar and rice flour to thicken the brew. The chocolate is chopped and melted with water or milk. An American friend of mind, who was crazy for Spanish hot chocolate when he lived in Spain, discovered that packaged mix for chocolate pudding and pie filling, made with extra milk, produced a reasonable substitute for thick Spanish drinking chocolate. My recipe uses real chocolate plus cornstarch to thicken it. Want to serve it as a dessert? Pour into shallow soup bowls and add a *buñuelo*, fritter (page 314) and a swirl of whipped cream.

SERVES 4

6 ounces bittersweet chocolate (at least 58 percent cacao)

¼ cup sugar

2 cups milk

¼ cup cornstarch

¼ teaspoon vanilla extract

Chop the chocolate and place in a heavy saucepan with the sugar, milk, and 2 cups water. Heat the chocolate over medium heat, whisking frequently, until the chocolate is melted.

Stir the cornstarch into 1 cup cold water until smooth. Whisk the cornstarch mixture into the chocolate. Cook, whisking constantly, until the chocolate begins to bubble. Reduce the heat and cook for 2 minutes, whisking.

Remove the chocolate from the heat and stir in the vanilla.

Serve the chocolate hot in mugs or large cups.

 # SOURCES

Many foods from Spain, such as extra virgin olive oil, Manchego cheese, and saffron, can be found in your favorite supermarket. Here's where you can find specialty foods imported from Spain—smoked pimentón, serrano ham, hard chorizo and soft cooking chorizo, saffron, piquillo peppers, *ñora* (dried peppers), *membrillo* (quince paste), and *torrefacto* (dark-roast coffee). Most of these sources have retail as well as online stores.

CASA OLIVER
www.casaoliver.com
Toll free: 18 88 80 SPAIN

DESPAÑA BRAND FOODS
www.despanabrandfoods.com
86-17 Northern Boulevard
Jackson Heights, NY 11372
(718) 779-4971

DESPAÑA NEW YORK CITY
www.despananyc.com
408 Broome Street (Lafayette Centre)
New York, NY 10013
(212) 219-5060

LA ESPAÑOLA MEATS
www.donajuana.com
25020 Doble Avenue
Harbor City, CA 90710
(310) 539-0455

La Tienda

www.tienda.com
3601 La Grange Parkway
Toano, VA 23168 (greater Williamsburg)
Toll-free: (888) 472-1022

Olé Olé Foods

www.oleolefoods.com
54 Schuyler Street
Belleville, NJ 07109
(973) 759-0333; toll-free: (800) OLE-8279

The Spanish Table

www.spanishtable.com
The Spanish Table Seattle
1427 Western Avenue
Seattle, WA 98101
(206) 682-2827

The Spanish Table Berkeley

1814 San Pablo Avenue
Berkeley, CA 94702
(510) 548-1383

The Spanish Table Mill Valley

123 Strawberry Village
Mill Valley, CA 94941
(415) 388-5043

The Spanish Table Santa Fe

109 North Guadalupe Street
Santa Fe, NM 87501
(505) 986-0243

BIBLIOGRAPHY

Aguilera Pleguezuelo, José. *Las cocinas árabe y judía y la cocina española*. Málaga: Editorial Arguval, 2002.

Alimentos de Castilla-La Mancha. Bimonthly magazine. Ciudad Real: Periodistas Asociados.

Alimentos de Castilla-La Mancha. ECOS CLM, Consejería de Agricultura y Medio Ambiente, 2002.

Álvarez Cobelas, M., and Cirujano, S. *Las Tablas de Daimiel*. Ecología Acuática y Sociedad. ICONA, 2002. Excerpts from accounts of Julio Escuderos.

Aradillas, Antonio. *Las Rutas del Quijote*. Madrid: Libro-Hobby-Club, 2004.

Ashtor, Eliyahu. *Jews of Moslem Spain*, volumes 2 and 3. Philadelphia: Jewish Publication Society, 1992.

Calduch, Enrique, and Gómez, Roberto. *Los Ajos de Castilla–La Mancha*. Madrid: Junta de Comunidades de Castilla-La Mancha, 2002.

Cervantes, Miguel de. *Don Quijote de la Mancha*. Barcelona: Editorial Ramón Sopena, 1978.

CLM Castilla–La Mancha—La Tierra del Quijote. Bimonthly magazine. Ciudad Real: Periodistas Asociados.

Cuéllar Tórtola, Javier, and Pardo Domingo, Pedro. *La Cocina Tradicional de la Manchuela*. Iniesta (Cuenca): Centro de Estudios de La Manchuela, 2004.

Díaz, Lorenzo. *La Cocina del Quijote*. Madrid: Alianza Editorial, 1997.

Falcó, Carlos, Marqués de Griñón. *Entender de Vino.* Madrid: Ediciones Martínez Roca, 2004.

García, L. Jacinto. *Carlos V a la mesa. Cocina y alimentación en la España renacentista.* Toledo: Ediciones Bremen, 2000.

García del Cerro, Carlos, and Alonso Madero, Francisco Javier. *La Mancha y el Queso Manchego.* Consejería de Agricultura, Junta de Comunidades de Castilla–La Mancha, 1986.

García Moreno, Enrique, and Agentes Femeninos del Servicio de Extensión Agraria de la Conserjería de Agricultura. *Recetario Gastronómico de Castilla–La Mancha.* Junta de Comunidades de Castilla–La Mancha, 1985. Book is out of print, but recipe database is online at *castillalamancha.es/turismo/SP/contenidos/Gastronomia.*

González Muñoz, Domingo. *La Cocina Tradicional en la Provincia de Toledo.* Diputación de Toledo, 1999.

Gregorio Arriaga, Carmen de. *Costumbres y Cocina Manchega.* Ciudad Real: Biblioteca de Autores Manchegos de la Diputación de Ciudad Real, 2002.

Macías Kapón, Uriel, and Benarroch de Bensadon, Ana. *La Cocina Judía, Leyes, costumbres, y algunas recetas sefardíes.* Girona: Red de Juderías de España, 2003.

Osa, Manuel de la. *Cocina Castellano-Manchega.* León: Editorial Everest, 2001.

Racionero Page, Joaquín. *Guisos, Viandas y Otras Pócimas.* Avila: J. Noticias, 2000.

Repostería Monacal de las Hermanas Clarisas. San Sebastián: Ardatz, 1999.

Rivka Cohen, A. *Los Placeres de mi Cocina Judía.* Barcelona: Parsifal Ediciones, 2003.

Sanjuán Vicens, Gloria. *Ollas, Sartenes y Fogones del Quijote.* Madrid: Libro-Hobby-Club, 2004.

Shaul, Moshe, Aldina Quintana Rodríguez, Zelda Ovadia. *El Gizado Sefardí.* Zaragoza: Ibercaja, 1995.

Useros, Carmina. *Mil Recetas de Cocina de Albacete y Su Provincia.* Albacete: Carmina Useros, 2001.

INDEX

bean(s):
  fava, eggs with, 59
  fava, with escarole and mint, 257
  with garlic sauce, 115
  green, Castilian red peppers and, 250
  green, salad, with grapes and anise, 46–47
  hearty vegetable soup with sausage and,
    107
  lamb shanks braised with, 239
  partridge with, 185–86
  pinto, chicken with pasta rags and, 172–73
  salad with chorizo, 37
beef:
  "altogether" stew, 207
  cutlets in adobo, 206
  and ham salad, 38–39
  hearty stew with sausage, 208–9
  one-pot feast, 120–24
  roast (variation), 203
  -stuffed peppers with chunky tomato sauce,
    210–11
  stuffed roll, 204–5
bigger-than-ladyfingers, 292
black-eyed peas with tomato sofrito, 114
bloodless blood sausage, 222–23
bonbons, chocolate-fig, 336–37
bread crumb(s):
  with chocolate (variation), 276
  shepherds' garlic-fried, 275–76
  and spinach stuffing, roast lamb with, 231–32
breads, 50
  basic dough, 80–81
  crisp croutons, 108–9
  hornazos para Pascua (variation), 83
  picnic rolls, 82
  polenta and crunchy croutons, 279
  Roscón de Reyes (variation), 306
  sweet cinnamon dumplings in caramel sauce,
    317–18
  sweet potato buns, 307–8
  sweet roll, 304–6
  sweet toasts, 316
  toast crisps, 30
  toast with olive oil, 85
  tortas, 196–97

bream, roasted, on a bed of potatoes, 138–39
broccoli with golden garlic and almonds, 255
broth, 6
  duck, 179
  simple chicken, 94
  simple fish, 135

cabbage:
  one-pot feast, 123–24
  pan-sautéed with cumin, 253
cakes:
  layer, with apricots and marzipan, Toledo style,
    296–99
  sponge, 296–97
  walnut, 295
Campillo de Altobuey, saffron harvest, 160–61
candied sweet potatoes in grape syrup, 332–33
Capuchin tortilla with asparagus, 55
caramel sauce, 318, 322–23
caraway seeds, eggplant with tomato and, 261
cardoons, 248
carrots:
  minted, 256
  sauté of fresh peas and, 258
Castilian green beans with red peppers, 250
cauliflower:
  batter-fried, 254
  with golden garlic and almonds, 255
  -potato soup with cheese flan, 95–96
cazuela, 7
chard:
  cazuela of potatoes and, 269
  and cheese pie, 74–75
  lamb roll wrapped in leaves of, 241–42
  sauté, 251
cheese:
  artisanal, 71–73
  baked eggplant with, 262
  baked eggs with, 65
  and chard pie, 74–75
  cheesy artichoke gratin, 248–49
  crispy, cheesy chicken breast with quince sauce,
    156–57
  eggplant timbale, 67–68

crispy leaves (pastries), 309–10
Cuenca-style honey-almond nougat, 334–35
custards, *see* puddings

denominación de origen (DO) 7–8, 349–50
Don Quixote's Friday lentils, 112–13
"double" eggs, 24–25
double garlic soup, 104
doughnuts, anise-flavored, 311–12
duck braised in red wine, 178–80
duck broth, 179

eggplant(s):
    baked with cheese, 262
    char-grilled, with lemon dressing, 264
    fried, with a drizzle of honey, 263
    meat-stuffed, spiced with nutmeg, 212
    medley of summer vegetables (variation),
        245
    pan-grilled vegetables, 265–66
    pickled, Almagro style, 280
    timbale, 67–68
    with tomato and caraway, 261
eggs:
    baked, with cheese, 65
    baked in spinach nests, 64
    Capuchin tortilla with asparagus, 55
    crackly fried, 57
    custard pudding with meringue topping,
        320–21
    "double," 24–25
    eggplant timbale, 67–68
    with fava beans, 59
    "Friday pie" with fish, 66
    garlicky asparagus and, 61
    garlic soup, 102–3
    glaze of egg whites, 286
    molded Manchego cheese flan with caramel
        sauce, 322–23
    picnic rolls with pork, sausage and, 82–84
    poached in tomato puree with cheese, 63
    potato, and garlic scramble, 58
    Saturday bacon and, 60

Spanish potato tortilla, 51–52
    tortilla with artichokes and ham, 53–54
empanadas filled with spicy chicken, 76
equivalents, 12
escabeche:
    chicken wings in, 170–71
    fish in, 132
    pickled mushrooms, 281
escarole, fava beans with mint and, 257

farmhouse rice with fish and greens, 142
fifteen-minute fish soup, 101
fig(s):
    -chocolate bonbons, 336–37
    figgy fritters, 315
    frozen mousse, 341–42
    poached in vanilla syrup, 327
    rabbit with Mudéjar spices and, 193–94
fish, 126
    baked stuffed trout, 131
    codfish balls with walnuts, 145–46
    farmhouse rice with greens and, 142
    fifteen-minute soup, 101
    fillets of sole with white wine sauce and grapes,
        140–41
    "Friday pie" with, 66
    olive pickers' cod and potato stew, 143–44
    poached hake with saffron sauce, 134
    roasted bream on a bed of potatoes, 138–39
    salt cod with roasted peppers, Manchegan style,
        147–48
    sea bass with garlic, pine nuts, and chile, 136–37
    simple broth, 135
    in tangy marinade, 132–33
    trout, Jewish style, 129
    trout and mushrooms in cazuela, Guadalajara
        style, 128
    trout fisherman in Cuenca, 130–31
    trout stuffed with ham and mushrooms, 127
flaky pastry dough, 79
flame-roasted garden vegetables, 246
flans:
    cheese, cauliflower-potato soup with, 95–96
    cheese, with ham, 69–70

eggplant timbale, 67–68
molded Manchego cheese, with caramel sauce, 322–23
"Friday pie" with fish, 66
"fried milk," 324–26
fritters:
almond, 313
figgy, 315
puffs of wind, 314
puffy shrimp, 19
frozen desserts:
fig mousse, 341–42
lavender honey ice milk, 338
orange ice, 345
quince sorbet, 343
red wine granita, 344
saffron ice cream with pine nut praline and chocolate syrup, 339–40

game, 152
braised partridge, Toledo style, 183–84
duck braised in red wine, 178–80
hunters' rice with rabbit, 191–92
hunters' stew with hare, 195
and liver pâté, Cuenca style, 35–36
partridge, 181–82
partridge with beans, 185–86
quail in "slipcovers" of red peppers, 189–90
rabbit with figs and Mudéjar spices, 193–94
shepherd's stew with, 196–98
squabs stuffed with raisins, apricots, and walnuts, 187–88
venison cutlets in adobo, 206
garlic, 105–6
char-roasting, 238
double, soup, 104
egg, and potato scramble, 58
garlicky asparagus and eggs, 61
garlicky salt cod dip, 29
golden, cauliflower or broccoli with almonds and, 255
green, potatoes mashed with, 270
lamb chops sizzled with, 240
pork chops in garlicky sauce, 215

sauce, beans with, 115
sea bass with pine nuts, chile and, 136–37
shepherds' fried bread crumbs, 275–76
soup, 102–3
spinach Iniesta style with, 252
glossary, ingredients, 6–11
goat, herb-roasted kid, 233–34
granita, red wine, 344
grapes:
chicken braised in spiced verjuice, 166–67
fillets of sole with white wine sauce and, 140–41
green bean salad with anise and, 46–47
varieties, 349
grape syrup, sweet potatoes candied in, 332–33
greens, farmhouse rice with fish and, 142

hake, poached, with saffron sauce, 134
ham:
beans with garlic sauce, 115
and beef salad, 38–39
beef-stuffed peppers with chunky tomato sauce, 210–11
black-eyed peas with tomato sofrito, 114
Castilian green beans with red peppers, 250
cheese flans with, 69–70
and cheese sandwiches, crisp, 86
"double" eggs, 24–25
eggs poached in tomato puree with cheese, 63
fat (tocino), 11
fifteen-minute fish soup, 101
garlicky asparagus and eggs, 61
garlic soup, 102–3
green pea soup, 100
Ibérico, 11
Manchegan soup with asparagus, 92–93
one-pot feast, 120–24
picnic rolls with pork, sausage, and egg, 82–84
Saturday eggs and bacon, 60
sauté of fresh peas and carrots, 258
serrano, 10–11
sheepshearers' rice salad with cheese and, 42
tortilla with artichokes and, 53–54
trout stuffed with mushrooms and, 127
hare, hunters' stew with, 195

Villalba de la Sierra, trout fishing, 130–31
vinegar, 11

walnut(s):
  cake, 295
  chewy cookies, 291
  codfish balls with, 145–46
  squabs stuffed with raisins, apricots and,
    187–88
  sweet bread roll, 304–6
  turnovers with honey glaze, 302–3
watermelon sangría, 360
wedding stew with chicken and meatballs, 163–65
wines, 348
  -cinnamon rings, 285
  denominations of origin (DO), 7–8, 349–50
  elements needed to make, 357

grape varieties, 349
local choices, 352–53
pairing food with, 351–52
red, duck braised in, 178–80
red, granita, 344
red, sangría, 359
single-estate (tour), 356–58
sweet spiced, 361
watermelon sangría, 360
white, Manchegan cooler, 354
white, sauce, fillets of sole with grapes and,
  140–41

zucchini:
  macaroni with chorizo sausage, 221
  medley of summer vegetables, 245
  pan-grilled vegetables, 265–66